The American Social Experience Series

GENERAL EDITOR: JAMES KIRBY MARTIN

EDITORS: PAULA S. FASS, STEVEN H. MINTZ,

CARL PRINCE, JAMES W. REED & PETER N. STEARNS

*1. The March to the Sea and Beyond: Sherman's Troops in
the Savannah and Carolinas Campaigns*
JOSEPH T. GLATTHAAR

2. Childbearing in American Society: 1650–1850
CATHERINE M. SCHOLTEN

3. The Origins of Behaviorism: American Psychology, 1870–1920
JOHN M. O'DONNELL

4. New York City Cartmen, 1667–1850
GRAHAM RUSSELL HODGES

*5. From Equal Suffrage to Equal Rights: Alice Paul and
the National Woman's Party, 1910–1928*
CHRISTINE A. LUNARDINI

*6. Mr. Jefferson's Army: Political and Social Reform
of the Military Establishment, 1801–1809*
THEODORE J. CRACKEL

*7. "A Peculiar People": Slave Religion and
Community-Culture Among the Gullahs*
MARGARET WASHINGTON CREEL

*8. "A Mixed Multitude": The Struggle for Toleration
in Colonial Pennsylvania*
SALLY SCHWARTZ

9. Women, Work, and Fertility, 1900–1986
SUSAN HOUSEHOLDER VAN HORN

WOMEN, WORK, AND FERTILITY, 1900–1986

SUSAN HOUSEHOLDER VAN HORN

NEW YORK UNIVERSITY PRESS
NEW YORK AND LONDON
1988

Library of Congress Cataloging-in-Publication Data

Van Horn, Susan Householder, 1934–1987
Women, work, and fertility, 1900–1986.

(The American social experience series ; 9)
Bibliography: p.
Includes index.
1. Women—United States—History—20th century.
2. Women—Employment—United States—History—20th
century.   3. Family—United States—History—20th
century.   I. Title.   II. Series.
HQ1410.V36   1988   305.4'0973   87-24018
ISBN 0-8147-8759-2

Book design by Ken Venezio

*To Elizabeth Rodriguez, Patricia Van Horn,
Lynda Graziano, and all the other women who will span
the transition to the twenty-first century.*

Contents

Foreword

Changes in women's roles and perceptions constitute one of the truly great watersheds in twentieth-century American history, along with the growth of the state and the nation's emergence as a world power. In this study, Susan Van Horn captures the basic features and the inevitable complexity of the women's revolution. Taking a relatively long span of time, which is essential if major change is to be assessed, the author blends statistics, anecdote, and interpretation to sketch a series of collective experiments by twentieth-century women to find a new voice and meaning in an advanced industrial society.

The commitment to new kinds of work and work settings represents the most fundamental change. While this is no surprise, the author delineates clearly the several factors that went into this new development, including the still-recent reduction of other more traditional work outlets and the competition of men in several "feminine" work sectors. Assessing and often combining a number of diverse interpretations of the causes of new job initiatives, she confirms the durability and significance of work commitments by showing their varied base. Wider economic developments, such as the rise of the service sector, new material expectations, new personal strivings and ideologies—all enter the mix, as the author weaves a far more nuanced tapestry than is available from most existing efforts to define causation. Nor are women treated as a monolith with regard to work: she shows clearly how social stratification differentiated women's responses to work and how, in turn, women's diverse work roles have in some ways heightened social gaps among women and in American society as a whole.

Work is not the only focus of this study, however. The book provides a welcome corrective to some teleological accounts that suggest an inevitable, single-minded march toward jobs and independent earnings. Twentieth-century women, and even late-twentieth-century women, still in the main juggle work and family commitments. A central feature of this study is to show how, in three key time periods in our century, three different balancing acts have been attempted. It is certainly possible to emerge from this book believing that the current equation, in which substantial work roles play off against relatively low birth rates, is the "logical" end result, the result with the greatest chance for durability. Even to accept this position, however, requires an understanding of the motives and experiences that went into different, and quite recent, patterns. The author's depiction of the baby-boom era, in which many women tried, for good if complex reasons, to combine comparatively high fertility with new work initiatives, forms one of the most compelling sections of the book. The experiment may not be renewed, but understanding it as something more than an anomaly or a strange retreat into domesticity remains vital to our assessment of women's present and future prospects.

This is, quite properly, a book about women. It is also an optimistic book. Without offering a conventional feminist account—in noting greater complexity of motive and result than some feminists emphasize—the author certainly shares an enthusiasm for women's initiatives and their outcomes, particularly in the work-force gains. Yet the book also reflects some of the tensions and sacrifices that have accompanied change at various stages. Some readers may also wonder about possible drawbacks resulting from the shifts that are described, ranging from a possible decline in domestic civility and esteem for children to some issues of economic productivity, to the heightened divisions among women (as well as men) in demographic experience and economic success, to the consequences of demographic stagnation for the larger society. We know, in essence, that a revolution has occurred, but we are far from having a grasp of its longer-term effects, particularly from vantage points other than those of successfully employed adult women. This book does not, as a primary purpose, attempt to fathom these effects. It is, however, written with an awareness of pitfalls as well as of gains. Its very success in showing what women's change has entailed—and what has not changed—provides a basis for wider assessments: for anguish at a revolution not yet completed; for worry about some larger outcomes; and, to be sure, for rejoicing at what has been gained.

PETER N. STEARNS
Carnegie Mellon University

Acknowledgments

This book brings together the ideas, advice, suggestions, grievances, criticisms, contributions, and efforts of many people. I can identify only a few, but I hope that all the others will understand my appreciation of them.

Carnegie Mellon University, more than any other institution, shaped my life and sharpened my skills during the fifteen years that my husband and I spent there. During that period my three daughters each received one or more CMU degrees, and I earned my doctorate in history. CMU was and always will be my intellectual base.

Dr. Peter N. Stearns, Professor of History and now the Head of the Carnegie Mellon History Department, served as advisor, critic, and friend. With Peter as a role model, writing a book, if not easy, at least seemed possible and natural.

The middle period of writing a book, from first sketches to final copy, recalls the dark ages—the bright ideas survive, but their luster seems lost amid the drudgery. Special thanks in those difficult days go to Patience Evans, who carefully and imaginatively edited drafts and researched weak areas; to Kay Knight, who typed flawless copy faster than anyone I have ever known; and to Patty Van Horn, for creating the graphs and charts.

While they are acknowledged in the notes, I also wish to recognize some of the other historians and social scientists whose writings informed and inspired me: Carl N. Degler, Leslie Tentler, Lois Scharf, Gerda Lerner, and Richard Easterlin.

Finally, I wish to thank my husband, Richard L. Van Horn. He introduced me to the wonderful world of word-processing, a major benefit for all authors, especially new ones who need to revise frequently. While sometimes borrowing ideas from me for his own papers and speeches, he gave in return a wealth of ideas and suggestions from a different perspective.

CHAPTER I

Introduction

Today in the United States women appear to be enjoying greater freedom of action than at any time in the past. Entry is permitted into a wider range of jobs, careers, and domestic arrangements than at any other time in history. A woman may reject marriage or child-rearing and pursue only a career. She even may select single parenthood, with little loss of status. The traditional option of full-time marriage with child-rearing at home remains available, but increasingly women combine paid work outside the home with marriage and child-rearing.

This diversity is in marked contrast to the limited choice of jobs and professions available to women throughout most of the twentieth century. The usual domestic arrangements open to women before 1960 included marriage and homemaking, with a possible job after the children had grown, or spinster status, with a slightly wider career choice but severely limited social and sexual options. Most young women of the 1980s would find these older choices unacceptable.

Most people in the early twentieth century would have rejected today's emphasis on paid work outside the home as damaging both to women themselves and to the stability of society. In the preface to Bessie Van Vorst's *The Woman Who Toils*, President Theodore Roosevelt wrote in 1903, "If the women do not recognize that the greatest thing for any woman is to be a good wife and mother, why, that nation has caused to be alarmed about its future."[1]

President Roosevelt's concern with the future of motherhood may
have been a result of the rapid decline in fertility rates in the nineteenth century. The historic peak of fertility in the late eighteenth
century gave way to a steep decline that showed no sign of change
until 1900, when the pace of downward movement slowed down
slightly. Figure 1.1 shows the changes in fertility rates in the United
States in the nineteenth and twentieth centuries.

A decline in the number of children did not lead to rejection of
motherhood. The new options for women came, not from a sudden
revolution, but from a history of gradual, erratic evolution. Already
in 1900, many women worked for pay in the marketplace. The great
majority were young single women, and most of them hoped to marry
and leave their paid jobs before they reached thirty years of age. The
gender-segregated labor market limited the range of jobs available to

FIGURE 1.1
Birth Rates, 1800 to 1983.

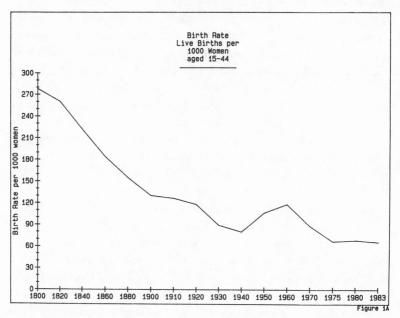

Sources: U.S. Bureau of the Census, *Historical Statistics of the United States: Colonial Times to 1970*
(Bicentennial Edition, Part I), Washington, D.C., 1975, Series B 5-10, p. 49; U.S. Bureau of the
Census, *Statistical Abstract of the United States: 1986* (107th Edition), Washington, D.C., 1986, p. 57.

women in 1900 almost exclusively to clerical work, some areas of factory work, domestic service, teaching, and nursing. In contrast, the
potential choices available in 1986 span the full range of jobs open to
men, including such former male bastions as police, mining, construction, and corporation management. Women, however, still find substantial barriers to their entry into the more desirable jobs.

The change from the limited role of 1900 to the more extensive
choices of 1986 included innovative effort by women themselves to
respond to new circumstances in politics and the economy. Women's
individual decisions throughout the twentieth century created the elements of a clear trend toward greater participation in the work force
and improvements in their position. Society's attitudes were sufficiently flexible in practice to permit some changes in women's roles
despite strong ideological constraints.

Change in women's lives depended upon neither ideological consistency nor political action. Women's lives, family roles, jobs, and attitudes changed substantially during the twentieth century. Much of
this change resulted from their efforts in their own lives to find satisfactory roles in an advanced industrial society, and in so doing to
redefine, in operational terms, women's proper place. By 1980 women
had acquired a visible and extensive role in the mainstream of modern
society.

Family and Work in Historical Perspective

The goal of this book is to explore and analyze the relationship between women's work and career choices and those of marriage, fertility, and child-rearing. Such an analysis is realistic and appropriate
because women work and rear children at the same time, and their
concept of self includes both roles. Historians have emphasized the
importance of what Daniel Scott Smith has called the "critical relationship of family structure and roles to the possibilities for full participation by women in the larger society."[2] Carl Degler, in his major
work on the history of women in the United States, has examined the
degree to which family roles are "at odds" with women's complete
and equal participation in work, politics, and power structures within
American society.[3]

Throughout most of history, women have pursued both family and work activities in combination. In preindustrial societies women performed both roles simultaneously in the home, but the requirements of each activity differed markedly from modern work and child-rearing norms. At a time with intensive requirements for neither work nor child care, a premodern woman could diminish her attention to one or the other activity. Work hours, although long, were more flexible than those of most modern employees; and, in turn, the requirements of child-rearing did not conflict markedly with the requirements of work. While premodern life often was harsh by modern standards, it did offer a central role for women that blended work and family.

With the emergence of industrial society, child care and economic production for the first time took place at separate locations and forced a separation of roles. The specialization of modern society changed a historic role for women into a contemporary problem. The separation of the workplace from the home required a long period of transition. Even in 1900 almost half the population still produced at home. The final phase of this shift occurred only in the twentieth century. Women's role as the keeper of the home remained intact, but the home itself changed markedly in function from economic production of goods and children to consumption of goods and nurture of children.

The shift of work from the household to modern centralized workplaces imposed the need for new adaptations for work and child-rearing. The most frequent practice in the nineteenth century left married women in the home and moved men and single women to the modern workplace. Women in the twentieth century retained their traditional role of special involvement with the home and family, but their role in economic production changed as this function moved out of the home into the modern workplace.

Women's twentieth-century experience called forth a search for a modern version of their premodern dual role. Although concurrent child-rearing and homemaking have dominated women's lives during child-bearing years in this century, paid work outside the home has become increasingly important. The growth of the women's labor force since 1920 has resulted largely from the increased participation of married women. Between 1900 and 1980 the percentage of married women employed outside the home increased from a small 5.6 percent to a substantial majority of nearly 60 percent.

The increasing importance of paid work for women complemented rather than replaced the importance of fertility. Less than 15 percent of married women have remained childless in the twentieth century, and marriage itself became increasingly popular, at least until 1970. Although the prevailing trend of fertility rates (number of births for each 1,000 women of child-bearing age) has been down, fertility rates from 1940 to 1960 showed substantial increase at the same time that work participation was increasing rapidly.[4]

By the end of the 1970s women's orientation had shifted toward a strong emphasis on paid work, clearly at the cost of a decline in fertility. In the two most recent decades, married women increasingly chose paid work outside the home, and correspondingly they limited, postponed, or rejected child-bearing and maternal child care. Low fertility rates coincided with a massively expanding female labor force.

In the later years of the 1980s both work and fertility curves appear to be finding a new equilibrium that includes high work rates for married women and low but no longer declining fertility rates. This stability of work and fertility rates is new in American twentieth-century experience. As work participation becomes the new norm for women, the fertility choice must often adjust to the demands of women's work, a relationship new in the 1980s. The normal pattern in most of the twentieth century has been the dependence of women's work on the requirements of fertility.

Historical Change

Women's work and fertility behavior in the twentieth century can be arranged in three periods of change in both fertility rates and work-force participation. The first period, starting with the U.S. Census of 1900 and ending with the census of 1940, began with high fertility rates and low work rates and was characterized by an inverse relationship between work and fertility—increasing work and declining fertility. In the second census period, the years between 1940–1960, rapid increases occurred simultaneously in both fertility and work rates. Work and fertility rates resumed their inverse relationship in the third period between the censuses of 1960 and 1980. In the last period, women achieved work rates higher than ever before in American history and low fertility rates that approached the zero population growth rate. Figure 1.2 illustrates graphically the three periods of different relationships between married women's paid work and fertility rates.

The importance of the variables of work and fertility in defining women's daily lives justifies their use in an analytic framework in women's history. Women of all social classes can place themselves within this framework, based upon their roles as mothers and workers. The dual framework is important because women pursue both activities. The changing relationship between the two variables thus offers a basic insight into change within women's lives.

Change between the periods exceeds change within them. In the most recent period, the decline in fertility as work rates increase re-

FIGURE 1.2

Trend Comparison: Birth Rates and Labor Force Participation.

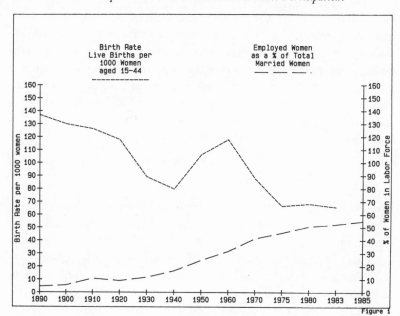

Sources: Historical Statistics, p. 49; Statistical Abstract of the United States: 1981, p. 57, p. 398

veals at a glance the scope of change in the last two decades. The continuing strong emphasis on work in the 1980s suggests that women may redefine their lives to include yet further reductions in fertility. Future prediction would be rash without assessment of the periods in which work and fertility did not correlate so "logically"—the middle period, for example, when work and fertility moved upward together. The middle period and the most recent period, between 1940–1960 and 1960–1980, provide a strong contrast, and relate closely to public policy issues and personal role decisions for contemporary women. However, the first period, from 1900 to 1940, sets the stage for understanding women's whole experience in the 20th century.

Some change within periods and consistency between them also describes the twentieth-century history of work and fertility. The long historical perspective highlights the length of trends and the tenacity of behavior patterns in family and gender roles. For example, fertility has never declined below the replacement level, despite the gradual, persistent emergence of women out of the home and into the work force. Marriage rates throughout the twentieth century have stayed higher than those of Western preindustrial society. Women have retained a strong identification with family roles even today, when paid work appears to be women's major preoccupation.

Women in the twentieth century have been concerned about both parts of their traditional role: the rearing of children in a family setting and the search for economic productivity—in modern times a paid role in the workplace. Women in their search for their proper place in the twentieth century have tried many combinations of work and fertility.

Both work and child-bearing also allow married women to achieve goals based on assumptions of right behavior or future satisfactions. Paid work and the raising of children both create resources for the future, or, in economic terms, they create human or financial capital. Since fertility requires consumption, and work provides resources for consumption, work and fertility directly complement each other.

Choosing between work and fertility represents a complex decision process involving personal goals, economic factors, consumption choices, and appropriate family and sex role behavior. Individual decisions for both work and fertility result from a complex set of inputs including events, attitudes, and trends, and are affected by personal utility, desired goals, and, of course, constraints, both external and internal.

Despite the occasional impact of a major event upon women's work and family roles, a perspective of the whole twentieth century shows both the importance and the consistency of long trends. Married women's work participation has moved steadily upward. Successive groups of women have chosen to work for widely varying reasons during the long period of eighty-six years. With the exception of some workers in World War I and II, no recognizable group of women workers has won entry into the work force only to disappear in later years. Women's long progress in work behavior is characterized by incremental changes always in the direction of increasing participation in the work force.

Fertility rates have shown less consistency, particularly during the baby-boom period, but even here patterns emerge. The lowest rates have never fallen below replacement level. The highest rates occurred in the early part of the twentieth century, a part of the long process of decline from the high rates that characterized premodern societies. Despite the fascinating aberration of the twenty-year baby boom, fertility rates have moved relentlessly downward throughout the twentieth century.

Married women who chose to work always had to find accommodations with the demands of marriage and family. Women today are still searching for a satisfactory way to pursue their historical dual role of mother and worker. The experiences of women throughout the twentieth century provided the values, norms, expectations, practices, and ideology that define women's varied roles today.

CHAPTER 2

Women in 1900

A study of women at the close of the nineteenth century provides a basis for comparison with twentieth-century changes. Although full-time motherhood occupied most married women in 1900, fertility rates continued the long downward trend from the high levels reached in the 18th century. But the more visible decline in fertility that would be the prevailing pattern in the twentieth century was about to begin. Married women's work rates reflected the same lack of immediate dramatic change, for the 4 percent rate of 1890 was followed by 5 percent in 1900. Here too the pattern of slow growth would soon be replaced by new developments in women's work in the twentieth century.

In the larger context, society had changed significantly. The United States had been recognized as a mature industrial society committed to urbanization and modernization. The capital base for industry, which would soon produce the greatest volume of goods of any industrial country in the world, had been created by 1900. The emergence of the United States as an industrial power of the first rank had a major impact upon women's work and family role. Women's traditional roles, already seriously undermined in the 19th century, would soon become even more visibly inadequate. Twentieth-century women would need to seek new behavior more appropriate for industrial and urban life.

The balance between urban and rural residents was shifting rapidly in favor of urban residents. Already in 1900, 45 percent of the population lived outside rural areas, and the economic value of urban industrial production had long surpassed that of rural farm production. A new wave of immigrants flowed into the cities; their numbers would reach a peak of over one million new entrants in 1907. The rapid process of urbanization was a well-recognized trend by the late nineteenth century. Thus, most change for women would occur within an urban world.

Another important change affected women directly. By the late 19th century, society had established the basis for eliminating the immense legal and medical gap between the genders that had developed in earlier centuries. Married women acquired the legal right to keep their own earnings and to control their own property. To be sure, most married women did not actively exercise these rights. However, the acquisition of a legal existence afforded women the possibility of assuming a more economically independent role within marriage.[1]

The medical establishment itself proved the fallacy of women's biological inferiority. In 1894 researchers at Harvard Medical School disproved the theory that women breathed differently from men and thus had weaker brains. Despite the new evidence, the assumptions of psychological and biological gender differences continued to define women as inferior. However, science had at least opened the way to recognition of women's physical and biological potential and made possible a more favorable context for the development of new roles for women in the future.[2]

A few persistent women achieved at least token representation in a diverse range of occupations, professions, and leisure pursuits hitherto totally dominated by men. The emergence of some female physicians, lawyers, professors, journalists, and a bank president suggested that women had more extensive intellectual capabilities than had been accepted earlier in the twentieth century. The occasional woman sea-captain, lumberjack, union leader, or mountain climber challenged the assumption of the female's inherent physical weakness.

One of these urban pioneers, Elizabeth Seaman, intrepid journalist of *The New York World* in the 1880's, is discussed by Lois Banner in her history of women in modern America. Elizabeth's pseudonym of Nellie Bly (from the well-known song by Stephen Foster) allowed her some anonymity in her role as exposer of corruption and exploitation in factories, insane asylums, and jails. Editors found her stories compelling and published them despite their female authorship. Nellie Bly is most famous for her journey around the world in seventy-two days in 1889, surpassing the eighty-day record of the fictional Phileas Fogg.[3]

By the end of the nineteenth century some women actively participated in politics at a high level, despite the handicap of being nonvoting citizens. Women served in juries in several Western states, and in 1900 the Republican National Convention admitted them as regular delegates. Two major contemporary political movements, Populism and Prohibition, welcomed not only female participation but also women's leadership. In addition, the long and active campaign to secure the final ratification of the women's suffrage amendment to the U.S. Constitution occupied the efforts of many women.

Women, then, on the eve of the twentieth century, did not live in a society characterized by rigid separation of gender roles. They had begun to assume visible public roles that included occupational diversity and political activity. As women succeeded in nontraditional pursuits and as laws protected women's rights to their own property and earnings, the insistence that women were the inferior gender started to abate.

In 1900, however, most women still remained in the private sphere where they had made their greatest gains in the nineteenth century. Their power in the home had grown as life styles changed. The functions of domesticity and sanctuary provided by women had become primary concerns for families. The home developed as women's separate sphere when men left home for the workplace. Women managed the home on a daily basis, and they alone provided most of the direct parental care of the children. This was a profound change from traditional and preindustrial society. Previously men had worked at home and supervised everyone's activities at the same time; husband and wife jointly tended the children's needs.

During the nineteenth century economic responsibilities within the home shifted. Women made many of the consumption decisions. Frequently working men turned over their pay to their wives, who then bought goods and services for the whole family. But, at the same time, patriarchal authority remained strong; men defined the basic setting in which the family functioned. At all levels of society the father brought home the bulk of the family's economic resources. The wife and children showed him the deference owed the symbolic head of the family, but the husband's daily absence left a power vacuum that only the wife could fill.

Daniel Scott Smith underscored the increasing power and auton-omy of the wife and mother within the upper-middle-class Victorian family. He showed that women gained greater control over sex and reproduction within marriage. He argued that the declining fertility rates in the nineteenth century and women's increasing use of contra-ception showed that women had achieved greater control over their own bodies. The emphasis on the importance of female enjoyment of sexual relations in nineteenth-century marriage manuals furnished ad-ditional support for this hypothesis. At the same time, women wielded more power within the family. Less burdened by frequent childbear-ing, they retained their health well into middle age. True, these ex-periences were far from widespread among all social classes. But some of the practices of the middle class, especially the reduction of the birth rate, afforded a model that other classes would eventually emu-late.[4]

The new family style allowed increased discretionary time for lei-sure. Women used these extra hours for activities that still harmonized with the concept of separate spheres. However, they did not neces-sarily remain within the home. The woman's club movement peaked in 1900. Clubwomen worked at reforming the world as well as man-aging their own homes. The idea of "municipal housekeeping" ex-tended women's domestic and nurturing traits into the public sphere. Applied to such problems as factory abuse, resource conservation, child labor outside the home, and sewage disposal, municipal housekeeping became part of a search for moral and domestic perfection in the larger society. Thus, women could still operate within the approved limits of their separate sphere and include new activities and new roles. All they had to do was extend the boundaries of their traditional realm.[5]

The concept of a separate sphere posed no obstacle to women's substantial educational achievement. On the average, women at the turn of the century had more years of formal schooling than did men. To be sure, more men continued their education beyond secondary school, but women, too, could attend college. They could choose between one of the women's colleges, such as Mount Holyoke, founded by Mary Lyon in 1837 in South Hadley, Massachusetts, or one of the many state universities and land-grant colleges founded after the Civil War. The University of Texas, created by a provision in the state constitution of 1876 and founded in 1884, soon had almost as many women students as men. Additionally, many women attended "normal schools," posteducational institutions that offered two to four years of teacher training.

Some male educational bastions still remained resistant to female attempts at admission. Many graduate schools and most professional schools that taught medicine, law, and engineering either refused to admit women or limited their numbers to miniscule minorities. But, even here, women managed some minimal success. In 1900 male medical schools allowed admission to women, who soon comprised almost 10 percent of the student body. This percentage declined as female medical schools closed their doors in the belief that regular medical schools were now easily available to any women who could qualify for admission. Even at a 5 percent rate, however, women medical students exceeded the number of law students. In 1891 only 200 of the 100,000 practicing lawyers were women.[6]

Society valued educational achievement for women precisely because they were the custodians of the home and trainers of the young. How could a woman who was unable to seek, read, understand, and act upon the advice given to her properly rear her children? This important function required knowledge. Women needed more than skills in arithmetic to manage the family's consumption efficiently. They had to be able to decide judiciously between conflicting claims made for competing products.

Society also recognized that many women would spend as many as ten working years between completing school and getting married. Girls who prepared for clerical jobs or positions as schoolteachers passed this time productively. Schooling for immigrant women and blacks was also viewed as essential because these groups needed to be instructed in the dominant value system, including their appropriate gender roles, and in the rudimentary knowledge that enabled unmarried women to get jobs.[7]

The private sphere, however, remained women's primary domain, although many women became involved in modern society in novel ways for short periods. These new roles encouraged or required women to leave the home temporarily to be students, paid workers, consumers, or reformers. By 1900 women's preindustrial activities had changed extensively, although not always to women's advantage.

For example, black women had moved into the labor force in much higher numbers than white women. Although most of them pursued the traditional occupations of domestic service and agricultural labor, some black women did find jobs in factories. Even in 1900 studies have shown that in some areas almost 20 percent of black households had women as heads of household. Thus many black women had substantial responsibilities as primary providers, an exceedingly difficult role in a society that did not encourage married women and mothers to leave home for paid work.[8]

On the other hand, farm women who worked at home as an integral part of the work force of the family farm were beginning to find their work lives less harsh than they had been throughout the nineteenth century. Home spinning and weaving were no longer necessary for many families, for cloth could be purchased at reasonable prices. The responsibility of preparing meals for family and farm hands had been eased in many farm homes by the purchase of cast-iron stoves with ovens and small iceboxes that permitted short-term food storage. The kitchen garden maintained by the farm wife also could be a source of cash that was used to benefit the family.

The major changes in farm life, however, awaited further technological and organizational change that would not occur until after 1920. The twentieth century would also see a substantial decline in the number of family farms. But in 1900 the work of a farm wife still occupied almost half the married women in the United States.

Married women in 1900 still spent most of their time in the home; with few modifications they would remain there for the next forty years. Provision of basic services to a husband, childbirth, and childrearing remained the common denominators of women's activities, be they rural, urban, immigrant, native, middle class, working class, black, or white. But, beyond this central and crucial similarity in activities, tremendous variations in all other dimensions characterized the lives of women at the turn of the century. In fact, 1900 may be the peak year for extremes in the distribution of income, multiplicity of national origin, diversity in occupations, and differences in fertility rates among different groups. For this discussion the most relevant of these factors is the differential fertility.

Fertility and Family

On the average, fertility rates from 1800–1940 showed continual decline. However, in the years between 1870 and 1915 we find extremes of differential fertility among different groups within the society. This pattern reflects the high fertility of traditional groups such as native rural farm residents and recent immigrant groups, in contrast with the declining fertility of modern groups. Differential fertility peaked in the early twentieth century in response to the variations in the levels of involvement with an industrial society.[9]

White native urban residents, particularly the middle class, had cut their birth rates in the nineteenth century. Native white working-class parents followed similar behavior only a bit later. In 1910, 25 percent of the completed urban families had only two children, and if we look only at cities in the Middle Atlantic and Great Lakes states the percentage of families with only two children rises as high as 40 percent. In strong contrast to this decline, the high fertility patterns characteristic of traditional societies remained intact in some rural areas, especially those most recently at the frontier. Fertility rates of the wives of farm owners, however, had already turned downward in the 19th century, but on the average rural fertility remained high until after 1920.[10]

At the same time, the fertility rates of immigrants and blacks substantially exceeded those of native white Americans throughout the period between 1870 and 1915. As Figure 2.1 shows, black fertility peaked in 1885, and the birth rates of immigrant groups showed the greatest variation from the fertility of native white Americans in 1915.

Rural and urban fertility maintained a wide and relatively constant gap throughout this period that spanned the turn of the century.

Richard Easterlin identified further refinements in the variation between rural and urban fertility. He showed that the highest birth rates occurred in rural frontier societies, the lowest in the older established cites. Between these extremes lie the old rural societies and new, fast-growing cities, both of which have moderate birth rates. The urban areas show slightly lower rates than the older rural locales.[11]

Perhaps the most satisfactory explanation for these particular variations can be found in an examination of economic factors. Availability of cheap land on the frontier and the presence of economic opportunity in the newer cities offered positive conditions for producing children. Children were perceived to have the greatest economic value in frontier societies and the least worth in the older cities. Economic

FIGURE 2.1

Differential Fertility: Birth Rate Trends by Population Group.

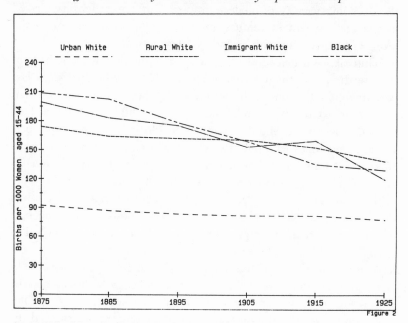

Sources: Richard Easterlin, *Population, Labor Force and Long Swings in Economic Growth* (New York, 1968), Tables C-3 and C-5, pp. 226, 228; *Historical Statistics,* p. 54.

opportunity is perceptibly more abundant on the frontier and in the newer cities, and children represent a more useful labor source on the farm than they do in any urban setting.

The American experience, however, included some unique features that accentuated the causal relationship between the differential pace of entry into industrial society and the corresponding variation in fertility rates. A wide diversity of urban and rural patterns in the United States described this period. Old cities, new cities, stable agricultural areas, and frontier agriculture existed simultaneously within one country. Successive waves of foreign immigration during the nineteenth century had maintained a continually diverse population at varied stages of modernization. Immigration, primarily from the eastern and southern European countries, reached its peak in 1907. The later immigrants often retained intact their preindustrial and rural value system that included high fertility. Immigrants had left their homelands out of a desire to achieve a new life in the United States, but they clung to traditional behavior.

The high fertility of blacks at the turn of the century may have been related to their rural origins. In this reasoning, the high birth rates among blacks resulted more from their occupations and residences than from a unique racial experience. A possible alternative is that blacks, only a generation removed from slavery and still segregated, saw family life as a refuge from an uncaring society. The usual relationship between the emergence of modern attitudes and a decline in fertility suggests a third interpretation for the high black birth rate. Fertility might have remained high because blacks lacked experiences similar to those of the white population. Few blacks lived in cities in 1900 where they might have acquired new fertility norms like those of the white population. Most blacks remained in rural environments that in the early twentieth century still included high fertility for most whites as well as for blacks.

Differential fertility at the turn of the century related closely to the larger social changes in the United States. The frontier remained in a few places in the United States along with older agricultural areas. A wide diversity of urban centers included older established cities and new, burgeoning ones. Perception of economic opportunity, be it in the form of cheap land or jobs in the city, supplied a crucial variable that explains the persistence of relatively high birth rates for some groups. Economic opportunity encouraged both parents and children to expect future prosperity.

The diversity in fertility behavior peaked in the first decade of the twentieth century because of the wide variety in the composition of the population and of their livelihoods. The largest number of immigrants arrived during that period. At the same time, over half the population remained rural, either in older areas or on the frontier. In contrast, established urban residents, especially the white middle class, had already lived as many as three generations in urban society, where they had developed new attitudes toward family size.

Family size varied more widely in 1900 than at any later time in the twentieth century. Differential fertility accentuated wide variations among groups. Married couples who produced families of more than eight children in 1900 included those who retained traditional economic reasons for high child production or traditional expectations and values that prized large families. However, at the same time, these couples had arrived at a higher standard of living that included better nutrition and health than in earlier times. A family that included eight or more surviving children shows the results of improvements in health for mothers and babies but an almost certain absence of any form of explicit birth control.

A completed family size of five children required a conscious attempt at birth control, despite its resemblance to the average surviving family in the traditional society. By 1915, because of the decline in infant mortality, the creation of a family comparable to the premodern family in size and spacing required some effort at controlling fertility. Survival rates for children at the turn of the century showed improvement even in urban areas. This trend led to the need for new controls to stabilize families at the traditional number of 5 children surviving to maturity. The high birth rates of traditional society were no longer obligatory to produce a family of five children, still considered by some people to be the optimum size.[12]

Already, however, the urban middle class and some of the working class and many farm owners in the established agricultural areas were choosing a "normal" family size of two to three children. These groups were the first to develop modern attitudes. They chose a smaller family size because it appropriately matched the goals of their household in quality of child-rearing and increased capital formation. As early as 1820 a modernizing middle class, a group that had already developed modified roles for women within the home, became identifiable in eastern urban areas. By 1900, their ideas had spread throughout the white urban population.[13]

Wide divergences in family size in early-twentieth-century United States were symptomatic of the ongoing process of differential modernization. However, the differences were intensified in the United States, which had an unusually heterogeneous society composed of immigrants of peasant heritage, frontier farmers, and rural blacks as well as urban whites.

All the groups, however, emphasized the importance of an intense family life despite the other diversities. The vast majority of the population lived in families; marriage rates were high; and few married couples remained childless. In this period the family played a stabilizing role in a society undergoing rapid social change. The family offered a refuge for immigrants bewildered by a new and strange environment. Children still represented an economic asset and source of labor for many people. And, for the middle class, the Victorian family ideal remained strong even though women had increased their power within the family and had developed new roles in society.

In their book *Women in the American Economy*, Elliot and Mary Brownlee underscored the importance of the role of the family at the turn of the century. They recognized the family as a major unit of socialization, all the more vital since society appeared to be fragmented into many unrelated groups. In the "bewildering social flux" only the family could inculcate basic values in children in their early years. The need for stability required all institutions, including the family, to increase the emphasis on the important task of socialization.[14]

All groups in this period shared the belief that married women should stay in the household. The woman was supposed to be involved primarily with the family. This consistency provided a common basis for family strength and stability, but at the same time it limited the variety of roles that women could assume. The middle-class version of perfect homemaking, quality child-rearing, and family nurture presented only one possible model for family formation. Still, it was one that all groups could understand and one with which they could agree in principle. Native working-class women as well as recent immigrants stayed in the home except in drastic family emergencies that required them temporarily to leave the hearth and to bring wages home from the workplace. Yet, even then, families explored every other alternative before the wife and mother left home to work.

Women, then, remained at home; it was their common ground. But household activities varied greatly among groups. Women did not freely choose their activities according to their own private goals. Instead, the economic resources of the family and the husband's occupation determined each woman's individual roles.

Work at Home

At least four variables—social class level, rural or urban residence, degree of modernization, and the value system of individual families— defined the nature of women's work in the home at the turn of the century. A few American families still lived in the old traditional way and produced most of their own goods for home consumption. In these cases, usually in isolated rural or frontier areas, all family members participated in the production of goods. Women in this mode scarcely discerned any differentiation between family and work roles. Indeed, they lived integrated, if harsh and demanding, lives; they cooperated in the economic production of goods at the same time that they reared children. However, this was the rare exception. The family as an independent, self-sufficient microeconomic unit had almost disappeared in the years following the American Civil War.

A slightly different economic role for women was that of working at home to produce goods for sale in the marketplace rather than for household consumption. The family farm, producing for the market, appears as the most prevalent example of this production unit. All the family members worked together to harvest food to be sold. Farm women had serious and important responsibilities. They functioned either as partners to farmer husbands or as their necessary assistants. Without help from his wife, a man could not bear the extensive work load of farming. By 1900 women were less likely to work directly in the fields than they had in the nineteenth century. Still, care of animals, preparation of goods for the market, and maintenance of some of the equipment remained primarily women's chores.

Farm women worked at their tasks of housekeeping and child care without the sense of a clear separation from their economically productive functions as farm workers. In 1900 homemaking and child-rearing in such households as this remained closer to traditional customs than the newer style of domesticity and quality nurture so dear to the urban middle class. Nevertheless, farm and home production remained a dominant way of life at the turn of the century.

A few other occupational groups still lived in the traditional arrangement in which the family and the workplace were integrated. In 1900 some craft shops, such as blacksmithing and printing, retained this premodern form. Many small retail stores operated out of the household. Law and medicine could still be practiced at home, and, of course, many ministers even to this day practice their profession at home with the help of their families.

In the early years of the long trend toward separation of the home and the workplace, many workers found it distressing to be forced to leave home to work. Yet by 1900 the outside job had become an acceptable way of life. This trend continued inexorably throughout the twentieth century, although remnants of traditionalism are still with us. Small hotels and inns, an occasional Ma and Pa grocery store, and the country doctor and lawyer in isolated rural areas preserve the older pattern in which work in the household blended with the family environment. In these situations women pursued economically productive work without any extensive difficulties of integrating it with their family roles. Women and families have gained benefits from the newer style of separation, but they have suffered substantial loss in the economically productive work roles of the older way of life.

Work at home for pay offered women some replacement for the disappearing traditional forms of work. This was a transitional model between traditional and modern forms of work—traditional because it happened in the home and was integrated with child-rearing; modern because women worked for pay in an occupation separate from the work of their husbands. Descriptions of rural transitional work appeared regularly in contemporary fictional writing. Farm wives sold their own butter, chicken, eggs, vegetables. Willa Cather, in several of her semiautobiographical novels, described such work as a frequent and well-accepted activity for women, whereby they supplemented the family's resources with cash.[15]

Taking in boarders, a more urban form of transitional work, became a major industry for women at the end of the 19th century. A 1907 study of New York City by the U.S. Department of Labor revealed that half the working-class households in the city kept boarders. In 1923, a similar study of the 9,767 female "breadwinners" in Passaic, New Jersey (a group encompassing 45 percent of the total female population over fourteen years old in the city), showed that 19.4 percent of them still earned money at home by taking in boarders and lodgers. In this way, city women as well as farm wives managed to add cash to the family resources.[16]

An older form of transitional work for women, that of cottage industry, also persisted into the twentieth century. As late as the year 1923, 24,000 married women in New York state embroidered, sewed, and made artificial flowers at home. Many women did home laundering and sewing for private clients in 1900, but these occupations did not long remain as options. Steam laundries replaced home laundering by 1910, and home sewing for pay has shown a steady and long decline throughout the twentieth century.[17]

In 1900 transitional work for women in the home was still plentiful. However, economically productive work in the home—either direct production of goods and services for market or active assistance of the husband in family businesses—was only a temporary expedient. The trend of decline in work at home for pay was already apparent.

Women needed to replace these transitional activities. They usually chose full-time homemaking and child-rearing, a modern type of work highly valued in 1900. Homemaking and domesticity already had a long history by 1900, and they formed an alternative that in no way threatened the contemporary value system. The roots of domesticity reach back to colonial times. The urban middle class, the most modern group in the nineteenth century, had embraced domesticity enthusiastically and defined its major components.

The major elements of domesticity were quality child-rearing and a high standard of housekeeping. In households that included economic production, women had concerned themselves with more immediate tasks than decorating the home attractively. In the newer domestic style, meals, formerly interruptions in the work day, became more important, and women spent more time at food preparation and at achieving a more gracious style of serving meals. The new goal was to create an environment of beauty, warmth, and sanctuary. An integral element in this new life style was a level of child nurturing that focused the primary attention of the mother on the individual development and training of each son or daughter.[18]

This cozy portrait of domesticity described the ideal of the time, but many women probably fell far short of this paradigm not only in actual achievement but also in aspiration. Still, there was abundant advice for the homemaker. As early as the nineteenth century, women's magazines published weekly or monthly instructions for setting goals for quality homemaking and detailed methods for reaching them.[19]

In 1900 society defined the ideal woman as the wife and mother exclusively involved in homemaking. All groups aspired to this style of family life. Additionally, the association of this style with the upper middle class inexorably bound homemaking and domesticity into the universe of values associated with upward mobility. The farm wife who had a parlor in which to entertain her friends considered herself more fortunate than her neighbor who had only a large kitchen. The extra room implied attainment of an economic level that permitted this form of consumption. Working-class families could not always enjoy the whole domesticity package, yet they could at least have a mother who remained in the home to provide good meals and clean clothes.

The insistence on the importance of the home and a mother who remained there originated in economic necessity. The value system of traditional society recognized that the wife was an integral component of the joint economic production of a married couple within the household. The importance of mother's remaining at the hearth lost its original justification when the locus of economic production moved out of the home. Nevertheless, nineteenth-century society continually reinforced the imperative that women remain in the home, with the new modern emphasis on the importance of domesticity.

In the early twentieth century the two separate ethics of the past—

the traditional pattern and the modern one of the urban middle class, both of which emphasized the presence of the woman in the home— merged with the aspirations for upward mobility. The synthesis created an ethic that all social classes supported of the woman as mother and custodian of the home. Both past experience and hopes for the future required mothers to remain in the home, protecting and reinforcing its value.

The Modern Workplace

A few married women chose a more radical alternative to remaining in the home, or were forced by circumstances to do so. Such unwitting innovators began the long upward trend of married women's work for pay in the marketplace. Many of these women paid high costs in health and vitality in harsh, difficult jobs. They faced the added difficulty of living and working in opposition to prevailing concepts of women's proper place. Further, they assumed work for pay in addition to their household responsibilities. Women throughout the twentieth century have coped with the problems of this double burden.

Single women entered the work force in substantial numbers long before married women. Until after 1940 the majority of employed women were single. Between 1880 and 1910 the women's share of the total labor force nearly doubled. Single women entering the work force accounted for most of this remarkable growth from 14.7 percent to 28.8 percent.[20]

Few married women sought gainful employment, but their numbers increased too. The 1890 census showed 4 percent of married women to be working. Thirty years later, in 1920, the total was 9 percent. In this period single women not only made up a numerical majority but held a larger proportion of the high status jobs than did married women.[21]

Women's jobs remained strongly segregated by gender; nevertheless, they included occupations at varied income and status levels. Industrial expansion increased the demand for typists and filing clerks. Women captured clerical positions in addition to their gender-segregated factory jobs, such as spinning, packaging, cigar-making, textile work, and food processing that they had occupied for several decades.

Domestic service remained a major job classification, especially for married women, until after 1920. Young unmarried women worked as sales persons in the new department stores, and they also taught at elementary schools.

Professional women, usually of middle-class origins, served as librarians and nursed the sick. Although in 1890 these professions required only a little more than a high-school education, more stringent standards developed early in the twentieth century. This increasing professionalization encouraged women to greater educational achievement to prepare for specific careers.[22]

In 1900 young unmarried women made up the great majority of the female labor force in both professional areas and clerical and factory jobs. More than half of all women between twenty and twenty-four remained single; half of these were still unmarried at the age of twenty-nine. Since most girls finished school between the ages of sixteen and nineteen, frequently as many as ten years elapsed before they married. Many young women spent this time working for pay outside the home. They either contributed to their family's support or saved money for their own future families.[23]

In her loosely autobiographical novel, My Antonia, Willa Cather remembered the wage contributions made by daughters of immigrant farmers in Nebraska. The girls worked in neighboring towns as domestics and on nearby farms as laborers, to buy modern equipment for their fathers and pay off mortgages on their families' farms. Urban wage-earning daughters also provided benefits to their families. According to a Women's Bureau study, 60 percent of the unmarried women workers in Rhode Island shoe factories who lived at home contributed their full wages to the household.[24]

Some historians like the Brownlees have suggested that work experiences gave positive benefits to young women workers. They felt that the working girls increased their sense of independence and self-worth. A more recent observer, Leslie Tentler, in contrast, saw a gloomier result. Her study of the factory work experience of young women in the Eastern cities stressed the long hours of dull work that required no imagination or creativity. Marriage, according to this interpretation, beckoned—a future paradise where women would be free from drudgery.[25]

A contemporary observer includes elements of both these later interpretations. In 1902 Marie Van Vorst, a society woman from Boston, took a job in a factory "out of conscience and curiosity." She had puzzled over the attraction of factory work for young girls. Frequently they left their homes to live in factory boarding houses, only to work long hours in dreary jobs under unpleasant conditions. She decided that the "spirit of adventure" prodded them. The scope of their experiences in the home was so limited, she commented, that they ventured out to try something different, even if it was only factory work.[26]

Nevertheless, if Leslie Tentler is correct in her interpretation, the experience served only to glorify women's concept of home life in the future. It implied that the role of wife would be preferable to that of daughter, a belief that no doubt encouraged family formation and acceptance of life at home by married women of the working class.

Professionally trained women found the workplace equally hazardous and uncertain. Dorothy Richardson, a former country schoolteacher, chronicled her experiences in looking for work in New York in 1905. In her account, she lamented the narrow range of possible job choices and deplored the random hiring methods. She spent all her reserve funds searching unsuccessfully for a respectable job and finally resolved to take the best one she could find. A cigar factory rejected her as inexperienced. She could have worked an 87-hour week in a small store. Again, this time at a candy factory, her lack of experience cost her a chance for employment. Next she rejected a job in an artificial flower factory for $1.50 in weekly wages. Finally she accepted work at a paper-box factory for twice that amount. Soon a sign on a door led to a new job, making artificial flowers for the same $3.00 wage. Unfortunately the job was only temporary. At a laundry "shaking" job, she found that most of her coworkers had been brought in by a man in a cart who picked up job-hunting girls on the street and hauled them in to work.[27]

Not all professionally trained women, however, found their job search so onerous. Emily Quick, a young woman of twenty-five years from Indiana, in 1909 left home to travel to the newly developing Rio Grande valley of Texas. She had put herself through business college in Indiana and then earned a scholarship to Hanover College, where she acquired a B.A. degree in English literature. Accompanied only by her two degrees, she quickly found a job with a land and irrigation company in San Benito, Texas. A developing area, the Rio Grande Valley was in need of workers of many kinds, and Emily was attracted by the chance to be a pioneer. After two years of work, she left her job to marry a young civil engineer from the University of Texas. She raised two children and with her husband managed a ranch and an insurance business in north Texas for the rest of her working life. Like most women of the time, she no longer worked for pay in a separate job outside the home after marriage.[28]

Many of the older large cities offered few jobs to women, and smaller towns and country areas had even more limited possibilities. Pittsburgh, dominated by heavy industry, had the lowest proportion of working women of any large city. By contrast, textile cities in New England had high employment rates for women.[29]

Women's jobs at all levels of status and pay required attitudes, skills, and behavior harmonious with the homemaking role. Care of the sick or helpless, routine maintenance, task implementation and support for male decision makers, and the direct service functions embodied in sales work all strongly resembled the tasks of homemaking. Domestic service directly included all the homemaking tasks. Most women's paid jobs fitted neatly within conventional female role definitions. This fact permitted working single women to retain gender dignity despite their lack of achievement at what was perceived as the ultimate female role— wife and mother. Women's work for pay outside the home did not require substantial changes of attitude and outlook from the homemaking role, although it did sometimes require special skill and training. The similarity of necessary attitudes and qualities might in fact have encouraged women to work outside the home.

However, most married women worked outside the home only when they were economically deprived. A study of 140 wives and widows employed in the glass industry noted that 94 of them either had permanently disabled husbands or had been deserted or widowed. Another 13 had husbands who were drunkards and refused to work. The husbands of 10 were temporarily disabled. The remaining 17 women in the sample were married to men who worked at the lowest level of unskilled labor. Massive job insecurity for men was commonplace in this period; many wives worked only to replace the income of unemployed husbands.[30]

Black women, the most disadvantaged group of all women, flocked into the labor force in the largest numbers. A quarter of all black women worked in 1910, two and a half times the percentage of white women. Herbert Gutman's study of black women and other disadvantaged ethnic groups reported that only Italian women did not have higher work rates than the average in the society. All these groups had lower than average incomes and, thus, a more immediate economic motivation to go out to work. Even in the disadvantaged groups, however, only small minorities of married women worked outside the home.[31]

Married women's low rate of work participation resulted from a combination of economic and ideological factors. Early in the twentieth century, there was an adequate supply of single women to fill most of the jobs defined as women's work. Single women dominated most of the professional work and the service and clerical jobs accepted as suitable for the middle class. Only 5.7 percent of the already small percentage of married women who worked held the higher status jobs in the professions and clerical occupations. Twenty-one percent of the unmarried women workers occupied higher level jobs.[32]

However, economic factors alone cannot explain the low rate of married women's work participation outside the home. Although there was a sufficient supply of single women to satisfy the demand for higher status workers, married women still secured jobs at all levels. This suggests that the opposition to hiring them was not universal. In addition, the fact that many married women who were seriously disadvantaged did not work for pay outside the home casts doubt on the argument that economic need alone explains married women's choice of work for pay. Why, then, did economic need not encourage more poor women to work?

Strong ideological reasons prohibited married women from working, and these reasons operated effectively at all income levels. The intense importance of the home as a force for stability anchored the value system of the period. The invention of homemaking, the new occupation concerned with providing a better family environment, combined with the old traditional ethic that required that women be protected from the outside world. All these reasons played a part in convincing women from all social and economic levels to remain at home.

In 1893 a Labor Department survey showed that even in the worst slum districts of New York, Baltimore, Chicago, and Philadelphia only 5 percent of married women worked. The traditional norm of women-at-home exerted continuing impact in immigrant families. Also the norm coincided with the modern middle-class norm of industrial society in practice, if not in origin.[33]

Existent legal barriers do not explain the discrepancy between the rates of single working women and those of their married sisters. Few, if any, laws existed to prevent married women from working. Laws already on the books protected all women at work. Courts usually upheld state legislation that placed limits on work hours for women, reasoning that women's different biological structure entitled them to special considerations. Still, these laws applied to all women, regardless of marital status. Of all women professionals, only schoolteachers suffered overt discrimination solely because of their marital status. School boards usually refused employment to married teachers and demanded that a woman resign when she married.[34]

Realistically, married women faced formidable barriers to participation in the work force, but they were not primarily barriers erected by society through the legal structure. The inexorable demands of housekeeping, childbearing, and child-rearing barred the way to careers outside the home. If the increased work load was not discouragement enough, the prevailing ideology tended to idealize the homemaking role and castigate the rebel who found it unsatisfying. At the same time, the transitional options, which allowed women to work at home for pay, caused no radical departures in behavior. Society praised industrious women who took in boarders or sold chickens to supplement the family income.

In 1900 the married women's work force exhibited an unequal bimodal distribution by occupation. The lowest representation was in middle-level jobs. A few professional superstars—women trained as doctors, lawyers, librarians, college professors, teachers, or nurses—remained in the work force after marriage. Such a choice necessitated at least tacit approval from the husband and ample funds to pay servants to provide basic home services. These women also possessed superior physical strength to carry a double role, as well as the mental toughness and fierce internal motivation needed to resist the conventional wisdom of the day that confined women to the home.[35]

Not surprisingly, many upper-class and upper-middle-class women chose volunteer social service rather than the continued pursuit of a career. Charity work was acceptable socially, and it yielded personal satisfaction. Women who continued their careers after marriage encountered a mixture of great satisfaction and ambivalence in their dual roles.

Women who recorded their experiences tell of formidable difficulties coupled with massive satisfactions. Elizabeth Stern Morton was an ambitious Jewish woman with strong motivation to serve society in meaningful ways. She met her husband at a settlement house where she was employed as a social worker. He was a medical doctor, cosmopolitan in both experience and parentage. Her descriptions of the marriage indicated that it was endowed with sexual happiness and was harmonious spiritually and intellectually. But, despite these positive factors, during her years of childbirth her career languished. Only when her husband became ill and the family needed her income to maintain its living standard did Mrs. Morton return to work. She then worked steadily for a period of years. Anti-Semitism ultimately undermined her career, but, more important, when her husband regained his health, his career resumed its former dominance. Elizabeth agreed to move to another city, where her husband had an offer that included a position for her on his staff. She was ambivalent about this change. True, she was happy to be "side by side," but she was also disappointed at her diminished income and the unfamiliarity of the new work.[36]

Ultimately she found the greatest satisfaction in an independent career within the marriage. She became a writer working at home, still happily married but with her own identity and career that would not interfere with the marriage. Her predicament and solution cannot be typical of all married career women. The incredibly small number of women who combined careers and marriage suggests that Elizabeth's difficulties were not unique to her situation, and for many women Elizabeth's solution would have been unavailable.

The economically deprived women working at low-paying jobs to help their families survive found their way to the other much larger side of the bimodal distribution of the married women's work force. These women did not have "careers." They would probably gladly have remained at home had their husbands been healthy and able to provide for their families.

In retrospect, the roots of the twentieth-century development of women's roles in the work force are identifiable in 1900. Nineteenth-century women had an exceedingly small part to play, but it was a beginning. Economic imperatives justified work for pay outside the home, despite society's strong commitment to the ideal of women's remaining in the home. Some married women wanted both roles—happy marriages and productive careers. A few women combined the two, but they were gifted with strong motivation and supportive husbands. Most women skirted the ideology of the time or worked within it to find ways to attain their goals of heightened productivity or service to society without risking a direct confrontation with the dominant value structure. This practice of avoiding direct confrontation with the cherished value system was the key to women's success at increasing their work opportunities. Not until the later decades of the twentieth century would the value system itself be challenged, and this would not occur until after the development of a large committed female work force essential to the operation of the economy.

Single women developed modern work roles first. The most dedicated career women had to remain unmarried if they wished to pursue their vocations singlemindedly. They held and protected certain occupations and professions within women's domain, and their experience ultimately benefited all women, whatever their marital status. But at all economic levels the working women of 1900 showed that a modern work role was possible for women in the twentieth century despite formidable obstacles.

CHAPTER 3

Women and the Family:
1900–1940

Women of all social classes throughout this period chose to retain their primary commitment to the home. In 1940 the vast majority of married women were still at home raising children and pursuing domesticity. The number of children in the family decreased, but the occupation of homemaking still commanded the primary attention of 85 percent of the married women in 1940.

Fertility rates declined, but not because of any tendency by women to shift their priorities to paid work outside the home. Surprisingly, fertility rates varied little, if any, between working women and those of the same age who remained at home. Paid work might have been seen as an alternative to domesticity by some women; however, work was not viewed as an alternative to fertility. A far larger number of women than those in the work force participated in the fertility decline, and equally true, working women had not rejected fertility.[1]

Between 1900 and 1940, fertility rates declined from 130 births for every 1,000 women of child-bearing age to 79.9. This decrease of 60 percent over a forty-year period was especially significant because it was a continuation of the long trend of declining birth rates throughout the nineteenth century. But the decline in the first four decades of the twentieth century was more gradual than the rapid decline in the nineteenth century.

The birth rate decreased despite many factors in the early twentieth century that might have encouraged greater fertility. Marriage rates increased, and the average age for women at marriage lowered half a year, from 22.0 to 21.5. The median marriage lowered half a year, from 22.0 to 21.5. The median marriage age for men dropped two years, from 26 to 24. In 1940, 80 percent of the population married and were still married at age 34, in contrast with only 75 percent in 1900. More frequent and earlier marriage multiplied opportunities for conception; nevertheless, birth rates declined. In fact they decreased to the lowest rate in the United States before 1978: the 73.3 births for every 1,000 women of child-bearing age recorded for 1936.[2]

Other factors within marriage contributed to the heightened opportunity for conception, but the result was not positive for fertility. Sexual activity within marriage increased during this period because urbanization and greater geographic mobility allowed greater choice of marriage partners. Thus young people were able to choose a sexually appealing spouse. A rising standard of living permitted more married couples to have a private bedroom: both an opportunity and a stimulus to expand sexual activity. Women donned more provocative clothing at the same time that dating and courtship customs became less restrictive. This emphasis on a higher degree of eroticism contributed to the development of increased sexuality.

Improved medical care and better nutrition might also have encouraged more frequent conceptions and births. The female population was healthier. More people were able to substitute protein for starches, and the consumption of fruits and vegetables increased as the twentieth century progressed. Even more crucial, the survival rate for both mothers and newborn babies showed dramatic improvement after 1890. Even childbirth became less of an ordeal after 1915, with the use of new drugs.[3]

Despite such potentially positive factors as increased sexual activity, better health, earlier marriage, and safer childbirth, fertility continued to decline. Married couples, then, must have increased their efforts to control births. No new technical birth-control aids appeared in this period. The condom had been known for centuries, and both the sponge and foam method and the diaphragm were available by the middle of the nineteenth century. That people made greater use of existing methods assumes not only increased access to birth-control information and equipment but also a greater desire to limit births. In the early twentieth century persistent advocates of family planning like Margaret Sanger actively publicized the availability of birth-control information to new groups in the population. The declining fertility rates clearly show the success of these efforts.[4]

The reasons for this modified behavior lay in the gradual disappearance of the rationale for the high birth rates characteristic of traditional society. In the twentieth century women no longer had to suffer ten pregnancies in order to produce five living children. As childhood survival rates improved at the turn of the century, parents could reasonably expect to see the great majority of their children live to adulthood.

The economic benefits of large families declined as traditional society disappeared. Children no longer provided the vital labor services that they had contributed in earlier times. They could still earn wages outside the home, and even in the twentieth century many of them did. But in the first three decades of the twentieth century, child labor laws gradually removed this source of family income.

The decline of differential fertility after 1916 clearly shows the gradual disappearance of the traditional reasons for producing children. By 1940 fertility rates for all groups in the population had become more alike than before. All groups in the population had moved closer to the native white urban family size norm of two children per family. This change can be explained partially as the result of increasing urbanization, a variable that has, with few exceptions in modern times, correlated with decreasing birth rates. Richard Easterlin showed that the economic value of children declined in the city, and that a more urban population manifests lower fertility rates.[5]

The decline in rural fertility between 1916 and 1940 was more surprising, but, like urban fertility, rural fertility declined for primarily economic reasons. The disappearance of the frontier in the 1920s eliminated a way of life that encouraged high fertility even within a rapidly modernizing society. By 1920 owning and operating a farm required a larger capital investment and less labor than in earlier decades. In addition, a decline in the return on investment tended to discourage the choice of an agricultural livelihood.

The increased production of farm goods, made possible by improved agricultural technology, temporarily outstripped the need for food in the cities. The resulting short period of overproduction led to a gap between supply and demand that decreased the direct market value of the farmer's crops. In turn, then, this change decreased the economic value of the labor of additional children on the farm. In the 1920s a rural recession preceded the more general economic depression of the 1930s. Ultimately, further urbanization, mechanization of the farm, and increased world demand for agricultural goods mitigated the problem of rural recession, but between 1920 and 1940 the agricultural sector continued to produce too well for its own economic advantage.[6]

Other economic factors in the 1920s also discouraged urban fertility. Richard Easterlin identified the existence of an inverse correlation between unemployment for young men and fertility rates between 1920 and 1970. Growing unemployment among young men in this decade threatened their feelings of confidence and undermined their belief in the security of the future. These attitudes appeared to correlate with declining fertility.[7]

A rising level of national income in this decade might have modified the negative economic impact from unemployment, but increasing income can affect the taste for fertility in either direction. Between 1900 and 1930 national income rose during a period of consistent fertility decline. National income showed a slight decline after 1930 and remained almost level until the later years of the decade. In 1936 both income and fertility rates began to move slowly upward, anticipating the predominantly positive and rising relationship that would dominate the twenty-year period after 1940. These changes followed a period of more than thirty years, when national income and fertility rates were in an inverse relationship.[8]

The inverse relationship dominated this period at both the individual and the national level despite the aberrations of the 1930 decade. A study comparing the completed family size of married couples between thirty-four and fifty-five years old in 1940 with the rental value of their homes (as a measure of their income) shows the consistent inverse correlation between income and fertility at all levels except those at the top of the income measure who had larger families than those with slightly lower income. Since married couples in this age group would have been creating their families between 1905 and 1940, the study gives us information about the relationship between income and fertility throughout the whole period under discussion.[9]

The combination of rising national income and a declining birth rate has characterized not only the first thirty years of the twentieth century but most of the nineteenth century as well. This long trend of consistent negative correlation can probably best be explained because each variable had a separate relationship to the process of industrialization. Rising national income in the long period from 1810 to 1930 is the result of the transformation of a traditional agricultural society, augmented with small commercial and manufacturing sectors, into a modern industrial economy.

The relationship between differential fertility and differential modernization of individuals and groups demonstrates the negative impact these important changes in society had upon fertility. The most modern groups, the earliest participants in modern industrial society, show the earliest decline from the traditional fertility pattern. On the other hand, the groups that remained closer to the economic remnants of traditional society retained also its value structure, including the belief in the benefits of high fertility.

National income growth may be the most revealing and inclusive indicator of modernization between 1810 and 1930. A basic sectoral shift occurred in the mode of production and the components of national wealth. The variable of rising national income in this period represented modernization, a process that has usually correlated negatively with fertility.

Urbanization and increased involvement in public education are also indicators of progressing modernization. Both of these processes accelerated in the twentieth century from long steady upward trends in the nineteenth century, and thus they provide corroborating evidence for the strong positive relationship between modernization and fertility decline.

As modernization continued to spread in the 1920s, the impact of its effects increased. More groups became involved in the market economy, and the economic value of children as a source of labor further eroded. The result was an increase in the pace of fertility decline.

The advent of the consumer society in the 1920s also affected decisions about fertility. The appearance of a variety of mass-produced luxury goods for all social classes forced families to choose between buying the items touted by competitive advertisers and having babies. After 1920 massive advertising effectively stimulated the demand for luxury goods, a development that had a negative effect upon fertility. Children had to compete for their very existence with an ever-increasing range of consumer goods and services. Just as the economic value of children declined, the arresting new advertising techniques whetted their potential parents' appetite for gracious living through possession of nice things. Children, in effect, became only one possibility in a massively expanding range of luxury goods.[10]

Could an increase in the general level of prosperity for the society solve the dilemma of choosing between consumption of goods and having children? If household income increased, a married couple might be able to choose both babies and sufficient consumer goods. However, in the 1920s, the increase in prosperity was unevenly distributed, concentrated at the high-income levels. At the same time, the heightened desire for luxury goods stimulated by increased advertising occurred at all income levels throughout the society. Such rises in income that did occur were insufficient to satisfy all these wishes. The desire for children frequently remained a poor second to an automobile or a new refrigerator for married couples who could not afford new goods and babies at the same time.[11]

The laws prohibiting employment of children under age 16, passed in almost all the states by the 1920s, gave the final blow to what remained of children's economic value in the family. Thus the real cost of rearing children escalated for the urban working class, new immigrants, and blacks, groups who had so recently depended upon child labor to supplement family income. Consequently, economic reasons dictated a substantial cut in their birth rates. All these factors—the desire for new goods, the decline in the economic value of children to the household, the decreasing income in rural, agricultural areas, and the higher rates of unemployment for young men—contributed to the substantial decline in fertility in the 1920s.

Fertility in the 1930s

The most intense decline in fertility in the twentieth century occurred during the economic depression of the 1930s. Most of the negative factors present in the 1920s persisted, and new ones appeared. The prolonged economic decline throughout the nation that lasted almost the full decade was a new experience for Americans. It discouraged people of child-bearing age from forming families and even marrying. They looked at an uncertain future in which producing children appeared to be fraught with risks. One-quarter of the work force were without jobs in 1936, and the young suffered most from unemployment.[12]

In the 1930s fertility rates fell below the level that people said they preferred. A 1937 Gallup Poll showed that the respondents preferred the three- and four-child family, rejected childlessness, and found the single-child family of inadequate size. But these preferences were not translated into higher fertility. Demographic data for this decade show few families with more than two children. Childlessness increased well beyond previous levels. By 1940, 17 percent of the married women between forty and forty-four had never borne a child. In contrast only 10 percent of the same age group were childless in 1910. Young married people in the 1930s produced fewer children than any other cohort in modern times.[13]

The economic factors discouraging to child production in this decade further accelerated the fertility decline. At the low levels of national income prevailing throughout the decade, fertility and income showed a positive correlation, at first in decline, but after 1936 both income and fertility moved slowly upward together. This aberrant pattern reversed a 140-year trend. Income growth, a surrogate variable for modernization, correlated negatively with fertility for 140 years as fertility "modernized." In the unprecedented economic crisis, the income variable acquired new relevance, and it temporarily lost its earlier importance as a surrogate variable for modernization. Declining national income indicated a decline in the already established system of modern industrial production rather than a shift away from the long process of modernization. But the decline pushed fertility rates below a level that most people found acceptable. In fact, fertility sunk below desired levels to a subnormal or submodern rate.

The dominant trend in the relationship between individual income and fertility remains inverse, as the 1940 study showed. Increased modernity represented by higher income still affected completed fertility negatively. The more prosperous groups still produced the smallest families on the average and at most income levels, while the groups still producing the largest families remained on the fringes of the modern economy or were in their first generation of modernity. But the aggregate data from the 1930s suggest that for a period of six to ten years a different relationship dominated. Only those with access to resources could risk having babies. These aberrant years, however, did not comprise a sufficiently long period to affect substantially the completed fertility of the relevant birth cohorts in relation to their income level. The fertility of all groups declined, but its inverse relationship with level of income did not change.

Thus, two negative tendencies interacted to produce low fertility. The precipitous drop in incomes merely augmented the decline in fertility caused by ongoing social changes that had already been occurring for the previous 120 years. Independent of other variables, groups who had until recently remained in the traditional value system were undergoing fertility modernization when they entered the modern economy by way of urbanization, education, or employment in the modern sector.

The severe economic decline of the 1930s profoundly affected the decisions about fertility made by married couples, but it did not affect their desire for children. The real aberration of the 1930 decade is that people had fewer children than they really wanted. The fact that both fertility and national income moved slightly upward together in the final years of the decade supports the contention that the decline in fertility between 1930 and 1936 represented a submodern level. Even small changes in income prompted the return to more normal modern fertility behavior.

Why do people in a modern society have children when economic reasons are against child production? Once the traditional reasons for child-rearing disappeared, should childlessness not have been the truly modern choice? The cost of child-rearing, combined with the competition with consumer goods and services, might have made children obsolete. Instead, this ostensibly logical decision represents an extreme extrapolation from the trend of decline rather than a real historical change. The traditional reasons for having children had disappeared for all groups by 1940, but the impulse for fertility still showed enough vitality to respond to a very small improvement in the economy. Even in the 1930s fertility exceeded replacement levels. New modern reasons for child production developed even as the traditional rationale disappeared.

Modern Fertility

Modern societies still require child production to survive, but parents pay the costs and society reaps the benefits of population growth. The advantages of child-rearing in traditional society had been more direct. Individual goal seeking and personal happiness became more relevant to decision making in modern society. Therefore the reasons that people continue having babies have acquired new importance.

The continuation of family formation in modern societies suggests the emergence of a set of new and positive reasons for the production of children. The modern family developed within two or three generations after 1850. The smaller size of the modern family was a nineteenth-century innovation. Some of its roots go deep into the past, but the small modern family began with the upper-middle-class whites. It spread first to other white urban dwellers and gradually to other groups throughout society in the twentieth century.[14]

Middle-class families substituted new goals for family life as the need for the traditional functions of family economic production declined in the middle of the nineteenth century. Families began to operate more clearly and exclusively as affective units. The "home," no longer only an economic and living arrangement, took on new multiple meanings: domicile, sanctuary, nest, as well as micro-economic unit. Children replaced goods as the products of the unit, and they still retained their old function as a future investment in human capital. But children in modern families became consumer goods because parents had to expend resources for their "purchase" and maintenance.[15]

Modern parenting demanded an investment of time and resources with no clear material return. It became largely an emotional endeavor. The parents possibly reaped rewards in satisfaction, joy, affection, feelings of immortality, and linkage with the past and the future. Yet parents had varied expectations, and it is difficult to gauge whether they achieved these goals, either wholly or in part, because the possible rewards were abstract, psychological, and subjective.

In the society that invented capitalism and chose economic interest as its foundation, the invention of a family structure based upon parental love, altruism, and lifelong devotion offers an excellent example of the human ability to live with contradictions. The nineteenth-century family structure promoted love between a man and a woman and between parents and children. In the early twentieth century this model of domesticity still consisted of a nurturing mother, a providing father, and children who offered charm, cajolery, a contact with the future, and perhaps affection and gratitude. Some of these characteristics may have been present in traditional society, but they did not provide the basic rationale for producing children.

The concept of the modern family included an assumption of the importance of the mother's effect upon children. Society had earlier believed that children's health and survival were random, controlled by chance, fate, or divine intervention. Now middle-class parents, and especially mothers, had to accept responsibility for the survival and health of their children. Early death was tragic, the new ideology taught, because it might have been prevented by capable and loving maternal care. This responsibility burdened nineteenth-century mothers when no substantial progress had been made in curing disease and maintaining children's health, and mothers lacked information about even the basic facts of children's growth and development.[16]

The new responsibility redefined the potential satisfactions of childrearing. Mothers were able to feel productive in their role of raising children, and they could gain a sense of control over natural processes. At the same time the new demands on them made large families a practical impossibility. The requirements of increased investments of the mother's time and the father's money limited the suitable size of the family. In the middle-class home of the nineteenth century, quality child care supplanted quantity child-rearing. This pattern spread to other groups in the early 20th century.

Reduced family size meant rising rather than lowered standards for child care. In fact, the increasing emphasis upon the importance of the mother's role led society to expect more of her. In the twentieth century, with increased pediatric knowledge, quality child-rearing acquired new dimensions. Child-rearing could be based upon the foundation of greater information, but the requirements of maternal devotion and time did not decrease. The importance of providing the new child care again emphasized the significance of the role of the mother. She used the new effective techniques to put the assumptions of the nineteenth-century ideology into operation.

The child's mental health emerged in the twentieth century as another new parental responsibility. The theories of Sigmund Freud had profound implications for twentieth-century child-rearing. Child psychiatry emerged in the 1920s as a result of the discoveries of Freud and his followers. Freud had postulated the existence of a subconscious relationship between parents and children. The new ideas expanded parental responsibilities to include psychological health as well as the physical health of children. Massive difficulties were inherent in this new role for parents since there were no clear operational guidelines for the new theories.[17]

Only the highly educated segment of the population was directly effected by these ideas in the 1920s because the impact of child psychiatry lagged behind its invention. But the writers of child-rearing manuals translated the new psychology into "practical" advice that frequently tended to be confusing or ambiguous. Every fifteen years child-rearing theory shifted between the ideological poles of permissiveness and disciplined scheduling that further confused an already ambiguous science.[18]

Between 1900 and 1915, for example, the conventional methods of child-rearing included maternal love, warmth, and the building of character, a regimen that permitted a relatively permissive approach to children. After 1920, child-rearing experts recommended a more rigorous disciplined approach that featured scheduled feedings, early enforced toilet training, and minimal cuddling of babies. Child care principles returned to the more permissive style after 1940.

The experiences of parents in their family of origin provided additional input to child-rearing practices. These assumptions acquired in childhood inevitably were more traditional than any of the formal advice, and at least before 1940 contradicted the assumptions of both modern styles. Change in approaches to child-rearing lags between generations because of the impact of early socialization, and this, added to the shifts in formal advice, inevitably generated confusion.

Modern child-rearing, then, did not leave parents untroubled and secure in their role. Contradictions among guiding principles remained unresolved. Parents yearned for control and efficacy in their lives and a reasonable amount of certainty about the rationale and standards for proper child-rearing. But that reassurance was not available, and the new experts in quality child-rearing did not tolerate inadequacy. In a traditional society, parents suffered no such uncertainty about their role. They felt no need for personal pleasure as a reward for raising children, so they were less likely to be disappointed than modern parents. Earlier parents never experienced the level of tension and responsibility caused by the pressure to avoid all disasters that their modern counterparts accepted.

The new family norm widely accepted throughout society by the 1920 decade—2.3 children—resulted from a half-century of development. Since children were no longer closely spaced two years apart, as in the traditional families, the mother could concentrate her efforts upon one child at a time. Unlike both traditional families and families after 1940, the child in the 1920-style modern family could bask in individual maternal attention in infancy and early childhood. Wider spacing of children curtailed family size; it also diminished the possibility of close relationships between siblings. The relationship between mother and child remained the most intense within the family.

This family style created by the white middle class achieved wide dissemination in twentieth-century society. Although no other groups adopted its concepts so completely, working-class people who wished upward mobility were exposed to its values in numerous ways—primarily through the media and by observation. The data show clearly the changes in family size, spacing of children, and, by implication, the function of the family in working-class homes as well as those of the middle class.

It is difficult to prove direct effects of this norm upon maternal behavior, but studies suggest that some differences in style persisted between social classes despite the widespread acceptance of the new norm. For example, a study of women's use of household time between 1920 and 1970 showed clear differences in maternal behavior. In the 1920s, working-class women remained directly attentive to the child for only the first three years after birth. The middle-class women remained attentive to the child for a longer time. Household management, housekeeping, and budgeting occupied a larger share of the working-class women's time than did child-rearing. However, their task was less burdensome in some ways than that of the women of the middle class because they retained closer involvement with their sisters and mothers, who helped them with child care. Research by Mirra Komarovsky has shown that working-class women felt substantially less discontent with their domestic role than middle-class mothers, who experienced more uncertainty about acceptable standards of performance.[19]

However, working-class women had experienced a form of modernization that encouraged many similarities to the middle-class style in their way of life. Had all classes not cared adequately for their babies, the rapid decline of infant mortality in the twentieth century would not have been possible. Working-class women, like middle-class women, considered homemaking to be a primary, full-time occupation. They avoided paid work outside the home except in unusual cases.

Working-class families also used their homes as sanctuaries. But here, unlike the idealized middle-class version, the model was based upon a need for family cohesiveness from the still harsh economic realities outside the home. A lower level of economic security minimized the gracious amenities in the working-class home. On the other hand, it intensified the necessity for mutual family support.

By 1940 all groups in society had accepted the basic outlines of the middle-class family style: the smaller size, the wider spacing between children, the primary role of the mother in child-rearing, and the importance of quality child care. The modern family had become the norm. The widespread acceptance of a decrease in fertility and the family style associated with a declining birth rate included two separate processes. First, the traditional reasons for high child production disappeared. The second originated in the creation and dissemination of new modern reasons for having babies. By the 1920s we can identify the results of the interaction between the two processes after a half-century of differential modernization. In 1940 the process of creating a model for the modern family was substantially complete throughout the society; only remnants of traditionalism remained.

CHAPTER 4

Work at Home:

1900–1940

Women and children benefited greatly from the changes in family life in the early twentieth century. The advantages they gained cannot be dismissed as irrelevancies or as negative side-effects of a modernizing society. Any attempt to halt the inexorable process of modernization would only have been a quaint historical anomaly because of the concomitant improvement in standards of living. At the same time, however, women relinquished the high levels of productivity that had been theirs in traditional society and in the transitional early modern period. A realistic appraisal of women's total lives underscores the serious erosion in the value of their labor.

The spread of the modern family pattern throughout society in the first forty years of the twentieth century brought to women massive increases in survival, improved health, and greater vitality. Their expected life span lengthened from 48.3 years in 1900 to 65.2 years in 1940, a substantial gain. Women bore fewer children under much less hazardous obstetrical conditions, and in other areas their lives became less physically demanding.[1]

Children were more likely to survive childhood than in the past. Women's attention to child care and domesticity as a vocation partly explained the great strides achieved in protecting children's health.

Mothers who could devote full attention to homemaking lavished increasing amounts of intensive care upon their offspring. Children spent more years in school because they no longer had to work at home or earn wages in the marketplace at an early age.

The modern family pattern demanded heavy capital investment and altruistic behavior from both parents. Its focal point was the mother, who spent a great deal of time caring for the widely spaced children. The decline in fertility left women with a less extensive role in bringing up the young. Quality child-rearing partly filled the void, but the nurture of fewer children did not require as much pressing effort as before. Women needed to replace old activities if they were to retain the high level of productivity sustained by their more frequent childbearing in the past. They needed to substitute new kinds of work in the home or to maintain older, more traditional work forms.

Full-time work outside the home provided an alternative for only 15 percent of the women in 1940, a threefold increase from the 5 percent in 1900 but still only a small minority. Thus, changes in fertility and in the orientation of the family in the home affected women more profoundly in the first forty years of the twentieth century than did changes in paid work. Society's tenacious belief that women should remain the custodians of the home diminished not at all in the first four decades of the twentieth century. The history of women's work in this period, therefore, is largely confined to work done by women in household production, cottage industry, and homemaking and child care.

Household production was already dying in 1900 and showed no resurgence in the twentieth century. The number of women involved steadily declined, and at the same time their work diminished in importance. Farm women still produced goods for market, but this work no longer retained the value that it had held in the past. Growth in prosperity and technological improvements combined to encourage a shift to homemaking as a more highly valued role than household production. In 1880 a Texas rancher's daughter would often have known how to ride, raise calves, and even rope cattle. Forty years later, in 1920, custom dictated that she stay inside the house, learning to be a gracious lady before she went to finishing school in the East. Ultimately, the strongest deterrent to the continuation of women's role in household production was the insidious linkage of women's full-time role as homemaker with upward mobility and prosperity.

Humanitarian reform combined with improved technology to deal a death blow to many working-class variations of household production. Labor reformers sought to control working conditions and deplored the continued existence of work in the household. A 1920 report on women's household work in Pennsylvania enumerated its harmful effects and urged the shift of work to factories. Governments could not fully enforce legislation intended simply to regulate working conditions in private households. Increased governmental control of labor standards, however, together with minimum wage and maximum hour legislation, finally eliminated the last remnants of cottage industry.[2]

The combination of humanitarian attitudes with economic facts established new work norms for industrial society. In 1920, for essentially humanitarian reasons, the Women's Bureau of the Department of Labor attempted to enlarge the government's supervisory role toward women's work. It wanted to assure "the effective employment of women while conserving their health and welfare." The Bureau conducted studies of working conditions, collected information on women's work experience, and established work hours and sanitary conditions necessary for women on the job. The Women's Bureau had no regulatory powers, but its activities hastened the replacement of household production by work in the marketplace.[3]

Even when reform movements and improved technology did not accelerate its demise, household work declined in importance. After 1900 the number of small family businesses began to decline. More modern alternatives such as the large department store, the corporation, and the factory replaced them. The geographical separation of home and work increasingly became accepted modern practice. Even occupations and professions that had integrated both activities in earlier years conformed to the new trend. Workplaces distant from the home represented a necessary if unwelcome compromise in earlier years; now the division seemed normal and natural.[4]

All these factors contributed to the disappearance of women's traditional work roles. Improved technology, industrial concentration, and economies of scale increased economic productivity, but women paid for these improvements with the loss of the value of their labor in the home. Despite persistent efforts of nineteenth-century women to continue home production, in the twentieth century women finally lost the last remnants of their traditional work roles. Child care and homemaking became the only socially acceptable vocations for married women.

At the same time the inexorable trend of professionalization outside the home usurped the more urgent maternal functions of the past. Women no longer controlled the socialization of the children, made independent decisions concerning the maintenance of the family's health, or directly provided food and clothing for husbands and children. Homemaking in the twentieth century increasingly included more trivial tasks that would only slightly improve the quality of family life.

Homemaking was still a viable vocation in the nineteenth century because women retained enough of their traditional productive functions. Children would have died without capable maternal nursing care. Sometimes they died anyway in spite of devoted mothering. Women stretched the family income, substituted their own labor for cash outlay when they made clothing at home, canned and preserved food grown in their gardens, or prepared meals using natural and unprocessed foods. Women cleaned and decorated their houses, offered personal counseling to their families, and furnished many supportive services that enriched the quality of life in the home.

In the twentieth century women's homemaking efforts had to compete directly with professional services outside the home that were perceived either as less costly than homemaking or of preferable quality. The higher standard of living permitted more and more women to become full-time homemakers, but they found that the modern standards continually undermined the value of their home services.

Advertisements typical of the times frequently show the mother's homemade product to be inferior to the purchased product. For example, in *Good Housekeeping Magazine* for January 1936, a Campbell's Soup advertisement stated that children much preferred Campbell's Vegetable Soup with fifteen different vegetables to their mothers' homemade soup. The mother therefore should trust the children to know and say what was good and cease wasting time making homemade vegetable soup.[5]

Economic considerations more than effective advertising undermined the mother's role as seamstress for herself and her family. As
early as 1900, ready-made clothing advertised in *The Sears Roebuck Cat-
alog* appears to be similarly priced as the materials necessary to make
a matching garment at home. A customer could buy a woman's suit
made of "mixed goods" of silk and wool "lined with rustling taffeta
and interlined with crinoline," complete with "inlaid rolling collar and
extra full sweep skirt," for $9.00. A "bicycle" suit consisting of five
pieces—jacket, skirt, bloomers, leggins, and cap—of "knobby Aus-
trian covert cloth" required only $4.00 for complete payment. Even
the cheapest suit fabric of 36-inch width cost .50 to .85 a yard. At
these prices, the economies of home construction could not have been
substantial.[6]

At the same time, the prices for processed foods declined, and they
became more readily available. The increasingly landless urban residents had to buy processed foods because it was impossible for them
to plant gardens and preserve their home-grown produce. Owning a
house and garden offered the chance to retain some elements of rural
self-sufficiency, but those few families who managed to buy homes
did so only at enormous cost. Stephen Thernstrom describes the urgent desire to own real property that the working-class residents of
Newburyport, Massachusetts, expressed in 1870. But few had the resources to realize this dream.[7]

In the twentieth century, homemaking tasks became less satisfying,
less demanding, and more difficult to define. Only in the recent past,
nineteenth-century women had still been partly successful in finding
useful work in the home to replace the chores that automation and
professionalization eliminated. Homemaking became increasingly easy
in the twentieth century, but the search for new forms of productive
work in the home had virtually ceased. A continued reassessment of
the changing dimensions of the homemaker's declining work role should
have been undertaken to help her allocate her time optimally and replace obsolete tasks with functional new ones.

Economic competition in the 20th century more frequently forced
rational reassessment of work in the economy outside the home when
automation replaced old jobs with new ones. But the emotional ideology of Home and Mother, so important as a stabilizing force in the

early twentieth century, stood in the way of a realistic appraisal of homemaking alternatives. The radical proposals of Charlotte Perkins Gilman for joint family living arrangements in which women combined their efforts to care for children and prepare meals were never taken seriously. Society's response was the creation of Mother's Day, established by the U.S. Congress in 1914, a ceremonial reward for mothers, but without substance or specific assessment of what mothers do or should be doing.[8]

The central problem, of course, given the need to preserve the basic family structure, was society's implicit recognition that homemaking tasks could not be eliminated but only reduced to include the minimum child-bearing, child care, and provision of food, clothing, and agreeable housing. These two factors—the commitment to the basic family structure clothed with the emotional ideology of motherhood, and the irreducible minimum of tasks—prevented explicit recognition of the decline of homemaking.

Instead of replacing obsolete tasks with new ones, women raised the acceptable standards for old chores. Mechanical household appliances lightened the physical demands of house-cleaning and cooking; they also undermined the value of women's labor. The new technology encouraged rising standards for homemaking, and women acquiesced. They found "make work" projects to fill their available time. The quality of homemakers' performances reached higher levels, but women trivialized their own worth when they accepted this alternative.[9]

For example, homemakers did not use vacuum cleaners to maintain the same level of cleanliness acceptable in the days of brooms and carpet beaters. Instead, they used the new machine more frequently and extensively to keep the floors much cleaner. Women spent the spare time the new machines afforded them on other tasks—usually more intensive child care. They spent more of their time maintaining household furnishings than creating them. They vacuumed carpets made on factory looms instead of braiding rugs as they had done in the past. Home sewing had given many women satisfying creative outlets. Now more and more they washed, ironed, and mended ready-made clothing to keep up its appearance.

Technical and professional aids undoubtedly improved the quality of home life. Women's modified role became less onerous and less physically demanding. But these advances blinded them to the long decline in the value of their own occupation. Capital investment replaced labor as the major source of the improved quality of home life.

The decline of parents' educational influence on their children also contributed to the weakening of maternal roles. This trend traces back to the early nineteenth century, when sources of counsel and advice outside the family circle began to undermine the control parents had formerly exercised over their children's education. Increased public-school attendance in the twentieth century only accelerated the process; children entered school at younger ages and stayed there longer.

Women dominated the teaching profession at the elementary school level, but unfortunately they acquired this important career at the expense of the mother's viable educational role at home. Public education tended to substitute new role models, peer group identifications, and value systems for the parents' examples. These ideas frequently conflicted with family principles and further undermined parental authority. Maternal counseling and guidance could so easily be negated when children found information sources outside the home more interesting and relevant. The trivialization of their mother's work contributed to their perception of the greater value of the outside sources. After all, their mother had little contact with the mainstream of society, so what could she know about the world outside the home?

The choice of the smaller family also undermined women's work roles at home, even though the choice was rational and oriented toward positive goals. Nevertheless, this decision substantially reduced women's work roles. Quality child-rearing was an elusive and poorly defined concept. There were no means for evaluating progress along the way. The implicit assumption that maternal devotion was a crucial factor in the excellence of a child's upbringing could not be proved. Women shouldered a great emotional burden when they accepted the responsibility of quality child-rearing as an integral part of their homemaking work without redefinition of tasks, guidance in selection of activities, or any standards for measuring success.

The homemaker who worked at mother-intensive child-rearing full time could look forward to early retirement. She bore fewer children and they would be grown and gone from the home while she was still comparatively young. In the twentieth century, women on the average lived longer than at any previous time. Frequently their child-rearing period lasted only for two decades. Many mothers were still under fifty years old when the last child left home, and some lived as many as thirty years more after completing the job of rearing their children.

Quality homemaking in an empty house resembled the maintenance of an unused shrine. Older women regretted the swift passing of their productive years; even in later life housework and hobbies were inadequate substitutes. Middle-class women had more access to household technology and limited the size of their families more than their sisters in the working class. Therefore, more of them faced these problems.

Working-class women focused their child-rearing energies on intensive care of infants. Because they enjoyed fewer modern household conveniences, they had to spend more time taking care of the house after the need to tend the babies became less pressing. Working-class women were also more deeply involved in the lives of their extended families than were middle-class women. They helped married daughters bring up the grandchildren. They experienced a less abrupt transition to the years after child-rearing than did middle-class women.[10]

Homemaking in the twentieth century for all groups of women acquired a more intense emotional component than previously. This emotionalism cast a rosy glow of purpose and dedication that blinded women to the implications of the loss of old tasks and the rising standards of housekeeping and nurturing. Had women seriously considered alternative tasks or attempted realistic rational redefinition of their roles, they might have saved homemaking as a viable occupation.

Innovation in Homemaking

Emotional preconceptions about Home and Mother did not prevent all innovation in homemaking. In the twentieth century a few new tasks evolved from tentative nineteenth-century beginnings. However, individual homemakers had no control over these new chores because standards imposed from outside the home were used to evaluate their success or failure. Since women had to depend upon others for approbation, these jobs offered less potential for personal satisfaction than older forms of work in the home.

Women became the managers of family consumption. This was an important modern function because most household necessities now had to be purchased. Shopping was not new for women, but the importance of consumer management escalated with twentieth-century economic growth and urbanization. Women had to sharpen their buying skills to differentiate between the growing variety of products on the market. After 1920, advertisers used more effective advertising strategies for the creation of the image of the "perfect home," which had to be properly furnished and equipped. Advertisements implied that the homemaker had to purchase and use certain goods if she wanted her family to be happy at home. If she did not buy them, was she truly offering enough love and devotion to her family? This movement emerged strongly in the 1920s with the consumer society, and it is part of an increasing emphasis on domesticity by advertisers, who implied that successful homemaking required many manufactured products, rather than effort, imagination, and creativity by women.[11]

In practice, women had little control over how much they could buy. The determining factor was the husband's earning power. Thus, a woman's success at homemaking depended very much on the size of the family income and very little on her imagination or persistent effort. Women could manage to improve the quality of family life only marginally through astute consumer management.

Another possible alternative for a women was to direct more concern and energy toward her relationship with her spouse. One possibility is that more companionable marriages followed in the wake of the sexual revolution of the 1920s. A closer husband-wife relationship might have lessened the intensity of the bond between mother and child and changed the focus of the mother's concentration.

After 1920, experts in child nurture advised parents to adopt a more disciplined style of child-rearing. Although this fact might appear to support the contention that women spent more time working on their marriage relationships, contemporary advertisements still dwelt upon mother love. The maternal instinct, they trumpeted, was the most important determinant of women's behavior. At the same time when the sexual revolution should have created more companionable and sexually oriented marriages, the maternal role expanded to include the psychological nurture of children. Mothers still expected to lavish attention on their children. Any positive evidence of increased sexuality in marriage, then, is tangential to the possibility of substantial reallocation of homemaking tasks.[12]

Had husbands begun to spend more time at home, we could assume that women might have responded to their presence by changing homemaking activities. Although men's average work hours declined slightly in the 1920s, even the more substantial shortening of the work day in the 1930s was not sufficient to alter women's routine activities. Perhaps companionability within marriage increased, but love and sex remained evening and weekend activities, no matter how ardently pursued.

Perhaps even more important, increased passion in the marriage relationship would scarcely reinforce homemaking activities positively. Greater emotional commitment to children or husband was irrelevant to the problem of restructuring homemaking tasks so that they would satisfy the woman as well as fill her time. The emphasis on the development of greater marital happiness would only have further obscured rational assessment of daily homemaking tasks.

More extensive leisure-time roles, however, offered women new opportunities for productive activities. Women got the right to vote in 1920, and while there is ample documentation of their failure to use the franchise to change their own lives or to affect substantially the political process, they became passively involved in political activities. Women participated at least peripherally in political clubs and electoral campaigns. They formed the League of Women Voters immediately after enfranchisement—tangible evidence that women at least wanted more information about political affairs.[13]

Middle-class women emulated the upper-class model of membership in women's clubs sponsored by churches and synagogues. These organizations encouraged women to participate in traditional social service activities. Married women broadened their social circles and secured an independent sphere in their lives separate from their families. Women controlled these clubs; membership in them encouraged women to establish more definite personal identities and more active roles in society.

In the nineteenth century, social service clubs had strongly concentrated upon reform issues. The General Federation of Women's Clubs, founded in 1889, was an umbrella organization, an amalgamation of a wide variety of existing women's organizations dedicated to reform. Its components had included missionary societies as well as suffrage and temperance associations.[14]

New reform organizations appeared in the twentieth century. But as the club movement spread farther into the middle class, groups more frequently chose to direct their efforts toward the improvement of the home. The newly formed National Congress of Mothers, Parent-Teachers Association, Consumer's League, and Home Economics Association all emphasized the need for better child care and good homemaking. They had massive membership rosters. For example, the PTA claimed a million members in 1928.[15]

Women's clubs, then, while providing needed sociability, increasingly reinforced the emphasis that society placed on quality homemaking. In this way they cooperated in the effort to impose ever-higher expectations for acceptable homemaking performance. These new standards lay heavily on the shoulders of married women. More and more varied sources bombarded housewives with information—far more than they ever needed for accomplishing the tasks incorporated in their declining vocation.

Efforts to glorify homemaking reached new heights when the universities added professional programs in "Home Economics" to their curricula. Home Economics lacked any of the requirements for a true profession; it could not limit entry or provide professional advancement. Achievement of high standards of performance yielded neither external rewards nor job improvement. The only conceivable job advancement came as compliments from a pleased husband or curious neighbors. These compliments were intangible, rarely related to quality homemaking, and frequently dysfunctional to it.

Although women got less satisfaction from homemaking, this in no way implies decreasing quality in home environments. Family life visibly improved. More infants and children survived; families ate more nutritious foods; they lived in cleaner and more attractive homes. But resources from outside the home—increased capital investment, consumption expenditures, and expert advice—provided the improvements. The changes in homemaking negatively affected only women, and some of the effects were indeed positive for women too. In earlier times, women's labor had been a crucial factor in the survival of their families and in improvements in the quality of life. Now, in comparison with the roles of women of the past and men in the present, women's roles lacked urgency. The value of the homemaker's labor had seriously eroded.

Homemaking as an occupation could not simply disappear because its irreducible minimum of tasks—child-bearing, child care, and the provision of food, clothing, and lodgings—was a permanent fact of family life. Society insisted that women perform these functions and provided extensive capital investment to make the job easier—vacuum cleaners, refrigerators, and obstetrical and pediatric services, for example—without answering the profound need for substantial reassessment of the job itself. Instead of merely making the work easier, society idealized and glorified the role. The homemaker became increasingly dependent upon other people to set performance standards and congratulate her when she met them. Women found that they had to substitute symbolic rewards for the satisfaction of a valuable job well done.

Women faced a dilemma in which none of the limited options was satisfactory. Homemaking was not really a full-time job. Women spent hours on "make work" projects to fill their spare time. Still the irreducible minimum of child-bearing and child care would never disappear, even if women rejected the imposition of higher standards by outside experts and professionals.

None of the newer areas of homemaking allowed women any real power. Consumer power is widely diffused and relatively ineffective on an individual basis. Budget management is visible only when badly done. A woman's contribution to the quality of her family's life, circumscribed by her husband's income, over which she had no control, could be marginal at best even if she shopped carefully and wisely. Without comparative standards, her skill was likely to go unnoticed.

Only recently women's work had been urgently needed by the family. In the twentieth century, women's roles became more comfortable and less physically demanding, but there was less pressing need for their contribution. By 1940 women enjoyed a great deal of free time, but other people set their work standards.

At the same time, men's value as breadwinners retained all its vital importance. To be sure, men had also lost control of their own work standards and had undergone the effects of automation, but new occupations had replaced obsolete jobs as a matter of course. Men's work had now become more important to family survival than women's work. Women could contribute only slight improvements to the quality of family life. The decrease in the value of women's labor contrasted with the continued importance of men's work, and men's role as the providers of income accentuated the role differences between the genders. Women could hardly reject their new station because it offered dramatic improvements in family life. But women's place took on a new aura of inferiority as homemakers busied themselves with ever more trivial tasks.

CHAPTER 5

The Workplace:
1900–1940

Between 1900 and 1940 an increasing proportion of women chose to work for pay outside the home instead of remaining at home pursuing domesticity. In 1910 women made up only a quarter of the total labor force, but by 1940 36 percent of all workers were female. The increased percentage of women workers after 1920 largely reflected the greater participation rates of married women.[1]

Did these women consciously seek an alternative to compensate for the declining value of their production in the home? Were they looking for new and modern substitutes that would restore the value of women's labor? It is tempting to view these early twentieth-century women workers as a pioneer vanguard who recognized the decline of homemaking as a profession and successfully found another path to productivity. This interpretation of the rising work rates for married women would mesh neatly with the history of the home.

Unfortunately, the history of working women in the first four decades of the twentieth century does not conform to this logical pattern. In fact, the chronicle of increased numbers of married women entering the marketplace remains surprisingly independent of the history of the deterioration of the vocation of homemaking. Few, if any, women freely chose work for pay because it was preferable to domesticity. Married women chose jobs that did not challenge the prevailing concept of women's proper place. Compared with the changes in women's work in the final forty years of the 19th century, or the period between 1940 and 1980, very little happened in the early twentieth century.

In 1860 most women still raised large families and worked in economically productive ways inside the home. By 1900 married women had already drawn the perimeters, limited as they were, for the areas in which they would work for the next forty years.

Comparative figures clearly describe the entrance of married women into the labor market. In 1900 one in twenty married women worked outside the home; by 1980 three in five held jobs in the marketplace. Certainly, the numbers justify the argument that there has been great change in women's working patterns in the twentieth century. But by far the greatest increase, from 15 percent to 60 percent, came between 1940 and 1980. Thus, the increase of ten percentage points between 1900 and 1940 appears to be quite minimal. Equally important, the jobs women chose in the period under consideration differed little from those they filled at the turn of the century, and during the forty-year span work motivations remained relatively constant.

Nevertheless, any thorough study of women in the workplace must include an examination of their work patterns between 1900 and 1940, if only to provide an accurate historical context for the marked changes after 1940. Two interpretations are possible for the significance of the increase in the percentage of married women in the labor force between 1900 and 1940. One might emphasize the 300 percent increase in percentage points from 5 percent to 15 percent of married women working. But at the same time we might also note that women, in relative terms, lost gains they had already made because their progress lagged substantially in comparison to men.

The changes, however modest, were indeed significant indicators of trends that would continue after 1940. By 1940 a small but increasing proportion of married women had left home to work for pay. They joined a women's work force that had become more diverse in age levels, ethnic origin, and social class than it had been in 1900. The percentages of all age groups entering the labor force increased between 1920 and 1940, but the single largest age group continued to be women in the prime child-bearing years, between twenty-five and thirty-four. They comprised 32.7 percent of the married women's work force in 1920 and 38.6 percent in 1940. In the 1930s increasing numbers of older women between thirty-five and fifty-five also entered the work force—a trend that would accelerate after 1940.[2]

Disadvantaged and minority women made up the bulk of the women's labor force in 1900, but by 1940 this had changed. White women chose work outside the home in significantly increasing numbers. However, the percentage of working black women, still the significantly disadvantaged ethnic group, remained larger than the percentage of blacks in the total female population.[3]

More middle-range occupations opened up for married women in this period. This fact doubtless encouraged women from a wider sector of society to seek employment. In 1900 most married women who worked outside the home settled for low-level jobs in domestic service, agricultural labor, or in low-paying factory work such as textiles, paper, boxes, and cigar-making. At the other extreme of the spectrum of the female labor force, a small group of married women practiced professions.[4]

After 1930 the pattern changed. Employers began to accept for clerical and sales jobs married women who were not trained in the professions. This trend encouraged women who would not have worked at the lower-level jobs to seek employment. Thus, by 1940, a unimodal distribution skewed slightly toward the lower-level jobs replaced the bimodal distribution of married women's occupations typical in 1900.[5]

Earlier in the century single women had dominated the middle-status categories of clerical and sales work, but with the growing demand for workers to fill these jobs, work opportunities appeared for married women of the lower middle class and working class. Thus, after 1920 married women repeated the experience of single women, who had found "respectable" jobs available to them thirty years earlier, before 1900.

Important differences persisted between the married women's work force and that of single women, but the contrasts are less striking than they had been in 1900. Married women still retained their subordinate position in the female labor force. Furthermore, until after 1930, the divergences between the occupational distribution of married women and their single sisters remained virtually intact. Until then a higher proportion of married women remained in traditional or early industrial occupations. Single women had been moving away from domestic service as early as 1910, but even after 1930 more than a third of married women were still doing this premodern type of work.[6]

The contrast was equally remarkable at the upper levels of the women's work force. Twice as high a proportion of single working women as married women were following professions, and single women dominated the middle-range occupations until after 1930. The only exception to this pattern was in manufacturing jobs; between 1900 and 1930 similar percentages of both married and single women worked in factories.

The occupational differential between married and single women had decreased in the lower- and middle-level jobs by 1940. In the ten years before 1940 married women's participation in clerical occupations had more than doubled, whereas single women's participation had increased by less than a third. Manufacturing continued to furnish occupations for both married and single women, and paid agricultural jobs had almost disappeared for both groups.

In 1940, however, single women continued to dominate the higher levels of the work force. The traditional women's professions—teaching, nursing, librarianship, and social work—remained primarily the domain of single women. Married women achieved only a dubious equality with their single sisters in professions in which all women were substantially underrepresented—dentistry, veterinary medicine, newspaper reporting, and writing. Married women dominated the area of management and ownership of small businesses, but few women of any marital class pursued these occupations.[7]

The reasons for the gap between the status of married women and single women in the work force depended mainly upon the greater work commitment of single women. The greater numbers of single professional women than married women resulted from the frequent practice of women rejecting the pursuit of a career when they married. This trend of career rejection increased in the 1920s as a large proportion of women married, and most of them pursued domesticity exclusively instead of careers.[8]

Women, whether married or single, made very little progress toward occupational equality with men in this period. During the economic depression of the 1930 decade the gender discrimination in the workplace not only persisted but increased. In occupations such as schoolteaching, sales work, and light manufacturing, which had been characterized by some gender flexibility, male participation increased substantially, to women's detriment. Employers preferred to hire men or single women rather than married women in times of job scarcity.[9]

Another negative factor was the decline in women's entry into the higher status professions traditionally dominated by men—medicine, law, and college teaching. Women's numerical participation in these callings increased between 1900 and 1940, but their percentage of the total participation decreased substantially after 1920. The same pattern is apparent in women's educational achievements. Both men and women completed a greater number of years of school, and the totals of college graduates of both genders increased. A substantially higher percentage of all women received college degrees in 1940 than in 1900. Still, the increase lagged far behind that for men.[10]

Only an exceedingly small proportion of the population, either male or female, achieved professional careers or acquired higher education. Lawyers, college professors, and doctors made up an even smaller proportion of the population. Nevertheless, involvement in the upper levels of society offers a key indicator of women's status in the society. The decline in the relative position of women remains an important part of the history of women in the twentieth century. Women made no progress toward equality with men in higher educational achievement or professional success in the first forty years of the twentieth century.

However, women did make progress toward a more limited objective: that of developing a modern work role. The emergence of middle-level employment for married women was of immense importance. Middle-class women could leave home and work for pay without completely clashing with the prevailing ideology of the woman-at-home. Clerical work and much of the work in retail sales remained primarily women's areas. Married women in middle age who lived longer and spent fewer years devoted to child-rearing became a newly available labor supply.

This new behavior by married women was not recognized as a radical innovation because an explanatory rationale emerged to justify it. Society considered that women's pay was "pin money" to be used for small and unimportant luxuries. The implication was that women were working to keep idleness at bay and to indulge their small whims. The husband still remained the family breadwinner; bread was more important than pins.[11]

Some women of the time used the concept of pin money to provide a comfortable rationale that permitted them to work and to use their small incomes as they chose. For others, the pin-money designation represented a humiliating degradation of both the value of their work and the importance of the money they brought home to their families. Especially during the depression of the 1930s, a wife's income often furnished the only cash the family had to spend.

Under these dire circumstances, the pin-money concept expanded to include another rationale, that of "emergency" work. If the family faced an economic crisis, the wife could legitimately work, but only until the emergency ended. During the years of economic depression, the emergency justification for wives' working spread upward into the middle class from the working class. Appended to the pin-money concept, it further postponed recognition of the importance of the durable contributions some married women made to the family income.

Thus, more women from new groups joined the work force at the same time that the values of society altered to lend legitimacy to their choice. The increased participation of married women in the work force appears modest in this period of forty years, but it represented an important departure from past practice. The assimilation into the work force of women from the middle class, white women, older women, and women whose husbands could support them launched the new trend that would continue in the next forty years.

Explanations for Women's Increased Work Participation

Between 1900 and 1940 increased numbers of married women entered the workplace primarily in response to economic factors of both supply and demand. The increased number of jobs open to women combined with improvements in working conditions to encourage greater numbers of women to leave home for work. These factors operated with greatest effect after 1920.

Women held a large proportion of jobs in certain types of industries, especially textiles and food processing. These industries were frequently located in smaller cities rather than in the major population centers. Thus the geographical distribution of the female work force was uneven, but in some areas of great economic significance.

The expansion of commercial training and free public education created a larger potential labor supply of women qualified for white-collar employment. As more middle-range job categories appeared, there were corresponding improvements in wages and working hours. All these factors were part of a general trend of greater job attractiveness.

Higher wages and shorter hours encouraged more women to work. In 1914 a woman's normal work week included fifty hours on the job. By 1920 women worked an average of forty-three hours, and ten years later in 1930 the work week for women had decreased to only forty hours. Women with domestic responsibilities valued the extra ten hours per week that they acquired between 1914 and 1930. Equally important, wages in constant dollars rose from an average of $.15 per hour in 1914 to $.39 in 1930. Most of this gain was not inflationary because the consumer price index remained fairly steady except for a brief period between 1919 and 1922. Continued improvements in real wages for women occurred during the 1930s. Wages rose steadily between 1934 and 1939 after a brief period of lower average pay between 1931 and 1933. In this decade the consumer price index was substantially lower than in the 1920s; therefore women's average real wages rose more in spending power than the actual dollar increase suggests.[12]

The rise in average wages and the shorter work weeks that women gained between 1900 and 1940 make a persuasive case for an increased demand for women workers. At the same time, the supply of potential single female workers declined. The average period of formal education rose from eight years in 1900 to ten years in 1940. Not only did young women remain longer in school but more of them married and at an earlier age. Thus the supply of single-women work years diminished as the marriage age dropped from 22 in 1890 to 21.3 in 1930. By 1940 the percentage of adult women who had ever married and who were still married at age thirty-four reached 72.5 percent, in contrast with 69 percent in 1910. Married women increased their participation in the work force partially because the supply of single workers declined.[13]

Consistently between 1900 and 1980 about half the total adult population of single women worked in the marketplace. The rates of participation range from a low of 43 percent to a high in 1944 of 58.6 percent, a result of the emergency demands for additional workers arising from World War II crisis conditions.[14]

In 1940 the total female labor force numbered 8,055,000; this number could be used as a representation of the demand for women workers. If married women's employment rate had remained at the 1910 rate of 10 percent, only 2,997,000 of them would have been working in 1940. To meet the demand for women workers, 5,058,000 single women would have been required in the workplace. This number represents 1,678,000 more working single women than we could predict from the established work pattern, and it would lead to a participation rate of 57.5 percent. Theoretically possible, this rate is inconsistent with the historically limited participation rates for single women. A more likely possibility was that the demand for women workers would be met by the more elastic supply of married women, specifically 4,675,000 married women at a new and higher participation rate of 15 percent.[15]

Valerie Oppenheimer in her economic factor analysis hypothesized that continued sex-stereotyping of jobs prevented the use of other potential labor pools. She based her argument on the assumption that as demand increased for new workers to fill women's occupations, married women, the most similar labor supply, replaced the depleting supply of single women. Alternative labor sources, particularly young men and older men, either were not available or were not appropriate for many of the jobs women held, given the existence of separate labor markets for each gender.[16]

Although Valerie Oppenheimer applied her thesis primarily to the period after 1940, it may explain some of the changes in the composition of the women's labor force before this date, as suggested by the above analysis. The restrictions imposed by the separate labor markets encouraged employers to hire married women when single women

were not available. In this way the gender distinctions of the labor markets worked to the benefit of married women's increased participation in the work force.

At the same time, the concept of pin money and the justification for temporary emergency work in times of crisis emerged to furnish a rationale that harmonized with conventional values. The rationale provided a protective coloring for new behavior by married women, new behavior encouraged by new factors of labor demand.

Many women, of course, continued to work for the traditional reason—to surmount poverty. In 1940 the inverse correlation between husbands' income and women's work participation persisted. The 1940 census shows this strong negative relationship in metropolitan areas where the average rate of work for all married women with a husband present in the home was 16.7 percent. But at the lowest category of the husband's income, 24 percent of the wives worked. Only at the middle range and upper levels of male income does the rate of women's participation in the work force fall below the average. This suggests that economic need remained the primary motivation for a woman to work outside the home.[17]

Economist Clarence Long supplied additional evidence to support the continued importance of economic need as a motivation for women to work. He established a negative correlation between work rates of married women and their husband's income levels in three census years—1920, 1930, and 1940. By 1950 the negative correlation had diminished, and by 1960 it had disappeared. Thus in the period under discussion the persistence of this negative relationship indicates that the need for the basic requirements for sustaining life remained the strongest motivation for women to seek employment.[18]

Economic factors provide the primary explanation for women's increased work entry in this period. Other possible explanations are either of mixed impact, negative, or irrelevant. Public attitudes, for example, show continual inplacable opposition to married women working, particularly when jobs were scarce. Hiring practices and public opinion polls reveal clear opposition to married women leaving home to work. The number of school boards that employed married women as new teachers fell from 39 percent to 13 percent between 1928 and 1941, according to data collected by the National Education Association. In 1928 one-third of the school districts surveyed required single women who married to resign; by 1941 more than half of them insisted women relinquish their jobs. This unwillingness to employ married women teachers increased as the economic depression continued and jobs were in scant supply. Most people believed that jobs should be reserved for men or single women, despite minor loophole rationales.[19]

In 1937 the American Institute of Public Opinion conducted a poll on whether or not married women should work if their husbands could support them. Over four-fifths of the respondents (82 percent) answered unequivocably that they disapproved of a two-income family. Also in the 1930s, several state legislatures introduced bills to restrict the employment of married women if their husbands were employed. None of these proposals became law, but they failed only because of their doubtful constitutionality. Many employers openly stated their preferences for single women and women under thirty-five years of age.[20]

Feminism also failed to affect public attitudes in any substantial way in this period, and it provided only limited support for married women's careers. In the early part of the twentieth century, the main branch of the feminist movement ceased to demand gender equality and chose instead to focus on political reform. Thus, although the movement was not opposed to simultaneous careers and marriage, before 1920 it remained largely aloof from the career/marriage dilemma. Feminists reserved their primary thrust for the political goal of getting the right to vote. The ratification of the Women's Suffrage Amendment in 1920 justified their choice of strategy, but they won the battle with essentially conservative arguments that emphasized women's special characteristics and their roles as homemakers.[21]

Resurgent feminist arguments appeared again in the 1920 decade, emphasizing the need for recognition of gender equality. Feminists deplored the stultifying effects of homemaking on intelligent women and asserted women's right to pursue careers along with marriage. These contentions echoed the arguments of feminists at the turn of the century. They may have encouraged women's aspirations, but their influence upon female behavior was not apparent.

In her detailed study of feminism and work during the economic depression of the 1930 decade, Lois Scharf shows that women's primary work motivation was economic need rather than feminist ideology. Arguments that women had the right to seek their own identity through careers of their own choice had little effect on their behavior. The relative decline of married women's entry into the professions in the 1930 decade reinforces the contention that feminism had little impact upon women's decisions about work at that time. Feminism is more likely to motivate educated women at the upper end of the socioeconomic spectrum, the group who might have chosen professional careers. In the 1930s, then, when more women started to work than in any other decade in this period, we find little indication of feminism as a significant influence on their behavior.[22]

The positive views of women propounded in the 1930 decade fell far short of the feminist position. President Franklin Roosevelt praised women's abilities and appointed several unmarried women to positions in government. In her speeches and actions Mrs. Roosevelt strongly emphasized the capacities and importance of women. Her own activities, far more extensive than those of previous first ladies, were extensively reported and frequently admired. Still she remained within the parameters of the traditional system of values. Her primary role was as a wife and a mother. The value system for married women remained essentially unchanged from 1900 to 1940.[23]

Another possible explanation for rising work rates might have been as a response to declining fertility. Did women substitute work for babies during this period? The home-centered value system remained strong enough to make this explanation unlikely. Economic motivations led most women to work, and straitened circumstances dictated declining fertility as well. Decreasing birth rates did not directly precipitate increased work activity for married women. In truth, the relationship is indirect and peripheral.

Married people limited the size of their families, primarily for reasons other than the wife's desire to work for pay. They usually sought higher standards of living and a higher level of quality in child-rearing. A few women chose to combine low fertility and paid work as a temporary response to the 1930 depression. Nevertheless, they chose to do so for economic reasons rather than for motives of self-actualization. The data on preferred family size imply that most women would have chosen higher fertility if their economic circumstances had permitted this option.

The relationship between child-rearing and working for pay also appears to vary with social class and income level. Middle-class women were unlikely to work even if they were childless. The presence of small children in the middle-class home certainly was a strong deterrent to the mother's working; in the lower-income families the effect was sometimes in the opposite direction. Here the mother might have been strongly motivated to work in order to increase the family income. However, the ideology of mothers caring directly for the children remained strong for all social classes.

The only direct and relatively widespread illustration of the impact of the new fertility pattern on work rates is the increased entry of married women over thirty-five into the work force. Women had acquired a new life cycle, unlike that of earlier generations. They now had extra years in middle life after the completion of child-rearing. These idle years resulted both from the choice to raise fewer children and also from the continually lengthening life span of women in the 20th century. Older women chose work not as an alternative to fertility but rather as a way to spend productively the new stage of life that followed their child-rearing years.

The Impact of World War I and the Economic Depression of the 1930s on Women's Work

Major world events in this period affected the lives of women and provided a new context for women's work. World War I brought three million women into the work force temporarily. Most of them took clerical jobs, agricultural work, or support positions, but a few women performed hard physical labor in heavy industry. Women welded, blasted, and made steel. This temporary work mostly attracted single women, but some young married women whose husbands were away from home in the armed services took jobs in war industries.[24]

War work, however, appears to have had no permanent effect on women's joining the work force. By 1920 the war workers had returned to their homes. Women's participation in the labor force continued to increase between 1920 and 1930, but the pace of increased entry did not accelerate. The major contribution that married women made to the war effort came from their attempts to conserve scarce resources. They planted victory gardens and sold war bonds—activities well within the permitted limits of homemaking and social service.

Experiences in the 1930s offered more important anticipations of future trends in married women's participation in the work force. The impact of the economic depression was more important than its immediate effects might suggest. Although the need for additional income was the primary impetus for women's increased, if temporary, entry into the working population in this decade, the effect of work experience was positive for choosing work again in other circumstances.

Studies done in the 1960s indicate that previous work experience is a major determinant in women's choice to join the labor force. If a woman ever works for pay, she is more likely to take a job later in life than is a woman who has never worked. Women in the low-income groups who were forced to go to work in crisis situations might return to work later in their lives, even without the impetus of an emergency. Some of the young temporary women workers of World War I may have returned to the labor force in the 1930s for economic reasons, and later in World War II, when the need for women workers far exceeded the requirements for the mobilization in World War I, they may again have rejected domesticity temporarily and entered the factories.[25]

Negative effects upon women's work were also prevalent in the 1930s. The belief that women who held jobs were threatening male employment discouraged some women from working for pay. Job scarcity led to more rigid and one-sided gender stereotyping of occupations. Few women were able to enter new areas of employment, but men increased their participation in two occupations, schoolteaching and light manufacturing, that had been primarily women's occupations in the past.

The economic deprivation of the 1930s stimulated resurgence in work in the home and restored the value of some of women's earlier productive activities. Home gardening and sewing, boarding, selling chickens and eggs—all briefly revived. For a time the emergency recreated some of the elements of an older society in which women's work at home had been urgently needed. The workplace seemed inhospitable in bad times that increased the need for sanctuary at home. When men lost their jobs and could no longer be the primary support of the family, they needed women for emotional support, emergency breadwinning, and work at home to bring in cash to support the family.[26]

The economic depression had a mixed impact on women's work. The positive effects probably exceeded the negative impact. Women responded to the emergency by working in new and old ways. The married women's labor force continued to increase, and women showed lower unemployment rates than men in the depressed economy. All these factors predicted a rising trend of employment for women in the future.

Hostile attitudes toward women's work provided a clearly negative impact upon the pace of entry into the work force, but this factor might easily be overemphasized because it is so visible. Its effects, however, cannot be measured accurately. The realities of the data on increased employment cannot be disputed, and the effect of negative attitudes could not eliminate the less visible positive factors that influenced more women to take a job. Even if a particular married woman could not find a job because of negative attitudes toward women's employment, she would not have been likely to be seeking work if the economy had maintained high employment for men. This woman and others of her sex who were successful in finding work shared the same motivation—economic necessity.

The invention of "pin money" and "temporary emergency work" for married women allowed women to work in new ways without a clash with home-centered values. The process of combining new behavior with small modifications in the prevailing value system would continue after 1940, an accommodation that allowed new behavior to occur concealed within old ideologies. The outlines of future growth were anticipated before 1940 as women made a tentative beginning at developing a modern work role.

CHAPTER 6

Ambivalence, Nostalgia, and Transition

Women's roles in the first forty years of the twentieth century remained essentially unchanged, despite the important social, economic,
and political shifts that defined the context in which women lived.
Such change that did occur in women's lives included either a loss of
some function important in the past or a decline in the importance of
roles that had historically been in their area of expertise. The lowering
of the birth rate, the loss of traditional work roles and the decline of
homemaking as a productive vocation affected women's lives in important ways.

At the same time, the first forty years of the twentieth century
included profound changes in the economy, in politics, and in social
organization. In these years the United States became a fully modernized nation. Even by 1900 the United States had become a mature
industrial society, but it took another four decades for this process to
permeate the whole society, and for its effects to become fully realized. The involvement of the vast majority of the population in at
least one of the modernizing process—education, participation in the
modern workplace, or urbanization—indicated that the process was in
its final stages by 1940.

Women had indeed participated in all these processes. By 1940 the median years of education had reached a new high of ten years for both men and women, and women had maintained steady increases in their participation in higher education. However, as their participation had increased, they had been diverted more frequently into educational programs that were less directed toward careers, and a more distinctively feminized form of higher education had emerged. This had the effect of decreasing women's already slow pace of entry into fields dominated by men, and increasing the movement of the college-educated portion of the female population into domesticity, child-rearing, and homemaking. A liberal arts education was justified for a woman as an important addition to her effectiveness in the home and in social service. Society viewed her education as the acquisition of knowledge of a heritage that she could transmit to her family.[1]

The increasing popularity of marriage after 1920 accentuated the relative decline in women's pursuit of careers, and in effect it left women's careers pursued largely by unmarried women. Home Economics remained a popular educational choice for college women, and many educators strongly espoused its direct relevance to the pursuit of domesticity. The number of strong-minded career women of the earlier twentieth century had been small, although their influence exceeded their numbers. But, despite their earlier visibility, their impact upon the increasingly large group of women who pursued higher education after 1920 was minimal compared to the outspoken new advocates of relevant education for women in their separate sphere.[2]

Thus education tended to confirm women's domestic role after 1920 instead of encouraging women to move into greater mainstream participation. The movement to cities from rural locations had a similar effect. Women had to change the location and sometimes the nature of their domestic pursuits, but urbanization provided no new stimulus to change their domestic orientation. For men, on the other hand, movement to urban locations provided a major career alteration.

The shift to the modern workplace had more effect on women's roles than either education or urbanization, for it provided a new set of job choices, and for the married women who worked for pay this change was important. However, domesticity remained the major pursuit for most married women, and a part-time pursuit for all of them, and its stability meant that women's daily lives changed less than those of men, who experienced modernization more directly.

Women's primary experience of modernization came through the modernization of the family, a process that had begun early in the' nineteenth century. The first suggestion of domesticity emerged in the colonial period, but its spread throughout the population required more than a century. A slow, sometimes inconsistent, process, the pace of transition to the modern family temporarily declined at the end of the nineteenth century, when women tenaciously held fast to many elements of their traditional roles. At the same time, the persistence of the frontier, the large rural sector, and the flood of immigrants from traditional parts of Europe temporarily increased the proportion of people holding traditional views of family life.

These factors held back the pace of family modernization, but women's commitment to many of the elements of the traditional family did not include the continued production of large numbers of children. The decline of differential fertility between 1916 and 1940, and the widespread acceptance of the modern family model by 1940, indicated that the process had reached the final stages.

Modernization had many different implications for women. The preservation and dissemination of the ideal of the modern family was a crucial element, as was also the mechanization of housework. Family medical care, especially childbirth technology, improved. Formal schooling became available for wider segments of the population. But the massive improvements in the quality of family life that accompanied the inexorable process prevented society from recognizing the need for innovation to preserve the value of women's work.

Some observers have suggested that the benefits of modernization include the increase in the sense of efficacy and the ability to exert control over one's life.[3] These important benefits completely eluded women in the early twentieth century. Women lost efficacy and acquired a whole plethora of outside sources to judge their performance. The modern school system, the medical establishment, women's magazines, women's clubs, the advertisers for products for the home—all stood ready to judge mothers wanting in some important activity. This judgment was always after the fact. No group, including women themselves, was able to provide practical innovative guidelines for domesticity in this long period of decline in women's roles.

Why were women not able to achieve innovation in the home at this time? What prevented women from providing the more imaginative efforts that had appeared in the nineteenth century and that would appear again after 1940? Women's control of the daily operation of the home in the preceding century had led to the invention of sanctuary, the pursuit of quality child-rearing, and the maintenance of old work roles within the home plus the invention of some that were new.

Some part of the answer lies in the persistence of the nineteenth-century ideal after its practical usefulness as a guide to activity had declined. In the twentieth century the nineteenth-century ideal of domesticity prevented rational adaptation to the changing conditions. Attempts to deal with women's problems under its aegis yielded ambivalent results.

For example, if rising marriage rates and popular rhetoric are trustworthy indicators, society still strongly valued the home. Yet contrasting indications suggest that the old sanctuary was becoming merely a temporary resting place on the path to modernity. The nineteenth-century ideology insisted that women be primarily concerned with homemaking and child care; twentieth-century women were finding this model increasingly confining and inadequately productive.

Different aspects of the role of the modern homemaker proved contradictory. Society insisted that she be the docile homemaker, but also the smart aggressive shopper; the submissive wife, but informed voting citizen; the sheltered mother at the hearth, but at the same time a strong machine operator at work. Sentimental glorification of the mother image prevented women from making rational choices. They were confused about what tasks needed to be done to keep a proper home, how they could use their own human resources productively in a modern society, and what potential satisfactions they might reasonably expect in their roles as homemakers.

Women expressed their own ambivalence in various ways. They became nostalgic for the traditional family, but at the same time they chose to have fewer babies. Housewives remained in their "place"; simultaneously they admired strong-minded working women. They rarely challenged the adequacy of an outmoded ideology or the assumption that marital happiness offered ample fulfillment. Instead, they either ignored these crucial problems or smothered them with emotional rhetoric.

The popular films of the time failed to portray vignettes of marriage as a creative form of mutual involvement for both sexes. Films about romance and dynamic relationships between males and females typically ended before marriage began. They never showed the marital paradise. Furthermore, reviewers dismissed films about marriage as "women's films" and wrote scorching criticisms of them. This inferior genre characteristically wallowed in various forms of female suffering and sacrifice—careers abandoned for love, children tearfully given up by mothers for their own good, or a woman giving up her own life for the good of the family. On the screen, maternal or marital martyrdom appeared to be women's inevitable lot. The immense popularity of these films raises interesting questions. Did they suggest that a happy marital role entailed only remote risks? Or did they represent exaggerated images of the sacrifices women felt that they already had to make?[4]

A sense of ambivalence about modern family life bred nostalgia for the traditional past when families were large. Public opinion favored politicians who had large families; voters felt they embodied important American values. Franklin Roosevelt recognized that his five surviving children were an important political asset.[5]

The 1937 Gallup Poll that showed actual contemporary family size lagging substantially behind people's desired family size demonstrates the existence of a strong yearning for a lost family model that it was no longer possible to attain. The persistence of higher birth rates for the small group with extremely high income suggests that more married couples preferred to have more children. Apparently many married couples modified their fertility behavior because they felt the constraints of inadequate resources. If they could have chosen more freely, they might have selected the option of plenty.

Articles in women's magazines in the 1920 and 1930 decades reflected this ambivalence about the role of the woman in the home. On the one hand, they discussed the jobs and goals of small modern families and suggested standards appropriate for quality homemaking and child-rearing. On the other hand, they addressed the boredom and discontent inherent in the vocation of homemaking. The writers' advice to dissatisfied women implied that they should be happy but recognized that happiness continued to be elusive for the homemaker. Maternal nostalgia conflicted with the desire for a productive life; the ambivalent outcome underscored the widespread dissatisfaction with the existing role.[6]

In the popular literature of the 1930s, enthusiasm for work roles outside the home appeared side by side with maternal nostalgia. Here the longing for lost activity took on a more modern guise. Articles in women's magazines discussed women's jobs in a positive manner. Stories told of heroines who worked as reporters, copywriters, lawyers, and secretaries who advanced in the organization to become executives. Films in the same period frequently focused on women's careers; Katharine Hepburn, Bette Davis, and Joan Crawford all made popular, successful films about career women. Not radically feminist, these films showed women who were subordinate and deferential to men, but who worked hard at their jobs. They were motivated, competent, frequently single, but not usually young. Rarely did they occupy a "female" occupation, and thus they were in no way representative of the realities of women's working world.[7]

At the same time, these popular views on working women strongly conflicted with other prevailing popular opinions and practices. Public opinion polls of the time reflected widespread public disapproval of working women. Potential employers frequently rejected women over the age of thirty-five and placed the women they did here in sex-stereotyped jobs. These attitudes blatantly contradicted the popular portrayals in the media. This further confused women, who sensed the decline in the value of their roles and recognized the difficulty of finding new ones.

Married women seemed to want more satisfying work lives than the twentieth century offered. Had homemaking still demanded strength, determination, and skill, women might not have yearned so intensely for a different role. Had homemaking not still demanded an unavoidable minimum of work, there might have been a more forthright movement toward new activities. Women continued to be nostalgic for the past and ambivalent about what they wanted; this fact implies that they found increased leisure unsatisfying and declining productivity unacceptable.

By 1900 women had acquired the leading role in the life of the home. This triumph might have set the stage for women to be the leaders in starting a major twentieth-century trend toward innovation in the vocation of homemaking. Women might have developed new kinds of home activities or emphasized the importance of motherhood by maintaining stable, high birth rates. At the very least they could have fought a strong holding action to preserve the nineteenth-century gains. Although such innovations might have been possible, none of them came to pass.

Women were caught in the gap between ideology and reality—the ideology of the nobility of motherhood and the reality of declining productivity in the home. Their response was to internalize this ambivalence and to live with nostalgia for lost activity. The improvements in living standards created by capital improvements and higher quality services from outside the home concealed the dilemma women faced. After all, some people might have said, "Why should they complain? Look at the improvements that have made their lives much easier than their grandmothers' had been."

At the same time, the major upheavals in a society completing the transition to a fully industrialized, relatively homogeneous nation by 1940 prevented a primary focus of attention on women's problem in the home. Integrating new immigrants within the society, building cities that could hold the burgeoning urban population, completing the construction of the industrial base, experimenting with the demands of a new national role as a major world power—all took precedence over changes in the family. In fact, stability in the family was viewed as an absolute necessity in a society undergoing major external change.

Thus as women's practical creativity was undermined by their ambivalence about their role and their nostalgia for lost activity, the distraction of a major transition within society prevented any outside help for women in the home. The history of the home in this period is primarily one of praise without and loss within, as the home's symbolic value increased but its practical importance declined.

The major innovations by women in this period were in their achieving new work roles outside the home. The innovative group were the small minority who moved into the workplace, the 5–15 percent who found work for pay outside the home. But, even here, the achievements were disappointing if success is measured by the extent of participation in paid work by married women, progress toward equality with men, or major expansion of the women's share of the labor market. Nor had women won the support of society to seek new activity forthrightly. With only a few modifications, married women's role in the workplace in 1940 strongly resembled that of 1900.

Despite the aura of nostalgia, old roles had become obsolete; new ones had not yet emerged. Women enjoyed greater freedom than they had in earlier decades. They could select the option of family limitation, and they had more leisure time, but the price for these benefits was lost productivity. Women's ambivalence about new roles and nostalgia for traditional activities emerged from the basic irony—they lost productive roles although they gained a higher standard of living.

This interpretation of the period as one in which modernization dominated provides a useful approach in analyzing the position of women in the society. Modernization explains the ambivalence and nostalgia experienced so profoundly by women, as change occurred more rapidly and in a manner that prevented easy adjustment. Recognition of this larger process and its effects on women's lives also prevents an inappropriate emphasis upon a few unusual individuals who did succeed in retaining productivity, as well as too easy a dismissal of these forty years as merely another long period in which women were exploited.

Women had to wait until after 1940 to find substitutes for their lost productivity. When rapid transition ceased and the society stabilized, to define the context in which women could experiment with innovations in their roles would prove less difficult. But, in the meantime, women felt a pervasive discontent with their proper place as it was evolving in the early twentieth century. Although this dissatisfaction seemed irrational, given the immense improvements, in truth it resulted from transition and its accompaniments: nostalgia and ambivalence.

After 1940 society would move toward the resolution of the conflict between the ideology of women's place as custodian of the home and the reality of declining productivity. Women would discover other values that they could borrow to increase their options in the future. The major change would come when society allowed women to internalize the work ethic. Already emergency situations rife during World War I and the depression of the 1930s had forced society to hold the old ideologies in temporary and partial abeyance. Women had sampled new jobs, and it would become impossible to convince them to return to the old order without questioning it. The stage was set to develop new patterns that would ultimately encourage women to make more diverse choices.

After 1940 the outbreak of World War II heralded increased marriage rates and a changing industrial structure. Society offered women a different framework in which to adapt their own desires to the major changes that were occurring. The economic and historical circumstances were not the same as before, but the problems to which women responded were already inherent in their experiences earlier in the twentieth century. They had to cope with the loss of traditional work and of child-bearing roles and the gap between ideology and reality. The process of establishing women's place in the modern world was still incomplete.

CHAPTER 7

The Baby-Boom Family

The census year 1940 marks a point of a major shift in American history: in the economy, in social relations, and in the history of the American family. The return of economic growth in the later years of the 1930 decade was quickly revealed to be only the tentative beginning of a thirty-five-year period of sustained economic growth after 1940. Stimulated at first by the requirements of war and defense, improvements in the standard of living soon became an expected part of national life in the 1950 decade of almost full employment.

Women found new opportunities to become involved in society through greatly increased participation in work outside the home. Negative attitudes toward women holding jobs bowed to the need for increased wartime production. And after the war adherents of the ideologies defining women's proper place in the home responded, albeit slowly and incompletely, to the need for women workers generated by peacetime economic expansion.

The involvement of all groups in society in at least one of the modernizing processes—public education, work participation in the modern sector, and urbanization—led to greater homogeneity in society than had been present in earlier decades of the twentieth century. This softening of sharp differences in society afforded a more stable context in which women could make innovations in the institution of the home. The "bewildering social flux," so widespread in 1910, had moderated.

All women in society began to recognize the similarities in their new experiences and their responses to them. Both fertility and work patterns in the two decades between 1940 and 1960 reflected increasing social homogeneity. Increases in birth rates and in women's employment appear throughout the social and economic spectrum.

The change in women's roles did not challenge the prevailing ideologies. On the contrary, the belief in the importance of women's remaining in the home received strong positive reinforcement in this period. The increase in fertility in all social classes revealed the tenacity of the belief in home and family. The increase in women's employment began primarily as a response to emergency requirements. This time the crisis was a national war rather than straitened family circumstances, as in the depression decade, but in both cases the justification of emergency provided an acceptable rationale for women's work.

Women's work participation remained within society's acceptable parameters. It was important that most of the women who chose to work were either younger or older than the prime child-bearing years of twenty-five to thirty-four. This encouraged society to accept women in the work force, or at least to tolerate their participation. This pattern was already apparent, if still tentative, before 1940, and it meant that some women could work for pay without directly confronting the cherished value system.[1]

After 1940 women began to develop a more productive role in modern society. They expanded their activities at home and at work. There had been little innovation in homemaking and child care before 1940, but after World War II homemakers found new tasks. They produced larger families, but at the same time their work participation increased. The expanding economy encouraged women to look for jobs. This work, although limited by conventional guidelines for women's place, offered unexpected scope for new activity, and the expansion of the family increased women's productivity in an old and traditional way.

The rising birth rates of the period between 1940 and 1960 (a two-decade aberration midway through the twentieth century) pose challenging questions. Since the early nineteenth century, birth rates had declined. Why did they rebound during this twenty-year period? Observers have suggested explanations ranging from a relatively simple demographic change or innovations in family life patterns to more complex underlying psychological concerns in society. But the impulse to have more children may have resulted from attempts to dispel the sense of loss endemic in the American people before 1940. The effect of the change was a mass movement toward more plentiful fertility and enriched family life.

Until recently the consequences of the demographic break have obscured much of the simultaneous shift in work roles for women. As the large baby-boom birth cohort (the children born between 1940 and 1960) moved through the life cycle, pressure was exerted on different institutional and economic resources every few years. In the middle of the 1960 decade, institutions of higher education felt the effects when the first wave of the baby-boom children entered college. They also went into the work force, and by 1978 the baby boom had become the "worker glut."[2] In the 1980 decade some of the baby boomers were given a new nickname, the "Yuppies." These young adult urban professionals rejected the life style of their parents, who had grown up during the depression and had chosen high fertility and mother-intensive child-rearing.

The worker glut of the 1970 decade and the emergence of the Yuppies in the 1980s brought renewed interest in the baby boom. More data have accumulated, and perspective gained with the passage of time has invited new interpretations based primarily on economic factors like employment rates, the changing level of expectations, and a recognition that children have become consumer goods. The return to declining fertility after 1960 also provided a new contrast with the baby-boom period that allowed more meaningful comparisons of the fertility behavior of modern birth cohorts.

The rising birth rates of the twenty-year period were not anticipated. As birth rates unexpectedly rose for twenty years, they approached levels reminiscent of the early twentieth century. Only the return to declining birth rates after 1960 quelled the speculation that the United States had reached a new stage in demographic modernization. The baby boom in the United States was unique in modern societies, far exceeding the brief and minimal rise in European birth rates in the same period.[3]

Fertility: 1940–1960

Women of all child-bearing ages, ethnic groups, and income levels participated in the baby boom; it was a mass phenomenon. At its peak in 1957 the fertility rate reached 122.9 births for each 1,000 women of child-bearing age. This rate, the highest since 1916, was 50 percent higher than that of 1940. Not until 1958 did the fertility pattern resume its slow decrease, the more "normal" curve of exponential decline.

Although average family size increased, parents did not return to the family size of traditional and premodern society. The new family had 3–4 children rather than the 5 or more that had characterized the families of traditional society. Still, this represented a significant upward shift from the family size of 2–3 children, the widely accepted norm of the 1920 and 1930 decades.

Another important divergence from the patterns of the traditional families and the modern families of the early twentieth century was the closer spacing of children. After 1940 many women, unlike either their mothers or grandmothers, chose to have children less than two years apart. Premodern mothers had produced children at least two years apart, due to prolonged lactation periods. Parents of the 1920-style modern family had chosen to produce their children with intervals of three or four years between them.[4]

However, despite the higher fertility rates and the new spacing intervals between children, fertility still conformed in other ways to trends of the earlier period. Differential fertility continued to decline after 1940, and as average family size increased the standard deviation from mean family size continued to decline. Differential fertility kept decreasing as the new norm was adopted by all groups in the society. Specific fertility, measured by race, religion, residence, age, and educational level, stayed closer to the general average of fertility in this period than in any previous or subsequent time span.

Figure 7.1 illustrates the changes in fertility behavior for different groups. Here we see graphically that the magnitude of modification varies among groups. For example, black fertility increased more than white fertility. The black birth-rate curve turned upward sooner and peaked at a higher level in 1957. Although rural fertility followed a pattern of increase similar to its urban counterpart, it remained continually higher.

Fertility of the younger group of mothers (those between twenty and twenty-nine) showed the greatest change of any age group during the baby-boom years. The rates for young women, who have always had the highest fertility rates, rose substantially more than the rates for all other age groups. But older married couples also had significantly more babies than their counterparts in earlier years. Only white urban mothers of the lower-middle-income levels showed a relatively low increase in fertility rates from similar groups in earlier periods.

Completed fertility for all baby-boom parents, most of whom were

FIGURE 7.1
Birth Rate Trends by Population Group, 1920–1960.

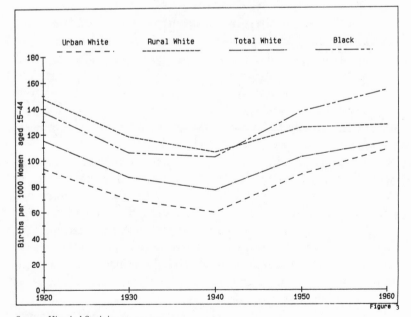

Sources: *Historical Statistics*, pp. 49, 54.

born between 1920 and 1940, exceeded that of their own parents, the birth cohorts of 1890–1910. Completed fertility for both groups correlated negatively with income level, the standard pattern observed throughout the twentieth century and in much of the nineteenth century. But the negative relationship between income and fertility for the parents of the baby-boom children was much less striking than it had been for parental cohorts earlier in the twentieth century. The reduction of the magnitude of the negative correlation between completed fertility and income level indicates in another way the increasing homogeneity of fertility behavior during this period.[5]

Correlation of fertility rates with income level, measured yearly between 1950 and 1960, reveals still another pattern that appears to be in contradiction to the results of the comparison of income with completed fertility. The annual birth rates show a distinctly different re-

FIGURE 7.2
Birth Rate by Age of Mother, 1940–1983.

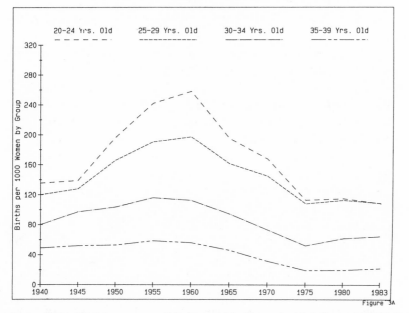

Sources: Historical Statistics, pp. 50, 51; U.S. Bureau of the Census, *Statistical Abstract of the United States: 1986* (107th edition) Washington, D.C., 1986.

lationship between income and fertility. Plotting the yearly figures yields a U-shaped curve instead of the expected linear relationship. The middle-income groups, those at the bottom of the U, have lower birth rates than either the upper- or lower-income groups. These data suggest that the most striking aberrant behavior is that of the upper-income segment, those who in the recent past had produced fewer births than those of lower and middle income, and that this aberrant behavior describes a relatively short time span, that of only one decade.[6]

The scope of the changes in fertility rates suggests the need for analysis of demographic hypotheses that lead to a more precisely defined problem, if not a complete solution. A list of explanatory demographic hypotheses might include the following possibilities.

1. An increase in the proportion of the population in child-bearing ages caused the birth rate to increase without any real change in individual behavior.

2. If most births occurred within marriage, a rise in the proportion of married people of child-bearing age led to higher birth rates.

3. Births were concentrated between 1940 and 1960 that "normally" would have occurred either before 1940 or after 1960.

4. Special circumstances increased the fertility of enough specific groups so that the total fertility rates increased.

Women of Child-Bearing Age. The first hypothesis—that an unusually large concentration of women in child-bearing ages existed in the population—would offer a simple explanation for rising birth rates. However, between 1940 and 1960 women of child-bearing age made up an unusually small proportion of the total population. In the 1950s there were 4 percent fewer women between twenty and thirty years old than in the preceding decade. In fact, although there were more women born in the 1920 decade (women between thirty and forty in the 1950 decade, thus still in child-bearing age) than in the 1930 decade, the combined number of both groups comprised a smaller proportion of the population than normal. The end to substantial immigration and the low birth rates between 1920 and 1940 significantly curtailed the number of possible mothers. Longer life expectancy led to an increase in older people; the high birth rate elevated the percentages of young people in the population. Thus, the first possibility is inapplicable to the problem.[7]

Increased Marriage. The second alternative—increased rates of marriage—is more promising. A peak in marriages occurred in 1946, followed by a high rate for first births in 1947. But this was only a short-term result of the marriages postponed until after World War II had ended. Still, 95 percent of all babies were born within wedlock in the baby-boom decades. Few newborns were illegitimate. An unusually high proportion of the population in child-bearing years was married in the immediate postwar years, a situation that certainly encouraged higher birth rates in the later years of the 1940 decade.

The popularity of marriage continued to increase in the 1950s. In 1950, 59 percent of the people in child-bearing ages were married; a decade later this proportion had increased to 65 percent. The increased proportion of married people in the population is largely a result of earlier marriage, and early marriage correlates with higher fertility rates.[8]

John Modell has shown that this relationship is not simply a result of earlier marriage and thus increased "exposure" to the risk of pregnancy. On the contrary, young people who believed in the norm of early marriage also preferred high rates of fertility. Both choices are voluntary and result from strong belief structures, and they occur in combination.[9]

Most children were planned or at least wanted in this period, since accidental fertility varied little from other time periods. Most couples used some form of birth control to control spacing and completed family size. Early marriage is an important indicator of enthusiasm for family creation in this period, but it does not "explain" the high birth rates.[10]

Concentration of Births. A more useful analytical suggestion is that births that might normally have occurred before 1940 or after 1960 instead were concentrated between these years. Women began to marry earlier, started having babies sooner, and spaced their children closer together. These behaviors led to significant clustering of births in the 1950s. Many young women in this decade completed their families before they reached the age of thirty, unlike their mothers or grand-mothers, who had continued bearing children until they were thirty-five or older.

The upper-income groups, in particular, exhibited this fertility pattern. The U-shaped curve illustrates this. But the higher concentration of births in the 1950s only partially explains the baby boom. The women born in the 1930s still produced a larger total number of children than earlier or later birth cohorts.

Women born in the 1920s also had high fertility rates; this too contributed to the persistently high birth rates between 1950 and 1960. Most of this group of women started bearing children later because the disruption of World War II had led to the postponement of fertility. They were still having children in the 1950s. These older mothers spaced their children in more conventional patterns than did their younger sisters. They were still having third or fourth children when the women of the birth cohort of the 1930s began their families. The combination of high birth rates for both cohorts pushed fertility rates upward in the 1950s.[11]

Married couples chose to produce larger families. More third and fourth children were born in one year, 1957, the peak year of the baby boom, than in any other twentieth-century year. Throughout the 1950s birth rates were unusually high for women over the age of thirty, especially for women between thirty-five and thirty-nine. Many of these women were completing three- or four-child families. In 1957, 117 children were born to every 1,000 white women of child-bearing age. Of these babies, 25 (21 percent of the total) were third children and 12 (10 percent) were fourth children. These numbers provide a sharp contrast with 1940, when not only was the birth rate much lower (75 births per 1,000 women) but only 11 were third children (15 percent) and 6 were fourth children (8 percent). Births of third and fourth children increased in the 1950s, and at the same time the median age of mothers giving birth to third and fourth children was unusually high. Thus, more of the women born in the 1920s gave birth to third and fourth children during these years.[12]

The extremely high marriage rates for the birth cohort of the 1920s between 1944 and 1947 were followed by successive concentrations of first-, second-, third-, and fourth-order births in the next fifteen years.

But by 1960 the median age of mothers giving birth to third and fourth children was falling, although the rates for these births was still high. This shows that the younger mothers (those born in the 1930s) also chose to produce large families, but with their children more closely spaced. By 1965, when this younger group had completed their families, the rate of third- and fourth-order births returned to the level of the early 1940 decade. The peaking of the birth rate in the late 1950 decade, then, has two major components—the first, second, and some third births of the women born in the 1930s and the third and fourth children of the older parents.[13]

The concentration of higher-order births in the 1950s and the early years of the 1960s was essential to make the baby boom a unique demographic event. Two different birth cohorts—women born in the 1920s and those born after 1930—completed their families during the same fifteen-year period. Not only did parents choose large families, but the second group's decision to space their children closer together exaggerated the immediate rise in birth rates. If the younger group had spaced their children more conventionally, the surge in fertility rates would not have been so dramatic. The curves would have risen more gradually, but a less remarkable baby boom would merely have continued longer.

Data collected by the Gallup Poll suggest that baby-boom parents produced the number of children they said that they preferred. Parents could realize their desire for more children in this period, a result that contrasted with the depression years, when straitened economic circumstances had dictated low fertility, and the early part of the 1940s, when war separations prevented both marriage and child-bearing.

In 1936 and again in 1960 poll interviewers asked sample populations what they considered the ideal family size, and the two groups responded quite differently. In 1960 none of the respondents found childlessness or even one child to be acceptable. Eighteen percent of the respondents found two children as the most desirable; 28 percent recommended three children, and by far the largest group (43 percent) believed that four children represented the perfect family size.

The 1936 respondents preferred smaller families. Only 22 percent of them advocated the four-child family as opposed to the 32 percent who favored two children and the equal number who chose three babies as the ideal. But in the 1930s actual family size lagged behind even these more modest wishes. Thus, the gap between the number of children parents wanted and the babies actually born was much greater then than during the baby-boom years, when parents both preferred and produced large families.[14]

Births in the 1940s. The intervening decade of the 1940s included some special circumstances conducive to rising fertility. Fertility rates rose between the depression decade of the 1930s and the prosperous 1950s. They increased even though many young men were absent in the early years of the 1940s. One explanation for some part of the rising birth rates between 1940 and 1945 is that older women who were still of child-bearing age and who had postponed having babies during the 1930s chose to have children when more prosperous times returned. Before 1940 women still under thirty waited until they could afford to have another child, and often they waited until they were at least thirty-five years old. The completed family size for women between thirty and thirty-nine years of age was larger in the 1940s than it had been for the comparable group in the previous decade. In the more prosperous war years, parents of the depression era who were still in the child-bearing years attempted to bring actual family size up to their desired levels. The result was a rising birth rate that occurred despite the absence of many of the younger men in the armed services.

Extra births in the 1940s can be explained more easily than those of the 1950s. Young married people in the 1930s had wanted more children, and they were able to remedy their feelings of deprivation when good times returned. The impact of World War II on the population of child-bearing age was also important. Together, these factors appear to explain most of the additional births of the decade. Both the depression and World War II might have increased the desire of parents in the 1940s to bring up larger families.

Birth rates usually rise after wars; societies turn to fertility, the creation of life, to replace the dead. There was a small baby boom in Europe immediately following the war. Amid the destruction and despite the severe shortages, people still had babies. The psychological relationship between birth rates and wars probably results from the restoration of basic human confidence that grows from the mere fact of survival.

But in the United States other positive factors further stimulated fertility. Savings accounts were padded from high wartime wages, but there were few consumer goods to be bought in the immediate post-war period. After 1945 children were "available" satisfactions, whereas alternative goods were not. This fact lent an economic stimulus to the increase in fertility.

Another economic stimulus unique to the 1940s also increased fertility. According to economists, the five years immediately following the war were the only modern period in United States history when the federal income tax deduction for children might have been an economic incentive to have babies. At all other times, the exemption has been only a minimal and almost irrelevant reduction of the costs of rearing a child. Before 1940 too few people earned large enough incomes to incur tax liability; after 1950 the deduction for children was so much less than the real cost of bringing them up that there was no true economic incentive to fertility.[15]

The reasons for the rising fertility in the decade of the 1950s are not so apparent. The direct results of World War II fail to explain the clustering of births, because the young parents had been small children during the war. The dramatic concentration of births in the 1950s, the crucial element of the baby boom, cannot be explained as easily as the extra births of the 1940s. And had these births not been clustered in these two decades and had taken place earlier or later, there would still have been a baby boom because people had chosen to have larger families. Instead of a steep rise in the birth rate in the 1950s, a more gradual increase in the birth curves would have spread over a longer period.

If patterns had been normal, amid altered goals, birth rates in the 1930s would have been higher, and in the 1940s they would have been more evenly spread over the decade. Still, fertility rates would have been high because the women born in the 1920s would not have waited until the 1950s to have some of their children. And, finally, had the women born in the 1930s followed the conventional pattern of spacing births at longer intervals, some of their third or fourth children would have been born later in the 1960s. The baby boom would have begun

earlier and lasted longer, but there would still have been a clear upward trend in fertility.

Fertility of Special Groups. The fourth demographic hypothesis suggests
that special circumstances affected different groups sufficiently to cause
a significant rise in the birth rate. A detailed breakdown of group
fertility in this period offers new insight on this problem. Special circumstances strongly affected several identifiable groups.

Religious principles affected fertility behavior. For example, during
the baby boom, the birth rate among Catholics appears to have been
higher than it was in other religious groups. Earlier, in the first two
decades of the twentieth century, Catholics had higher fertility rates.
Many were recent immigrants from southern and eastern Europe, with
traditional values about family life. Therefore, the premodern value
system, combined with religious beliefs, led to high levels of fertility.
After 1920 the impact of both religion and traditionalism declined
rapidly. In that decade, partially because of a lower marriage rate for
its adherents, Catholicism correlated negatively with fertility.

After 1930 the fertility of married Catholics began to rise; it remained high until 1964. The 1930 census showed the negative correlation, but in that year the Pope's encyclical *Casti Connubi* "firmly
labeled attempts to frustrate the natural power of the sex act to gen-
erate life as 'branded with guilt of grave sin.' " Thereafter, Catholicism correlated positively with fertility; the census results for 1940,
1950, and 1960 show this reversal. Catholics usually resorted to a
traditional method of birth control: the postponement of marriage.
Those who did marry earlier were likely to produce the few very large
families (five or more children) during the baby boom.[16]

Special circumstances then affected the fertility rates of Catholics
between 1930 and 1964 even though the rise in their fertility was also
part of a more general fertility increase in the population. Catholics
married later than other groups after 1940, an anomaly during the
baby boom, when early marriage was the norm. After 1960 Catholics
increasingly adopted artificial birth control, a practice that led to decreasing fertility after 1964. The Pope's encyclical of 1930 remained a
part of Catholic doctrine, but lay attitudes shifted, partially perhaps

in response to the more liberal pronouncements of the Second Vatican Council.[17]

Black fertility also varied somewhat from white fertility. Although there were only 21 percent more black mothers in 1957 than there had been in the base year of 1940, birth rates of blacks were 100 percent higher in that peak year of the baby boom. This dramatic increase coincided with the massive migration of the black population from rural to urban environments. The impact of urbanization on black fertility during the baby-boom years broke with historical precedents. Lower birth rates had been the predictable corollary to urbanization in the past for most white migrants; for the black migrants the experience was reversed. The newly urban blacks were escaping from rural poverty to perceived or expected improvement in economic conditions. If chronic privation had been the major deterrent to fertility in the past, the new circumstances encouraged a rising birth rate.[18]

Rural populations of both races showed rising fertility during the baby boom. However, neither rural nor urban populations returned to the premodern family size. The rural birth rate consistently has correlated with the rises and drops in farm income. This long-term pattern began before the baby boom, continued between 1940 and 1960, and persisted in the most recent period of the twentieth century. The increase in rural fertility during the baby boom fits consistently within this established trend.[19]

Native white urban birth rates remained relatively consistent with the precedents of the recent past. Fertility in this group increased less than in all others. This consistency is most pronounced for the middle- and lower-middle income groups. In the 1950s the white lower-middle class and the more prosperous segments of the working class tended to be more conservative in their fertility behavior than either those of higher or lower income.[20]

The more educated and higher income portions of the white urban middle class, however, changed their fertility behavior the most drastically. The birth rates for the educated middle class were higher during the baby boom than they had been before 1940 and would be after 1960. Between 1950 and 1960, the fertility of this group substantially exceeded that of the lower-middle income groups. High fertility among

upper-income groups was an aberration, a substantially different behavior from that usually characteristic of modern societies.[21]

College women of child-bearing ages during the baby boom had
significantly larger families than college women of older generations.
This difference is apparent for women who were in their twenties in
the decade of the 1950s. The higher income and higher education
groups were not identical, although substantial overlap occurs. Both
groups when measured separately show unusually high birth rates.
The clear and important conclusion of these data is that a loosely
defined well-educated upper- and middle-income segment of the population chose high fertility and concentrated this behavior in the 1950s.

During the baby boom this group of high socio-economic status
chose to marry earlier, bear children sooner, and space their children
more closely together. This combination, unprecedented in modern
times, gave rise to a particular kind of family that pursued some new
goals. It differed from the traditional family of five children spaced
two or more years apart, but it was not merely an extension of the
1920-style family to include one more child. The new modern family
included young parents and three or four closely spaced children.

Parents planned their child production; they used birth control extensively and could avoid accidental pregnancies. The upper middle
class strongly favored this family style, which contrasted with the
preferences of a similar group earlier in the twentieth century. The
upper middle class had pioneered the smaller modern family in the
nineteenth century. Again, a similar group defined the new guidelines—this time for efficient production of children in a later form of
modern family that featured closely spaced births and more children.[22]

The new family style was most clearly identified with the upper
middle class; nevertheless, families in other groups also chose the new
style. Fertility responded to an external environment stimulating to
increase and innovation. Many special circumstances converging in
these decades encouraged higher fertility for many groups; rural residents, Catholics, and blacks all experienced conditions positive to fertility increase. Many of these circumstances were consistent with trends
of the past. Only the upper middle class white urban residents broke
so strongly out of their past (and future) fertility patterns.

Innovation in the Baby-Boom Family

In many ways the baby-boom family resembled the modern family of the early twentieth century. The mother remained the emotional center of the family, and mother-intensive quality child-rearing still provided the basic method of family care. In the baby-boom period the experts on child-rearing shifted their views to emphasize permissiveness and the importance of the development of the individual personality, emphases that were strongly reminiscent of the views of child-rearing experts at the turn of the century. The child's needs acquired priority, superseding convenience and schedules.

A massive child-rearing literature appeared, led by Dr. Benjamin Spock, whose first book, *Baby and Child Care*, appeared in 1946 and exceeded all previous sales records for child-rearing manuals. He included the latest medical information and psychological insights. Mothers' belief in the importance, indeed the necessity, of taking correct actions led them to seek the advice of experts, often at the expense of trusting their own wisdom and insight. These attitudes, like the child-rearing theory of permissiveness, also resembled those of the turn of the century, another period when mothers searched diligently for expert advice.[23]

Despite these similarities to the older form of the modern family, the baby-boom family included important new features. The roles for all the members of the family changed in important ways. Parents now encouraged the development of warm sibling relationships among their closely spaced children. The new concept that emerged, that of the close family unit, did not displace maternal devotion; it enriched total family life in a new way. A loving and active paternal style replaced the distant and authoritarian patriarchal standard. And, finally, family leisure activities proliferated, and the home became a place for creative interaction and personal development.[24]

These were not totally new goals, but the emphasis had changed. Mothers found new tasks. They had to plan leisure-time activities for the family and to maintain recreational equipment. They spent many hours supervising groups of children at play. In the 1950 decade the popular architectural style for middle-class homes both encouraged and responded to the new family styles. Most homes included a "family" room integrated with either the kitchen or the more formal living room. The bedrooms were grouped together in a separate wing. The floor plans of the houses of the 1950 decade had encouraged very little individual privacy. The old nineteenth-century den, the private habitat of the father, disappeared from the newer houses, and the separate bedroom wing for the parents would be unheard of for at least twenty more years. Thus even domestic architecture fostered regular interaction between family members in their daily lives.[25]

The new family style flourished in the expanding suburbs. Here, the mother's homemaking role gained even more importance because home ownership became a prime goal for baby-boom families. The mother became responsible for maintenance of the house, landscaping the yard, and planting gardens. Home decorating also demanded new investments of her time. In this period home sewing again became an economically sensible choice for women because rising labor costs had made readymade clothing expensive. Traditional crafts like rugmaking, embroidery, needlepoint, and knitting reappeared. Fathers purchased tools for carpentry and repair, and frequently built furniture in workshops in the garage, a practice that revived an old tradition of homemaking for men and extended the concept of marital partnership into new areas.

Child-bearing took on a positive mystique, and family creation acquired new status. Young mothers, eager to prove themselves worthy, rejected the image of painful childbirth and emphasized it as a positive experience. Painless childbirth, rooming-in, and breast feeding became normal practices for mothers during the baby boom. This practice contrasted with the long anesthetized hospital recuperation in darkened rooms far away from their newborn babies that new mothers had experienced in earlier twentieth-century decades. Recuperative time following childbirth shrank to resemble that of primitive societies as baby-boom mothers returned to normal life as soon as lactation began.[26]

Suburban sociability kept loneliness at bay for women at least in theory. Morning coffee parties and after-school car pools replaced the afternoon tea and the women's club on social calendars. Hospitable housewives in suburban neighborhoods created daily enclaves of social interactions among mothers and children. The neighborhoods became communities in which families led active social lives.

Not all families could afford to realize the 1950s family dream of a well-equipped home in the suburbs, but a booming economy encouraged young couples to try to achieve this goal. Almost everyone could at least surpass the family style of their parents, who had struggled just to keep the home together in the depression decade of the 1930s. Employment levels remained high, and median family income increased at a constant rate. These facts meant that more children, more equipment, and more family activity were within the reach of everyone.[27]

The new family style predominated for about twenty years; family size showed clear decline by 1965. Families begun in the late 1950s and the early years of the 1960s continued to pursue the baby-boom style, but it was beginning its long decline. The devotedly nurtured baby-boom children grew up and found the outside world more exciting than home. Ultimately, men put away their carpentry equipment and bought tennis racquets or gold clubs instead. Again mothers were left behind, tending an empty shrine, but this time they left home for the workplace. Economic growth and an established female labor market offered them a productive role outside the home.

Betty Friedan called the baby-boom family style a "Victorian revival, a conspiracy to trap women in the home," but it can perhaps be more comprehensively viewed as an effort to integrate nostalgia for the traditional family with the benefits of modern life. Resurgent prosperity made this possible. The homemaker used new knowledge and more sophisticated theories of child-rearing; she seemed to feel that the home could still be an exciting and innovative institution for personal development.[28]

Young people between 1940 and 1960 made conscious choices to expand the importance of homemaking and child-rearing. The lower divorce rates between 1950 and 1968 suggest that married couples attained a certain level of success. The average duration of marriage was longer for the baby-boom parents during child-rearing years than the duration of marriage for similar age groups in later years. Perhaps more extensive criteria than a simple indicator like longevity should be used to measure marital and family success. Still, the numbers are starkly clear. New factors encouraged creations of families in a new environment. In quantity of children produced and in the stability of the families participating, the results were impressive.[29]

CHAPTER 8

Perspectives on
High Fertility

Explanations for the high fertility rates after World War II include a wide variety of popular and scholarly interpretations. Immediately after the war, high fertility appeared to be a natural and predictable reaction to past events. But as fertility continued to rise in the 1950s and a younger generation of parents pursued family rearing with new enthusiasm, speculation increased about the cause of this unexpected choice.[1]

Early in the baby-boom years, many psychologists applauded women's return to their biologically unique destiny. Remembering Sigmund Freud's views espoused fifty years earlier, they saw the true maternal nature emerging again and encouraging fulfillment for women.[2]

This observation offers little in the way of explanation, for it gives no reasons for the sudden emergence of women's "true maternal nature" in 1948 after a long period of decline. But the strong approval implied by this description of the imperatives behind the fertility resurgence is revealing of the widespread positive attitude toward family and child-rearing that characterized the baby-boom period. No neo-Malthusians marred the perception of a fertility paradise with warnings of crowded schools to come, or an inadequate economic pie for distribution in the future.

In 1962, after fertility had already started to decline, Betty Friedan offered an explanation for society's approval of the baby boom based on the need to keep women in the home. She suggested two reasons for society's encouragement of the formation of large families. First, women's departure from the work force after World War II to return to the home would leave jobs available for men returning from the armed services, a high priority choice in the society. Equally important, women who stayed at home and produced babies would increase consumer demand for a wide variety of goods. In a society that expected and feared a postwar depression, many people agreed with these beliefs.[3]

Though society might have approved, it is difficult to use Friedan's economic explanation to establish the causal link between the reasons for society's approval and women's actual behavior. Married women in child-bearing ages had always remained at home; thus their return there after the war had substantial precedent, a factor that challenges the adequacy of the fertility explanation that is based primarily on the need to stimulate the economy.

The positive attitude of society toward fertility and family provided only a supportive context for this decision by individuals. Explanations for fertility increase need to focus on the reasons for the private decisions of individuals. Societal norms play a part in this process, but the previous chapter has already described the new kind of family created by baby-boom parents, a family for which a societal norm was not already in existence.

The problems that need solutions are why baby-boom parents chose to have one or two more children than the number approved by the existing family norm; why did all groups participate in the fertility resurgence; and why did some groups, particularly the upper middle class, behave so differently from their counterparts in the 1920s and 1930s? In more general terms, why were the demographers of the late 1930s and early 1940s not correct in their prediction of fertility rates only slightly higher than those of the late 1930s?[4]

The problem that Betty Friedan seeks to explain—why women of child-bearing age returned home from the work force after World War II—should be replaced by the problem of explaining the new elements of their family behavior once they had returned. Going home was to be expected; women between twenty-four and thirty-five were the first age group to leave the work force even before the shift to peacetime production had begun. If this group had remained in the work force or even tried to remain there, we would have a real problem to solve, for women would have been behaving in a historically unprecedented manner. Understanding their return to the home requires no assumption of a societal conspiracy providing pressure in the interests of economic recovery.[5]

Women had not given up the home as an institution of worth and value. Their efforts in the direction of its rejuvenation through higher fertility and the addition of new family functions were innovations to reverse the trend of decline that had become apparent before 1940. What circumstances made this choice the preferred option? What made it economically possible?

Explanations for changes in fertility behavior can usually be divided into two basic types: those that deal with the availability of resources for rearing children (costs) and those that are concerned with the reasons why people want more or fewer children (tastes). If we assume that tastes remain similar over time, then changes in the availability of resources are the key to explaining variations, or, conversely, if resource availability remains similar over time, and fertility changes, we must assume changes in the taste for children. During the baby boom, resource availability increased in a period of rapid economic growth, and tastes also changed in an upward direction, as the Gallup Poll data cited in the previous chapter show so clearly. Thus both types of explanations—those of tastes and those of costs—are important for the baby-boom period.

The Cost of Children

The relationship between the changing tastes for children and the availability of resources for raising them was direct and consistent in the earlier part of the twentieth century. In the period between 1900 and 1940, resource availability increased throughout the society except for a few years in the 1930s. All groups participated in the process of economic growth, but fertility still declined because tastes for children were changing. The traditional ethic of child production gave way to the new modern family behavior, and the effect of this change was negative for fertility.

The inverse relationship between resource availability and fertility was primarily a result of the greater involvement of the more prosperous people in the modern sectors of society, where children had become only one of the available consumer goods for which resources could be used. Children were an old good, available to all, even those who had not yet developed an extensive involvement with the consumer society. But child purchase required resources, and this realization spread rapidly throughout society in the early twentieth century.

By 1940 the realization of the important relationship between resource availability and child production had become widespread. Fertility was clearly more dependent upon monetary resources in modern society than it had been in the days of traditional society. In earlier times expectations were lower, and children provided useful services to the family.

Gary Becker, Theodore Schultz, and other "New Home Economists" have done the major research on the theoretical relationship between fertility and available resources. They developed an economic model that applies microeconomic theory to the household, and concluded that children in modern society have become consumer goods that compete with other possible purchases for family resources. Parents "purchase" children and in return receive "child satisfaction."[6]

This view recognizes that the cost of child-rearing is an important factor in the fertility decision of potential parents. It assumes that fertility decisions are made rationally, and it defines the function of children in modern societies. A further implication of this theory is that income and fertility should correlate positively in a society in which families make perfectly rational decisions and have similar utility functions, or the same taste for fertility.

Evidence proves that after 1916 fertility behavior became ever more homogeneous, or, in Becker's terms, it revealed more similarity in family utility functions. Tastes for children became more similar throughout the society.

During the baby boom, society also moved toward less variation in fertility norms. Notably, even though there was a gradual upward movement in birth rates in this period, the standard deviation in family size continued to decline. The higher birth rates for the upper-income groups during the baby boom furnish additional evidence to validate the Becker-Schultz model of modern fertility.

However, other evidence suggests that there are substantial problems with this theory as a predictor of behavior. Completed fertility for all groups still correlated inversely with income at all levels during the baby boom, and although the upper end of the U-shaped curve fit the Becker-Schultz model, the lowest income groups still showed the highest fertility even in the 1950s.

Three conclusions are possible. First, fertility decisions are not made rationally. Second, tastes vary in some way unrelated to income, and, third, the cost of children is not perceived as the same for all groups. The first conclusion would undermine the discussion of fertility completely, by its implication that all fertility is in some sense accidental. The second conclusion is possible, but acceptance of it is in effect a rejection of the microeconomic theory of the household. Sufficient data exist to support the assumption that the taste for children and level of income bear some relationship, but not always consistently over time.

The third possible explanation is simpler and can be easily defended. Income effects alone are incomplete indicators of the economic impacts on fertility, and this factor may explain some of the deviations in behavior. The cost of child-rearing varies among social classes and income levels. Thus, dollar figures may not represent a consistent percentage of income at all levels. A family that chooses high-quality child-rearing techniques may anticipate much heavier expenditures than one whose requirements are more moderate. Food, shelter, medical care, clothing, and schooling are the basic cost items of raising a child, but these expenses can vary widely across and within social classes. Discretionary costs of child-rearing include college education, private school, summer camp, expensive toys and leisure equipment, private bedrooms, and playgrounds. The range of potential costs is indeed extensive. Some families will consider them necessary; others will find many irrelevant or unsuitable.

Each family considers its present economic conditions and future prospects, values for child nurture, and the rewards they assume will come with child-rearing. These and other crucial variables define the family's fertility equation. For each family it is different, and it may not relate to income level in any substantial way. The simplified rational model does not describe real life, because rational people of diverse social classes, educational levels, aspirations, and socialization make different assumptions about the costs of child-rearing. Even if we assume the rational model, uncertainty and imperfect information can lead to different decisions for people with the same intent, and this also hampers realization of the theoretical model.

These qualitative considerations might seem unnecessarily to complicate attempts to relate the model to actual behavior. However, they underline the importance of human perceptions, expectations, and goals. These qualities, difficult to measure quantitatively, may be more important in explaining changes in fertility than level of income alone.

One group may consider a society (or family) to be highly prosperous that another group would dismiss as scarcely above poverty. At the individual level or in cross-sectional comparisons the importance of these differing perceptions is obvious. But they may also be relevant at a macro level for the aberrant period between 1945 and 1960. Real income may have increased faster than the level of expectations. Measurements of people's changing perception of the minimum income necessary to support a family of four people indicate that improvements in actual family income exceeded the perceptions of the necessary minimum.

Figure 8.1 shows that the growing economy furnished resources that continually exceeded the perceived cost of child-rearing. The question of the minimum weekly income necessary to support a family of four people was included frequently enough on public opinion surveys over time that indications of trends in that perception can be compared to actual improvements in the level of family income. Both opinion polls and actual behavior indicated that the desire to produce more babies seemed to be economically viable during the baby-boom period and in the 1960s. The existing assumptions about the costs of rearing children fell within the constraints of resources available to families.

Rising income exceeded rising aspirations, an unusual relationship

FIGURE 8.1

Changing Perceptions of Family Resource Needs.

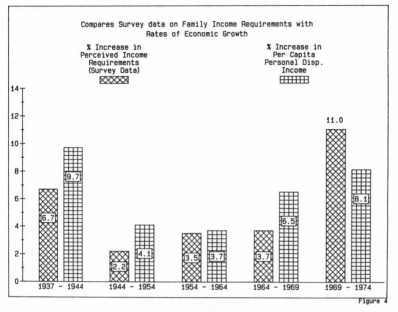

Compares Survey data on Family Income Requirements with
Rates of Economic Growth

Sources: Economic data derived from *Historical Statistics*, Tables 51-5 and F6-9; and survey data compiled from George Gallup, *The Gallup Public Opinion Poll, 1935–1971*, Volume 3 (New York, 1974).

in modern society. This convergence permitted parents to realize their fertility goals. Although families recognized that the necessary minimum income for family maintenance was rising, they also observed that general prosperity was increasing even more rapidly. In this period Americans achieved a higher fertility norm and less differential fertility, and at the same time the pace of economic growth exceeded rising aspirations.

Morris Janowitz collected data that reflect the same positive assessment of individual financial position seen in Figure 8.1. Janowitz studied public opinion polls on financial position and relative deprivation between 1938 and 1974. The pollsters had asked respondents a variety of similar questions. The more direct of these, "Are you better or worse off financially than in the last year?" was sometimes varied by the more general "Are people better off or worse off financially than one year ago?" or the more personal "Are you and your family pretty well satisfied with your financial situation?" Janowitz found a trend of rising satisfaction that moved continuously upward from 1938 when only 26 percent though they were better off than in the previous year. The peak year for satisfaction was 1956, when 40 percent of the respondents considered either themselves or people in general to be better off than they had been in the previous year. After 1956, the satisfaction trend turned negative, and in 1974, the final year of the study, only 31 percent felt more prosperous than they had in the previous year.[7]

The analysis by Janowitz shows the dichotomy between perceived financial improvement and the hard data on actual improvement in per-capita economic growth. As Figure 8.2 illustrates, real per-capita income shows continual improvement throughout the 1960 decade and the early years of the 1970 decade, the same years in which some

FIGURE 8.2
Trend Comparison: Birth Rates and Economic Growth.

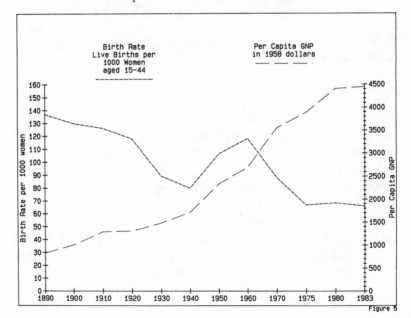

Sources: Historical Statistics, p. 225; Statistical Abstract of the United States: 1986, p. 433.

measures of the perception of improvement showed decline. Fertility appears to relate to the perception of income improvement more closely than to the real growth of income in the economy.

The New Home Economists have shown the important relationship between access to resources and child production, and the Janowitz data reveal the importance of income perception even if it is unrelated to the real financial circumstances. The relationship between economic perceptions and real economic improvement in the baby-boom period provides a strong contrast with other periods when perceptions were not so positive. Baby-boom parents perceived a growing economy that would provide plentiful resources for family-rearing at a level beyond basic needs, and this positive perception extended into the 1960 decade in the years of achievement of parity at relatively high levels.

Macroeconomists, like microeconomists Becker and Schultz, have also searched for the income and cost variables that correlate with changes in fertility. Their insights have shown the importance of economic factors as they related to fertility, but consistent and simple explanations do not emerge. Cross-sectional and longitudinal studies appear to show different results, as we have already seen in the fertility behavior of the 1950 decade. The *U*-shaped curve of yearly fertility suggests different results from the inverse and linear relationship observed in completed fertility. The parallel upward curves of income and fertility at the macro level do not match either the data on completed fertility by income or, consistently, the impact on fertility of higher family income at the individual level.

Microeconomists Julian Simon and Boone Turchi stress individual variation in fertility decisions based on income change, although Turchi emphasizes the importance of long-term income variables, and Simon showed that at any point rising income in individual families can affect in either a positive or negative direction the decision to have babies. Here is clear evidence of the importance of individual tastes for fertility. For some married couples, the new income allowed the realization of a desired pregnancy; for others, new income provided resources for newer consumer goods.[8]

Morris Silver suggested, however, that at a macro level and, on the average, income improvement during the baby boom encouraged fertility, or in effect allowed the implementation of already existing tastes for fertility. His work shows that the fluctuations of the 3–5-year business cycle explained 30 percent of the births after the first one. The upward blips in the fertility curve, plotted with a lag of one year, are in parallel with the upswings of the business cycle, clearly suggesting an economic impetus for the planning of pregnancies.[9]

Another income variable that relates to fertility realization has been identified by economist Peter Lindert. He showed the importance of the breadth of improvement in income distribution during periods of economic growth, and he suggested that this breadth is dependent upon a labor force of high quality, training, and experience. These factors he found to be present during the baby boom but not during the 1920s or in the period after 1960, both periods of economic growth and lower fertility.[10]

Presumably a broad income distribution encourages consumption of all kinds, and if child-bearing is only a special kind of consumption those who want babies could realize their goal. Since a larger group could be participating in consumption, on the average this should lead to a higher birth rate. When only a small group participates in the growth of prosperity, consumption is limited. Even if a substantial portion of the consumers choose child production, the growth of the birth rate is necessarily constrained by the smaller number of participants. The breadth of participation in economic growth that characterized the baby-boom years allowed widespread realization of the taste for fertility.

The effect of the breadth of participation in economic growth may have been accentuated by another income effect known as the relative income hypothesis. The premise of this theory is that perception of prosperity should be separated from the actual income level of individuals. People perceive income improvement (or decline) differently according to their comparative frame of reference. What might appear to be a good income for some workers might for others be inadequate because it is low for their peer group, or it might not represent a significant enough difference from groups perceived as deserving of lower income. According to the relative income hypothesis, an individual's income relative to his peer group or a group he believes is of lower or higher status affects his behavior more strongly than the amount he actually earns.

Richard Easterlin has suggested that the success of the baby-boom parents in achieving an income that surpassed that of their parents at a similar point in the life cycle created a perception of success in their lives. Relatively, their incomes were higher in the 1950 decade than those of their parents in the decade of the Great Depression. This perception of achievement appears to correlate positively with fertility at a macro level, although it has been difficult to show that this same relationship has validity at the individual or micro level.[11]

The relative-income hypothesis may provide insight into the reasons for the rising fertility of the upper middle class so apparent in the 1950s. In the 1940s income of blue-collar groups rose more rapidly than the income of white-collar workers. The reverse relationship appeared in the 1950 decade, when the professional and managerial segments of the white-collar group benefited from more rapid increases in income. This improvement in the income of the white-collar groups suggests a possible correlation between their high fertility and their greater improvement in prosperity in the 1950 decade relative to that of blue-collar workers. However, a straight income argument could also explain the realization of higher fertility tastes in this decade.[12]

Cross-sectional studies of the relationship between the occupation of the husband and the fertility pattern of the family also support the income argument. During the 1950 and 1960 decade, professionals, the highest income group, became fathers more frequently than managers or clerical workers. In blue-collar occupations, differences in fertility rates also appear. The birth rate in the families of laborers and operatives remained relatively high, but wives of craftsmen maintained intermediate to low levels of fertility. These data seem to be relatively consistent with the U-shaped curve of birth rates that continued into the 1960 decade, even if they conflict somewhat with the inverse relationship between the income of baby-boom parents and their cumulative completed fertility. However, gross occupational categories do not necessarily relate consistently to income. Examining fertility rates by income levels alone probably conceals some of the variety of behavior between occupational groups.[13]

Richard Easterlin identified another variable that may be the most important income effect on fertility. He showed the positive relationship between the employment rates for young men and fertility rates for young women. High employment rates do not always occur even in times of economic growth, although the reverse is almost always true—declining economies are characterized by declining rates of employment. The young are peculiarly vulnerable to unemployment, and they are also the prime source of child production.[14]

The employment rate for young men correlated with fertility rates throughout the twentieth century. In the 1920s employment rates for young men were low despite the continual growth of the economy. During the baby-boom period, employment opportunities abounded, but after 1960 unemployment rose and fertility declined. High employment rates for young men relate directly to high fertility because they indicate broad economic improvement for young married couples, the most important group for fertility measurement.

Easterlin suggested that the size of one's birth cohort is the crucial factor relating employment rates for the young with fertility rates. If the birth cohort is relatively small, their scarcity value increases their employment opportunities. Members of larger birth cohorts have fewer changes for employment at an early age because the supply of labor exceeds the demand. If the parent's birth cohort is larger, their offspring who are members of a small birth cohort not only will have greater employment opportunities at a younger age but will probably have larger incomes.[15]

This relationship is particularly important for explaining the baby boom. The small birth cohorts of the 1920s and 1930s entered the work force in good times. Their less fortunate parents had begun adult life in the 1920s, when they faced unemployment, or in the more limited opportunities of the 1930s. Easterlin argued that the positive economic experience of the small birth cohort stimulated feelings of confidence and a belief in future prosperity. These psychological factors provided an impetus to fertility, for the world appeared to be a positive place for rearing children.

With these suggestions, Easterlin moved from the income arguments that help to explain fertility realization to the more elusive concept of the taste for fertility. With the concept of cohort experience, he separated the effect of income on fertility from the taste for fertility. In his view, the economic variables affected the implementation of fertility tastes, but the desire for children depended in part upon the size of the individual's birth cohort and the resulting psychological factors that the size of the birth cohort engendered.[16]

The Taste for Fertility

The concept of cohort experience is a valuable tool for analyzing the phenomenon of the baby boom, offering a promising foundation for identifying other variables and experiences that also affected child production. Economic variables give us insight into the implementation of fertility choices, the timing of planned births, and the importance of the perception of the availability and adequacy of resources for child production. Nevertheless, even detailed and sophisticated income variables do not explain why individuals choose to rear children rather than to purchase other consumer goods.[17]

Tastes for fertility become more similar cross-sectionally after 1916 and remained similar until 1965, when differential fertility again appeared. However, tastes have changed longitudinally, and they did not maintain the same relationship with income levels in this fifty-year period, although the dominant pattern has been the inverse relationship between income and fertility.

The cross-sectional similarity of fertility tastes, combined with the pattern of longitudinal change, provides no challenge to the argument that fertility tastes relate to unique cohort experiences. A context like this would be precisely what one might predict from the hypothesis of unique cohort experience. The cross-sectional similarity suggests the emergence of common experiences that change over time as new birth cohorts move into adult life. The sixty years between 1920 and 1980 have seen three birth cohorts or generations that have had distinctly different experiences and have varied in size. The size of the birth cohorts is a crucial variable that affected their response to cultural, social, and economic change.

Cultural analyses of the fertility behavior of different birth cohorts offer new insights into the changing taste for fertility. The impact of the shared experiences of a specific cohort might be the key to understanding why there are variations between the birth rates of different cohorts. If the special experiences of a birth cohort distinguish it from others, fertility variation could relate to differences in experience.

The possibility of such a relationship is particularly high if the special circumstances of a cohort affect belief structures and attitudes. The process of differential modernization before 1940 was a cultural variable of this kind. It proved useful both in longitudinal and cross-cultural comparisons of fertility variations. To be sure, cultural factors are less quantifiable than economic variables, and thus the results offer less proved validity; in fact, the results are highly speculative. However, especially within a period like the baby boom, with its many aberrations from the past and the future, unique cultural factors provide insight into important factors that would be otherwise overlooked.

Social scientists frequently use cultural factors for explanatory purposes, although not without criticism from those who prefer hard data rather than "soft." Sociologists recognize that societal norms change over time. Anthropologists assume that change in any single dimension of life has a broad impact upon a total culture. And, of course, historians routinely describe changes between generations—a tacit acceptance of the importance of variations in cohort experiences. Cultural change is an important part of the historical record.

The next section suggests a possible scenario for the effect of cultural changes upon baby-boom parents, emphasizing the experiences that might have borne most strongly upon the upper-middle-class portion of the birth cohort of the 1930 decade. The fertility behavior of this group of young adults varied most strongly from past practice. As their fertility rates moved upward, their new behavior appeared to be unique when compared to other groups, historical precedents, and similar groups in later decades. The economic explanations reveal the conditions that allowed fertility realization, but the search for the elusive element of the "taste" for fertility depends upon a recognition of special experiences of the period.

The suggestion here is that the fertility choices made by the upper middle class of the birth cohort of the 1920s and 1930s, and the common experiences of the whole birth cohort of both decades, led to the widespread fertility increase throughout all groups in the child-bearing years. At the same time it provided the positive context for formation of home and family that appeared so strongly in the baby-boom period. The role of the upper middle class as innovator in family style has substantial historical precedent. This group had been the inventors of the new modern family by the late nineteenth century.

At the same time, special circumstances remained important for the taste for fertility increase in special groups, thus broadening the widespread increase in fertility that economic conditions permitted during the baby boom. For example, blacks who moved to the city perceived themselves to be in a relatively positive economic environment compared to the rural poverty they had left behind. Thus they could indulge their taste for fertility that appears to be on the average higher than that of the white population throughout the twentieth century. One important study on black fertility has shown that the periods of lower black fertility earlier in the century resulted from the widespread sterility caused by poor nutrition, not from fertility rejection. Blacks retained high fertility in the period after 1960 despite high levels of unemployment for young black men, a fact which suggests that the black population may have strong cultural norms supportive of high fertility regardless of economic circumstances.[18]

Other special groups include practicing Catholics, who during the baby-boom years chose to accept the possibility of high fertility by rejecting artificial birth control. And growth in rural fertility probably resulted in part from the movement of many farmers into the middle class in the years of high farm incomes. Thus many of the same factors that affected the urban middle class also affected farm owners.

The fertility analysis of the baby-boom period shows that the major innovations were those of the upper income strata. Their cohort experience led to the formation of a belief structure positive to fertility by emphasizing faith and confidence in the future. Thus child production appeared to be a reasonable investment of time and resources. The choice of a revitalized family life resulted from nostalgia for the lost golden age of the families of traditional society and a conviction that innovation could create a new modern family.

Patriotism, Prosperity, and Gender:
A Unique Cohort Experience

The birth cohorts of the 1920 and 1930 decades, those responsible for the baby boom, came of age in a period of stunning economic and political success. Society had overcome the economic stagnation of the 1930 decade, won the Second World War, and succeeded to an international role as the primary world power. The tensions of the Cold War in the postwar period did not appear at the time to be a serious failure for the United States. The high level of economic growth in the 1950 decade generated continual positive support for the economic and political system that had fostered success.

The context of massive success and growth provided a positive environment for family creation. In this period of high fertility some of the circumstances particularly affected the upper middle class, the group with the most striking changes in fertility behavior. A number of simultaneous events between 1940 and 1960 contributed to the diversion of the trend of fertility in a new direction. The changed environment incorporated many of the values of the past in a modern way.

Some of the experiences of the baby-boom parents that might have contributed to their eventual high fertility took place in their early lives. The parents of the babies born between 1920 and 1940 had felt constrained by the modern form of limited fertility. A nostalgia for the remembered joys of the traditional family grew out of their yearnings for a fully productive life. They recognized the limits imposed by economic deprivation, but they still cherished the memories of the family in traditional society, clothed in the golden patina of the passage of time. At the same time that these parents logically chose to sacrifice the quantity of children for "quality," they felt a sense of loss. Their children, the birth cohorts of the 1920 and 1930 decade, internalized the ambivalent feelings of their own parents.[19]

The existence of a relationship between depression experiences in childhood and later behavior has been shown by social scientists. Glen Elder concludes an article on postwar child-bearing with the following statement: "Depression experiences in postwar childbearing underscore the fundamental interdependence of social change and the life course." He also emphasizes the need for life span research on behavior change to define the dimensions of this relationship.[20]

Historical and economic concepts provide a guide to the nature of the relationship. Perhaps the scarcity of the children of the depression gave them added value to their parents and ultimately to themselves. The increased worth of children, juxtaposed with the remnants of authoritarian patriarchy and the disciplinary style of child-rearing, presents an oddly mixed context in the home, but not one that would necessarily be negative to perceptions of value by either parents or children. In this decade children learned that economic deprivation limited both the quality and the quantity of family life. As offspring of a one- or two-child family, they internalized a sense of the deep value of family life, with its potential for love and stability. But at the same time they recognized the contradictions between the potential for love and closeness and the remnants of dying patriarchy. And then they came of age in a time of growth and success. Might they not have chosen to fulfill their parents' wish for more children and to reenact the close families ties they had experienced, but without the limits imposed by the conditions of the 1930 decade?[21]

Some of them had experienced an economic rejuvenation within their own families of origin in the early 1940s as wartime incomes brought new prosperity and encouraged parents to produce the desired third or fourth child. The increased birth rates for women between thirty-five and forty for higher-order births offer solid demographic evidence for this argument. The nature of its effects on the future baby-boom parents, of course, remains speculative.[22]

Wartime children gained a sense of identification with the larger world that was much different from the more self-focused images of earlier cohorts. Children collected scrap metal for the war effort; they participated in war-bond drives. Children's work became important again—this time for a national purpose. Most of the males of the birth cohort of the 1920 decade joined in the war effort directly. Postponement and anticipation made them only more eager to create families.

Had these experiences not been further reinforced, they might have faded from memory and had a minimal impact later, when the young people became adults. But the wartime mentality lasted long beyond the end of World War II. The effects of subsequent events intensified the values imprinted earlier in their lives.

After World War II and during the Cold War a combination of new experiences reinforced the values of an earlier time. National effort and patriotic identification temporarily replaced the modern individualism of the previous two decades. Mobilization for war resurrected the older virtues of physical courage and obedience. Romanticism and emotionalism supplanted the more stringent rationalism and cultural innovation that had thrived in the 1920 and 1930 decades.

The nineteenth-century dichotomy between the good girl and the bad girl resurfaced in the films of this period. The goodness of June Allyson and Doris Day contrasted with the sensuality of Veronica Lake. In *Ruby Gentry* and *Duel in the Sun* a "sisters under the skin" theme showed the difficulty of ever crossing the gap between female stereotypes. As impossible in 1950 as in 1890, good women could never really relate meaningfully to "bad" women. Films concentrated on World War II in the 1940 decade, war dramas emphasizing courage and patriotism. In the 1950 decade costume dramas replaced the war emphasis, but the same values were emphasized.[23]

The lives of ordinary people reflected and reinforced these cultural patterns. A revival of nationalism and patriotism placed emphasis on the heritage of the past. The accent on patriotism and tradition, not an aberration in its existence but in its intensity, exceeded the emphasis that characterized both earlier and later periods. Society increasingly focused upon the traditional institutions—family, church, and the military. Church membership rose with birth rates, and the infatuation with the military extended to such high levels as the willing reinstatement in 1948 of selective service. Never before in peacetime had the United States seriously considered instituting the draft, but no effective opposition emerged to challenge the concept of a standing army.[24]

The distant threat of war reinforced patriotism. It interacted with increasing prosperity to buttress traditional institutions. The Cold War against the Soviet Union and the fear of the nuclear menace brought a further renewal of nationalism. Unrestrained individualism was too precarious a virtue in threatening times; tradition offered escape or defense from foreign threats. Reminiscent of nineteenth-century values, "home" again became the sanctuary. This time, however, it symbolized a refuge from distant danger rather than from a harsh industrial society immediately beyond the front door.

Revivals from the past proliferated in popular culture. In the 1940 decade women dressed like the Gibson girls of 1890. Their sisters in 1950 wore the full skirts, tight bodices, corsets, and crinolines of the antebellum era. Popular music borrowed from exotic locations: the rhumba, samba, and tango from South America. The representational art of Dufy and Utrillo replaced abstraction as the public searched again for familiar art forms.

In the United States of the 1940 and 1950 decades, the restoration of the values of the past and the reemphasis on strong distinctions between the genders encouraged young people to create families. Family creation is the quintessentially gender-distinct activity. American images of the ideal men and women contributed to the increased taste for fertility by emphasizing unique gender roles.

Men were supposed to embody the military virtues, and women to be concerned about the home and family while exemplifying the womanly virtues of nurture, devotion, and loyalty. Clothing styles emphasized women's breasts, small waistlines, and long legs. Men's hair styles were short, straight, and military. Women wore their hair long, curly, and flowing. Gone were the film plots about spunky career girls, who were now replaced by heroines who represented sexuality and femininity. Love, home, and mother took center stage.[25]

Women chose positive ways to emphasize their female qualities—strong and successful childbirth and perfect homemaking, and they always tried to remain beautiful. In the 1950 decade, the Mrs. America contest appeared on television. This pageant was a reflection of all the popular ideals, and it recognized the whole female gender package—beauty, motherhood, and homemaking.[26]

Men showed their masculinity through achievement at work as well as in the military. Union membership increased with economic growth, and men's wages rose more rapidly than those of women. High wages emphasized the traditional masculine role as primary breadwinner. Young men gained new self-confidence in their gender role when they surpassed the work achievements of their fathers. In the same vein, women tried to exceed the accomplishments of their mothers in female ways—triumphant childbirth, increased family size, and better homemaking. In the decades of the 1940s and the 1950s gender distinction reached its zenith. Never again would the contrast between feminine and masculine bodies, qualities, and activities be so vividly emphasized.[27]

Women returned in the 1950s to another activity of earlier times—social service, social activism in the interests of the community and the nation. To the older activities, including the creation of libraries, cooperative nursery schools, and volunteer programs in art museums, were added activities to protest nuclear war and to integrate lunch counters. Reminiscent of the early twentieth century, upper-middle-class women encountered new social issues to extend further the separate sphere into the world at large. Municipal housekeeping and domestic feminism emerged again, and this time they suggested the tentative beginnings of a movement toward more extensive participation in social activism in the 1960s.[28]

The emphasis on fertility and family creation were part of a combination of responses to national economic growth, accession to world-power status, and external threats to national survival. The emphasis on three institutions—the family, the church, and the military—suggests the chosen solutions to the problems of the time. The selections were traditional in nature, conservative choices to preserve the prevailing vision of the good and appropriate American society.

Without economic growth, the appearance of external threats would probably not have prompted such strong emphasis on the family. Modern family creation demands extensive resources in both household and human capital. But without nostalgia for the "golden age" of large, happy families, economic growth would have led to more emphasis on pleasure-oriented leisure, more open sexuality, less emphasis on work, and more innovation in human relationships. After 1950 western Europeans took this alternative path. The small European baby boom peaked early and ended rapidly. After that, western Europeans continued modernizing their life styles through economic and political innovation.[29]

Only in the United States did society experience the combination of nostalgia and strong gender identification. The cultural factors that had impact were related to the tension between external threat and

internal growth and success. The resulting environment stimulated the taste for fertility. In turn, the domestic ideal encouraged the return to a modern variation of the nineteenth-century family, a family with higher quantity of children as well as more concern for a high quality of child-rearing.

Many factors encouraged the taste for fertility in this period, and few negative variables appeared. Potentially discouraging factors appear not to have been negative in their impact. Concern with nuclear catastrophe, for example, strong enough to stimulate extensive building of bomb shelters, did not prove negative for the child-bearing decision. The Cold War only encouraged a fortress-America mentality and an implicit recognition of a need to develop human resources as well as natural and industrial resources.

The geographic mobility enforced by the policies of modern corporations for the upper middle class might have been another negative factor. Parents could have chosen to keep their families small, since families were transferred by corporations with great frequency to distant places. But, on the contrary, this pattern seemed only to reaffirm the growth of the family as a stabilizing force in society.

Ambitions to include immediate alternative roles to those of maternity and child-rearing appear not to have been strong in this period for young women in the upper economic groups. Many recent college graduates in the late 1950s disclaimed any interest in long-term careers and expressed high job satisfaction with brief early careers as clerks.[30]

But, at the same time, the baby-boom mother chose close spacing of children and planned to complete her own child-rearing at an earlier age with higher parity than her own mother. Might this not suggest that she cherished quiet or secret ambitions for the future? These ambitions did not undermine fertility, but the perception of prosperity and growth in the economy led women to hope for a more varied career than motherhood alone.

The emergence in the 1970s and 1980s of this same group in the work force and in career-oriented educational programs might have been a result of the rebirth of feminism in the 1960 decade, or this new choice might have been the result of ambitions acquired in the middle years of family-rearing rather than earlier in married life. But an alternative point of view—that these ambitions had always existed—can be supported by the recognition that this same group of women created the rebirth of feminism. Far from being passive observers reluctantly persuaded to develop ambitions, women of this social class led other women to accept the new ideology. Indeed, even their own daughters learned about feminism from them. Betty Friedan, one of the early leaders of the feminist movement, was a baby-boom mother of four who translated her perceptions of her own experiences into the first major American document of the feminist revival, *The Feminine Mystique*.[31]

Educated women could so easily have always cherished the concept of a second career, and finally recognized that the old ideology did not permit the realization of their ambitions. The concentration of child-rearing in the early years of marriage is difficult to explain if women were planning their whole lives around the marital and maternal role. And in the later years of the 1940s, many older women were already practicing the later stages of their dual role, including work and fertility in successive stages. Thus a model already existed for young women of the 1950s to emulate. But meanwhile this group of women concentrated strongly on the maternal role encouraged by economics, politics, social norms, and their own internal motivations.

In addition, the convergence of many unusual or often unique factors encouraged the taste for fertility in this period. Special demographic, religious, or cultural circumstances permitted many groups (Catholics, farmers, and blacks, in particular) to indulge in higher fertility. At the same time all groups benefited from high employment for young men and prosperity that rose beyond all expectations. The satisfactions of child-rearing increased when medical science found remedies for bacterial infections and, in 1956, prevention of polio epidemics. Fears of child abuse, adolescent drug addiction, and premarital pregnancy would haunt the next generation of parents, but during the baby-boom years, these hazards were still unrecognized or unknown.

In the mid-twentieth century the new family model of the upper middle class spread throughout society just as the first modern family model created by a similar group had spread (more slowly) in the nineteenth century. The second variation grew out of nostalgia for an earlier time and an emotional need to produce more children. Economic plenty encouraged rejection of the sense of limits that had pressed upon the parents of the 1930 decade and replaced it with a full and productive family life.

The baby-boom family style began to decline after 1960. The special circumstances that encouraged high fertility lasted for only twenty-five years. The relatively short duration furnishes additional support for the argument that the unique experience of relevant birth cohorts produced the unusual but brief pattern of family creation during the baby boom.

Cultural explanations depending upon cohort experience have an intrinsic limit of about a generation. Then a new cohort with different experiences reaches adulthood. Already during the baby-boom years, many factors had emerged that would undermine the transfer of this family variation to another generation.

The quantity of youth would undermine its scarcity value, and the baby-boom birth cohort would mature in a world in which youth's value at home exceeded their value in the outside world. The conservative values of home, church, and the military would suffer rejection in the later years of the 1960 decade as the young chose new institutions to value, those in which youth had more power and influence. Costs would rise, and new goods would compete with the decision for child purchase.

The pride engendered by the stunning success of the World War II victory would fade, and new problems would be discovered by the generation that was unaffected by the mystique of the 1950 decade. The new generation of young adults would have a different taste for fertility than their parents, and economic circumstances would provide less support for fertility realization.

But, before 1960, some of the same trends that positively affected family development—economic growth, war and defense mobilization, and a desire for greater productivity—also influenced women's work for pay. Work roles for women developed without challenging the maternal role. Fertility thrived in the same period that a strong women's work force developed, only to provide the base for the larger and more varied women's work force of the 1980s.

CHAPTER 9

Women's Work:
1940-1960

Productive roles for women in both work and fertility developed within the limits of the prevailing value system. The work force substantially expanded, but the ideological constraints of traditional gender definitions remained. Under special circumstances society began to approve of women working outside the home for pay. In 1940 only 15 percent of the married women had paying jobs, but in 1960 more than one in three had moved into the working world.

Greater employment of married women would ultimately undermine the taste for fertility, but the expansion of women's work began with women over forty years old who were not involved in the fertility innovations. Work increase for women did not challenge the dominance of the home role, but by 1960 an experienced female work force provided a visible and essential part of the nation's economy.

The key to understanding women's behavior in this period is the recognition of their success in increasing their productivity both at home and in the workplace, but they rarely pursued both kinds of work at the same time. Society would not have permitted this duality, and women probably would not have wanted it. They recognized that their life span was longer than in the past, and this fact gave them new opportunities in home and in workplace alike.

The innovators in the home were the women of the upper middle class, and they would be the leaders again after 1960; at that time they would be demanding new opportunities in the work force. But the pioneers in the work force in the 1940–1960 period were from a different group: women with high school education, women of the lower middle class or working class, primarily those over the age of forty. They did not invent any new ideologies to encourage work participation; they worked strictly within the existing value structure. Their success did not include a direct challenge to the male domination of key areas in the work force, but instead they quietly and inexorably proved that women were capable workers and that society needed their participation.[1]

The emergence of a committed female work force appears to be a strange accompaniment to the innovation in the home that reaffirmed the value of mother-intensive child-rearing. But between 1940 and 1960 women did, in fact, combine work and fertility in this unexpected way. How did work roles emerge that required no rejection of the increasing importance of the home, or that needed no new ideology to minimize gender differences in the work force?

New work roles developed in ways that did not challenge the primacy of the home, to fill in the gaps in women's life cycle that remained after (or before) the years of intense focus on domesticity. The jobs that women found provided easy entrance and exit to the work force, and they offered no challenge to the skills and qualities that were required at home. Even women's work motivations harmonized with their home role because they worked primarily to provide the family with goods and services that enriched family life.

As in fertility, the scope of participation was also extensive in women's jobs, creating a strong sense of gender in the work force as well as in the home. The work force showed a greater diversity of participation than had characterized it between 1900 and 1940. Women from all age groups, social classes, educational levels, and ethnic origins chose gainful employment. The women's work force not only was much larger, but it was more representative of the female population.[2]

The participation of black women in the work force more closely resembled their percentage of the population, as white women also discovered the importance of work. Married professional women showed higher rates of participation than they had in the previous period. Working women at all levels in the work force gained more experience and better qualifications, and they showed more commitment to work. At the same time, however, the central core of the new married women's work force was the group of women of high-school education and low fertility. These women worked longer before child-rearing and returned to the work force sooner after their children were raised, and thus they had the longest work lives and the greatest participation rate of any economic and educational group.[3]

Occupational Shifts

The expansion of job opportunities for women was largely confined to the standard female occupational categories. Men continued to dominate the work force in the upper echelons despite the increased participation of women and the more extensive range of their jobs.

For both genders, expansion of technical and service occupations and the relative decline of blue-collar work were the major factors affecting employment throughout this period of economic growth. Society needed a higher proportion of clerical and service workers than had been required in the earlier stages of capital development. The expansion of white-collar employment created new occupations for men, but the jobs demanding lower levels of skill and training still largely remained in women's province. The women's labor force provided the secretaries, stenographers, file clerks, and machine bookkeepers, but accounting, auditing, and managing positions were held by men.[4]

Married women had already entered sales work in increasing numbers in the 1930s. After 1940 more older women chose this type of work. Expanding service industries demanded more workers. Greater numbers of women became waitresses, operatives in laundry and dry-cleaning establishments, and clerical workers in banking and insurance offices. But, despite the high proportion of women workers in the services, men held the management positions.[5]

Factory work still continued to offer important and expanding employment opportunities for women, despite the decline of manufacturing relative to the service sector. More women acquired the skills necessary for these jobs, and a sophisticated technology opened opportunities to them.

Before 1940 most women had been confined to unskilled work in inspecting, packaging, small-parts assembly, textile work, and food processing. But during and after World War II, electronic assembly massively expanded. Women dominated this new semiskilled work because employers believed that they had greater patience with detailed tasks of assembly. Manufacturers preferred to hire women workers for jobs that required manual dexterity and quickness of eye instead of physical strength.

An interesting case study of women's increasing role in manufacturing is their experience in the knitted hosiery industry. Here was a marked occupational change. Women in this industry before 1940 had worked only at unskilled jobs—pairing, looping, seaming, and mending stockings. During World War II women operators replaced men at the knitting machines. Women found the heavy machines difficult to use, but with greater ease they operated the seamless hosiery machines, which required less strength. After the war, women lost the jobs operating the heavier machines, but they continued to operate the seamless hosiery machines. The new fashion of seamless stockings in the postwar period increased employment opportunities for women hosiery workers.[6]

Women also became adept "boarders." Before the war, only men had done this job, which entailed the stretching and shaping of stockings. After the war, both genders did this work. Boarding was unusual in its lack of gender stereotyping, but, since both men and women had proved competent at the job, the expansion of the hiring pool proved economically rational.

In the postwar period women succeeded in holding some of the jobs they had acquired in the heavy goods industries during the manpower shortage. Women joined unions and gained seniority; this gave them access to some of the higher paid skilled positions in the iron, steel, and automobile industries. Thus we can see several changes in women's position in manufacturing that offered the possibility of more gender flexibility in manufacturing jobs, despite the prevailing pattern of gender limits on jobs. The keys to this change included the appearance of more sophisticated technology to decrease the requirements of physical strength, a more positive perception of women's abilities by employers, and the admission of women to union membership on an equal basis with men.[7]

Changes also appeared in other areas of women's work. Increasingly, women in traditional professions chose to continue the practice of nursing, teaching, librarianship, and social work after their marriages. These service professions cared for the needs of children and families, and the higher birth rates increased the demand for women trained in these important areas. Both schoolteaching and nursing were directly affected by the expansion of the population. More classrooms were full, and hospitals needed larger staffs. The supply of single women who were professionally trained was inadequate to satisfy the needs of society. The shortage of workers encouraged married women to stay on the job or to return to work as soon as possible after child-rearing.[8]

Men remained in women's professional areas as managers, just as they did in clerical and service work. Most head librarians were men; male physicians set the performance standards for nurses. It was rare, even, to find a female principal of an elementary school. Only a few women rose to managerial levels in their own professions, and these were usually unmarried women with extensive work experience.

A few women penetrated the traditional male professions. Between 1940 and 1950 they entered these areas in increasing numbers. In the 1940s, the number of women dentists doubled; the number of women engineers multiplied by six times; and the number of women lawyers also increased, but only slightly. Women engineers found well-paying jobs between 1942 and 1952, in sharp contrast to their experience in the 1930s, when jobs were scarce for women engineers even in 1939.[9]

Also during the 1940s, a trend emerged toward greater diversification in women's professional participation. In 1940 three-quarters of all women professionals were schoolteachers or nurses. Ten years later only two-thirds of the professional women were practicing these two traditional professions.[10]

However, if we look at the total period between 1940 and 1960, women's relative participation in the male-dominated professions decreased. After 1950 women's participation in 28 of the seventy professional occupations listed in the 1960 census declined. In no major profession did women's participation increase more than that of men, and this disparity included even the traditional women's fields of schoolteaching, librarianship, social work, and nursing.

Figures 9.1 and 9.2 show the decline in women's share of participation in almost all professional areas, *including nursing and schoolteaching* after 1950. In the traditional male professions a small increase in women's participation appears in only one area, that of medicine. Many more men than women were able to enter professions traditionally held by the opposite sex.

During the 1950s demand increased for practitioners of women's professions. This trend temporarily concealed the implications of the change in gender flexibility in these areas because positions were always available for qualified applicants. Soon, however, the greater gender flexibility in women's professions would limit women's opportunities when demand declined, and the supply continued to include ever more additional participants from the opposite sex. More men than women benefited from the expanded demand in the professional areas.

At the same time that men were actively welcomed into women's professions, women were actively discouraged from attempting to enter the male professions. Medical schools enforced a quota of 5 percent on female entrants, with no regard for the qualified applicants they were rejecting. Most women physicians entered general practice, gynecology, or pediatrics after completion of medical school, the only areas viewed as appropriate for women. In the 1950s engineering schools had no incentive and little interest in opening their doors to women. A few exceptions to this attitude, however, included Carnegie Institute of Technology in Pittsburgh, Pa. (now Carnegie Mellon University), which instituted a special program offering admission to selected young women with strong aptitudes in mathematics and science, and Purdue University in Indiana, which accepted and encouraged qualified young women.

Law schools did not enforce a system of quotas on women, but in many cases they were actively discouraged from applying for admission. Law-school professors or practicing lawyers used entrance interviews to deter women by describing the difficulties they would encounter. Their descriptions were indeed accurate, for women lawyers

FIGURES 9.1 AND 9.2
Penetration of Women in the Professions—Traditional "Men's" Professions and Traditional "Women's" Professions.

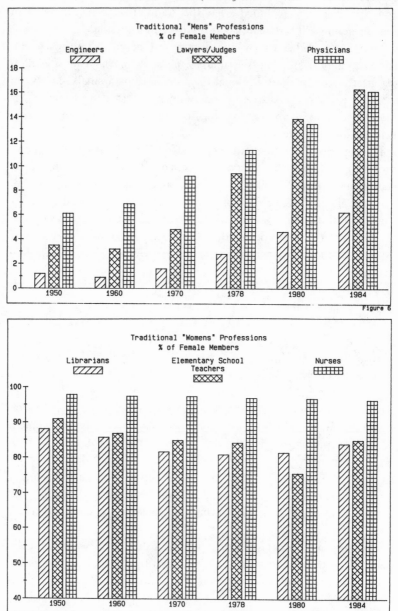

Sources: *Statistical Abstract of the United States: 1986*, pp. 400 and 402; *Statistical Abstract of the United States: 1982; Statistical Abstract of the United States: 1960.*

encountered frequent barriers when they attempted to practice their profession. Law firms rarely hired women, and those few who were accepted were shunted into research and case preparation rather than courtroom practice.

Women's educational preparation played a crucial role in their success at acquiring jobs. A study on employment for women who received their baccalaureate degrees in 1955, 1956, and 1957 shows that specialized training in fields where demand exceeded supply did, in fact, increase their job opportunities. Women statisticians, engineers, and mathematicians all found jobs immediately upon graduation. Most women still sought employment in the traditional areas of teaching, nursing, and clerical work, and these graduates also found jobs available.[11]

Women, however, were not successful in entering all professions in which there were serious shortages. Society urgently needed more accountants, pharmacists, doctors, and dentists, but women either did not choose to enter the appropriate professional schools, or were not encouraged or permitted to do so.

However, over half of all women college graduates disclaimed any long-term career plans, and in most cases had pursued academic interests unrelated to any employment areas that might have been available to women. This group of educated women who worked only briefly before child-rearing provided the bulk of the fertility innovators, the creators of the new baby-boom family. Ultimately this group would appear in the work force but not until the 1970s, when they were in early middle age.[12]

Women achieved the greatest success at the semi-professional level. This important new occupational category encompassed technical specialties, jobs that were not of professional status but still required special education and skill. Psychiatric social work, medical and dental technology, engineering drafting, and social science work suggest the range of these new careers. Since these jobs demanded more specialized training than either clerical or sales work, a fluctuating work force could not fill them. In the new areas, the work, pay, and managerial attitudes were more flexible than in either the male-dominated professions or the traditional women's callings, and they did not require the long training and massive commitment expected of entrants into law, medicine, or engineering.[13]

Concurrent with the creation of new occupational areas, the trend toward broadening the range of middle-level jobs continued from the 1930s. Also on a positive note, women at the lower end of the wage spectrum virtually ceased working in the lowest paying areas of domestic service and agricultural labor. The greater availability of more desirable modern jobs in manufacturing and service work made the old, traditional forms of work appear substantially less desirable.

Work Motivations

As the female occupational structure expanded, the groups entering the work force became more diverse. The labor force increased in size as more white women entered, and by 1960 the ethnic imbalance had disappeared. The percentages of black and white workers closely resembled the balance within the population as a whole. One important difference remained, however, between the participation of black and white women workers: many more black mothers of small children worked for pay than did white mothers in the same age groups.[14]

During this period, women workers came from a more balanced cross-section of educational levels than they had in the previous period. The work entry rates of women with higher education moved upward slightly after 1950, although high-school graduates still comprised the most numerous segment of the work force. This group of women also had the lowest fertility rates, and the highest rates of work participation during the prime adult years (between twenty-five and forty). This behavior is in contrast to the women of only grade-school education and those who had finished college. These other groups had concentrated more heavily on fertility in prime adult years and confined their work participation to the years before and after child-rearing.[15]

However, relating the data on women's education and work-force participation to the income of the husband proves to be difficult in this period, and this fact suggests the emergence of new work motivations as the work force expanded. Clarence Long showed the existence of a relatively consistent inverse relationship between the income of the husband and a wife's decision to work between 1930 and 1950. But in 1960 this relationship had disappeared. In 1951 and 1956

women's labor-force participation still showed a small inverse correlation with the income of the husband, but there was no pattern of
regular progress between income groups. The smallest percentage of
women who were working in 1951 (8.6 percent) had husbands who
made between $7,000 and $10,000. But 21.6 percent of the women
whose husbands had incomes over $10,00 held jobs. By 1963 a small
positive correlation between the income of a husband and his wife's
employment appeared, as work rates for women between the ages of
fourteen and thirty-four who had no children under eighteen were
higher, the greater their husband's incomes.[16]

These data suggest that more complex work motivations than those
of economic need were beginning to appear for women. But perhaps
most useful for understanding the confusing results that Clarence Long
has shown, by the middle of the 1950s, is a recognition of the age
distribution within the women's work force. Women worked at two
periods of their lives; one in early adult years and the other in middle
age. Most women chose to be occupied with homemaking and child-
rearing between the ages of twenty-five and thirty-four (allowing for
some shifts of timing in either direction). This bimodal pattern shows
that women's work participation clustered at the ages that corresponded to the lowest and also the highest levels of their husband's
income. In fact, the second age segment corresponded to peak earnings for some blue-collar workers, but for others to a time when their
earnings had begun to decline. For white-collar male workers, wom-
en's later work period corresponded to their maximum salary.

Income curves for different male occupations varied; this adds further confusion to the analysis. An income of $10,000 a year might
represent the peak earning for some males, but a relatively low level
early in the careers of professionals and managers. Therefore, a women
working after the age of forty might have been in phase with her
husband's peak earnings, his mid-career period, or his income decline;
the absolute levels varied widely. A young woman working would
probably always be in phase with her husband's lowest income but at
widely varying absolute levels. Long's study controlled for age; nevertheless, he used age categories that were too broad to recognize wom-
en's bimodal work pattern. A final difficulty with the analysis is the
variation in ages at which people reach similar stages in the life cycle.

Because of differences in the ages of women at marriage and at completion of child-rearing, the pattern itself can vary five years in either direction.

These data suggest that the husband's income had become less important a determinant of a wife's labor-force participation than her involvement in child-rearing. The age variable is important for what it shows about any given woman's position in the life cycle of motherhood. In this period, unlike the previous or particularly the later period, child-rearing provided a substantial deterrent to labor-force participation.

The study of the ages at which women chose to work also offers insights into the ideological constraints against working that they encountered because of their gender. Women over the age of fifty who had finished rearing their families had the highest rates of entry into the work force. The youngest group of married women—those between eighteen and twenty-five who had not yet started having children—had the next highest rate of entry. The youngest women had always worked, but in earlier decades they had been unmarried. Now, with both earlier marriage and higher rates of marriage, young married women provided a large share of the female labor force. Women over the age of fifty, however, were a relatively new addition to the work force.[17]

The bimodal pattern of the ages at which women worked underlines the prevailing social realities of the period. In prime adult years women were seen appropriately as devoted to the home and the rearing of children, but at the same time certain jobs were reserved for women as "women's work." This concept clearly reflected the prevailing view that female gender characteristics strongly affected behavior on the job. The tasks in many women's occupations closely approximated the role of housewife. Harold Wilensky listed these qualities: "routine, rapid use of fingers, patience, quickness of eye, sex appeal, attractiveness, and a distinctive welfare orientation toward other people (especially children)." Some men's jobs required some of these characteristics, but all women's jobs demanded most of them. Few, if any, women's jobs called for frequent decision-making, bursts of physical strength, or craft skills—factors that were often important in the jobs held by men. Women's limited work role was at least behaviorally consistent. Women's work for pay and women's role in the home were virtually mirror images.[18]

Throughout most of this period few women showed enthusiasm for long-term careers; instead, they viewed paid work as temporary. Thus, women who entered the work force frequently capitalized upon their already existing skills. If women perceived their gender characteristics to be work skills, using them on the job appears to be rational and consistent. Any group that expects to be absent from the work force for a long period has little incentive to invest time and money in additional training. Thus, surprisingly enough, even highly intelligent and well-educated young women who worked at routine clerical jobs expressed high levels of satisfaction with their work during this period.[19]

Married women derived some advantages from this similarity between gender roles at home and at work. They could easily move in and out of the work force. The similarity of tasks performed in the workplace and at home allowed them to adapt more smoothly to regular work outside the home. Sex-stereotyping of jobs may have been the crucial factor in creating wider employment opportunities for women. Society would tolerate women working outside the home for pay only if they remained "womanly."

Advocates of gender equality, who speak from the perspective of the 1980 decade, have often condemned women's work roles of the 1950 decade as exploitive and sexist. But the concepts of sexism and exploitation had no meaning in the 1950 decade. A work pattern that maintained women's child-rearing role may have been the only possible work role for the time. Society did not tolerate equality between the genders in the workplace precisely because it would have left the home untended and children without mothers present. Achievement of even a limited work role required the breakdown of formidable barriers.

Fertility increase and higher levels of work participation fit together in this period precisely because there was no question in anyone's mind as to which was the more important role. Women's home behavior matched their behavior at work. Women at work were still gender-defined. They accepted, or perhaps they approved, the limitations, because within this framework they could move easily between home and work. The prevalence of home and family, the high visibility of babies, toddlers, and schoolchildren showed with noisy clarity women's acceptance of their maternal role. But this very visibility concealed the importance of their developing work role.

Women's work motivations also reflected the same merging of roles: the recognition that at home and at work their goals were consistent. The new economic motivations for all groups included the implications of the same ideology that had encouraged a dedicated home life. In 1957 sociologist Daniel Bell, in a national magazine article on women's work, said, "The most significant factor in women's work participation is the hunger for the appurtenances of the good life that multiple incomes bring most sharply."[20] He might also have mentioned that the "appurtenances of the good life" consisted entirely of family goods rather than personal luxuries for the parents. Consumption data clearly show the emphasis on family-oriented possessions in this period.[21]

Especially in the later years of the baby-boom period mothers worked for family vacation trips, summer camp and college educations for their children. The baby-boom family style implicitly encouraged the substitution of capital for labor at home as children grew past early childhood. By 1955 this trend was providing a new "family" role for women as providers of family capital through modern paid work. Implicitly women were accepting a new role that included the function of providing capital instead of labor at home. By 1955 the work-participation rate for women with children between twelve and eighteen exceeded that of women with no children under the age of eighteen, data that strongly suggest the importance of older children as a stimulus to work participation, an even greater stimulus than leisure goals.[22]

Work entry was encouraged by diverse attractions; rising wages and sociability provided satisfactions unavailable at home. Survey of older married women workers showed that financial rewards did not always provide the primary motivation for work. The benefits of sociability found in the job situation far outweighed the financial rewards. Few women claimed to be working only for financial reasons. Work provided a productive source of sociability, unlike leisure activities that usually required investments of time and money.[23]

At the same time, rising real wages in the baby-boom period played an important role in encouraging women to work. During World War II and immediately afterward (1940–1948) women's wages reflected the increased demand for women workers. Between 1946 and 1960 real wages continued to increase for women, but men's wages increased at an even faster rate, a factor that had a strong impact upon the timing of women's decision to work. Women's median income increased 30 percent between 1950 and 1960, but men's median income rose 75 percent.[24]

Higher wages for men increased the levels of prosperity in families between 1945 and 1960. The steady increase in family incomes from the male side of the family might have discouraged female employment. However, the quality of family life was not sacrificed by women's work participation. Women in the work force were predonminantly in the age ranges when family demands upon their time were relatively low. The women's work force could and did expand without undermining the requirements of the home and family, and raising wages contributed to this achievement.

Several studies explore the nature of the relationship between women's work-force participation and other sources of family income. After a ten-year study, Marion Sobol concluded that the wife in families of falling income was three times as likely to enter the labor force as her counterpart in those families with constant income.[25] Jacob Mincer demonstrated that "an increase in the wife's market wage over time leads to a reallocation of work toward the market, although her likelihood of participation at any given point is decreased if family income increases from another source, and her own potential wage remains the same."[26]

The Sobol study also examined the factor of perceived economic insecurity in families. Whether or not the absolute income of the husband compared favorably with that of the recognized peer group strongly influenced the decision of the wife to get a job. In the context of rising national prosperity, families clearly yearned to share in the bounty at the level they felt was appropriate for them.

Other supply factors also operated to encourage women's employment. Valerie Oppenheimer defended the proposition that the close resemblance of married women to their single sisters was extremely important in encouraging married women to work. Demand increased for women workers just as the supply of single women declined.[27]

Since 1920 married women had gradually been replacing single women as the dominant group in the work force. Women over the age of forty who had completed child-rearing in the smaller 1920-style family were an expanding group after 1940, and these women had higher life expectancies, greater health in middle age, and more years available for work. Not only did the supply of single women decline, but the supply of married women who were available for work increased in the 1940 and 1950 decades. In a labor market in which jobs remained defined by gender, work opportunities for married women increased as the supply of single women declined. Here is an interesting example of an indirect relationship between the new emphasis on family and the increased work roles for women.

Women between 1940 and 1960 created the concept of a serial dual role in which work and fertility occupied their efforts in different parts of the life cycle. The diversity of productivity that this discovery engendered is shown in the rising curves of both work and fertility. Women's own motivations provided an important element in this success, but they were insufficient alone to have produced this important change. Exogenous economic and political factors combined to provide a fertile context in which women could realize their desires for greater productivity.

External Factors Encouraging to Women's Employment

Two important external factors promoted the rapid development of the married women's work force in this period. First, economic growth demanded new workers. The need for workers to fill women's jobs provided an economic context in which women could work for pay if they did not threaten the cherished value system. The demands of wartime mobilization, the second factor, led women to enter the work force, encouraged and required by the national need for increased production. After World War II the argument disappeared, buried under an avalanche of evidence to the contrary, that women over forty years of age could not maintain demanding work schedules. Women discovered the advantages of work for pay, and they remained at work after the emergency had ended or returned when the opportunity reoccurred.

Feminist ideology had little or no effect upon the decisions of most married women to enter the workplace in this period. The rebirth of feminism as an effective force would not occur until 1965. Indeed, the ideologies that emerged in this period were only updated versions of the nineteenth-century emphasis on women's distinct gender qualifications, especially those of biology.

The older value structure, with its emphasis upon maternity and homemaking, continued to dominate public opinion. Both the results of public opinion polls and women's own fertility behavior underlined the renaissance of the importance of home and family, and a major part of this belief was the assumption that a lifetime commitment to paid work threatened women's focus on the home. Public opinion continued to show strong opposition to married women working.[28]

However, some inconsistency of positions within the context of basic opposition suggests that ambivalent attitudes toward women working were beginning to appear. For example, although many people staunchly disapproved of women working, they also agreed that if a woman was working at the same job as a man, she should receive the same pay. Another prevalent opinion was that a woman should work only if absolutely necessary to support the family, but, if she should be so unfortunate, she should be allowed to deduct child-care expenses from her income tax. This ambivalence in the opposition lent flexibility to the principle of general hostility to work for married women. The development of a work pattern that held fertility, child-rearing, and homemaking primary contributed, in practice if not always in principle, to the toleration of women's work.

At the same time, economic change strongly stimulated women's increasing participation in the workplace. The clerical and service sectors, always bastions of female work, expanded significantly. In a growing economy, this expansion inevitably spurred growth in the female labor force. Unemployment rates for men were low, a fact that gave female workers greater opportunities for work, even though married. Otherwise, adolescent boys or men over retirement age would have had to work. Society chose instead to tolerate married women working.

Economic factors alone, however, even when combined with women's new work motivations, were not sufficient to explain the major increase in the numbers of working women between 1940 and 1960. War mobilization also played a major role in releasing women from the home, dramatizing their work capabilities and creating a more qualified and committed work force.

The Impact of War Mobilization

The massive production requirements of World War II, the Korean War, and the relatively continuous defense requirements of the Cold War increased employment opportunities for women. Married women became an important labor supply because industry needed temporary workers to join the national defense mobilization. Women's performance in the war emergency provided a strong counterweight to the prevailing negative views about their ability on the job, and it helped to identify women as visible and productive workers. Government policy encouraged women's work because this created a trained labor supply reserve for national emergencies.

Women first became a national job resource in World War II (1940–1945) and again during the Korean War (1950–1954). During both emergencies, national policy focused on efforts to attract women into the labor force. As men entered the armed forces, women filled their places in factories. Expansion of industries related to war production created the demand for additional workers who were female. Suddenly it was patriotic and appropriate for women to work; their country needed them. Temporarily, sex stereotyping of jobs disappeared. The only manual jobs reserved strictly for men required heavy lifting or handling the most dangerous machine processes. Female participation in the armed forces brought women into a new role—highly visible and socially approved—remote from the accepted female roles. The war emergency not only justified this new behavior; it encouraged women to accept their new status. Crisis temporarily minimized the importance of gender differences on the job.

The federal government supplied the ideology to defend paid work by women. The emphasis was always on the temporary nature of women's employment and on the continued commitment to women's true destiny as homemaker, but the tone and content of the public appeals irreparably undermined the assumptions of the past that had kept women out of the work force. The view of woman as weak, in need of protection, unable to perform difficult jobs, could not survive the contrary views continually propounded by government calls for help. The language in which the summons was expressed underlined the strength and capabilities of women—their ability to work hard and learn fast on the job while they still maintained the essentials of home life.

Six million women entered the labor force between 1940 and 1945. Four and one half million of these new working women had passed their fortieth birthday. Rosie the Riveter at age forty-two became the national symbol of women's war work. Older women comprised nearly half the total labor force, men included, by 1945. Here is one of the most crucial points about women's participation in the war emergency. Women in prime child-bearing and child-rearing years comprised an exceedingly minor portion of the work force.[29]

Most mothers of small children remained at home. Older women, with grown children, provided the major source of labor to fill war industries and keep the peacetime economy productive. A secondary group of workers included young married or unmarried women who had no family responsibilities. Thus the women's work force during the war showed a distribution of age levels similar to the peacetime work force of the 1930 decade and the postwar period, and like the peacetime work force, it accommodated to the demands of mother-intensive child-rearing.

High wages and patriotism were strong work incentives for women without strong and immediate family responsibilities, and industry enthusiastically received them. Already during the 1930 decade, older women had become increasingly prepared to move into the work force. Now women were ready to go to work, and they found their new

work role fully satisfactory. By September 1945 women strongly out-
numbered men in the civilian labor force.

During the war emergency women worked in many new job areas.
Expansion of the executive branch of the federal government alone
demanded an increase from 186,000 women workers in 1940 to one
million in June 1943. Women replaced men in many of the service
industries. They filled vacant positions in hotels, restaurants, retail
trade, and banking. Direct war work attracted many new women
workers; one-third of the aircraft assemblers were female. Women were
so valuable in the electrical machinery and radio industries that they
were able to negotiate union contracts, including equal pay for equal
work. In a time of war emergency, even this radical behavior was
approved. In the peacetime year of 1939 only 9 percent of workers in
heavy industry were women. By 1944 this percentage had increased
to 22 percent.[30]

The urgent need for women workers in wartime forced society to
dismantle many of the old barriers to their employment. After the
war most of the obstacles never returned. State legislatures repealed
laws controlling work hours for women. Employers modified working
conditions to make life on the job easier for women. They provided
women's restrooms and adequate ventilation; they installed new machinery more appropriate for women operators. These changes encouraged women to continue working after the war emergency had
ended.

During wartime, women benefited from government and industrial
training programs, the enactment of minimum wage laws, and the
opening of union membership opportunities. These changes integrated both genders in the work force, and some residual impact remained after the war. In 1946 rejection of female employment by the
old arguments that they could not work well was impossible. Government propaganda during the recuitment program refuted this view.
Even more important, women's war record spoke eloquently: women
performed well on the job, and employers recognized this. Women
created a significantly modified image of their ability in the workplace.

The changes in women's employment at the end of World War II
suggested the work pattern that would be developed in the next two

decades. The age levels of the work participants and women's movement into separate job status matched the major characteristics of the
early baby-boom labor force. Young women left the work force first.
By 1946 a lower percentage of this group held jobs than in 1949. This
group of young women would soon be mothers, as the birth peak in
1947 illustrates so vividly.

In contrast, many older women stayed in the work force although
their jobs changed to levels of lower pay and less skill. Two and one-
half million additional production jobs created during the war became
permanent; women held onto one million of these. Half of these jobs
were in the higher paying durable-goods industries. Seniority rules,
which applied to women as a result of their wartime union membership, protected those women who had been employed between 1939
and 1942. Thus they could remain at work if they chose.

In industrial work, the iron, steel, and petroleum industries had the
highest rate of layoffs. But the normal processes of employee turnover
in these and other industries account for the loss of many women's
jobs. Women voluntarily quit two and one quarter million jobs after
August 1945; employers laid off one million additional women. Still,
two and three quarters million women were hired in production in
the same period (between August 1945 and June 1947). Women who
were rehired, however, moved to the unskilled and semiskilled jobs.
Men returning from the war filled the skilled jobs.

Women kept most of the clerical jobs and increased their representation in sales positions. In 1940 women held only one-fourth of the
sales jobs; by 1947 they had garnered two fifths of them. More fluc-
tuation occurred in the service industries, but economic expansion and
the absence of a postwar depression softened the impact of the transition to peacetime.

After the enactment of the G.I. Bill of Rights, war veterans frequently chose to take advantage of the new and unexpected opportunities for additional schooling. This postponed their return to work,
and large numbers of them never went back to industrial production.
In the long run, this additional schooling increased the educational
gap between men and women and provided men with a substantial
advantage in the job market at the upper levels. The declining percentages of women in managerial and professional positions in the

1950 and 1960 decade showed the results of the postwar educational gap. The short-term effects of widespread veterans' education, however, were beneficial to women workers who wanted to keep their jobs. The demand for production workers still exceeded the supply, and the shortage significantly reduced pressure on women to leave the labor force.

A new emergency followed closely behind the relatively smooth transition from war to peacetime. Only four years passed before the Korean War demanded another massive effort to recruit workers. Again the United States Labor Department spoke in strong support of women's work. The labor recruiters made statements like "Women are the chief reserve work force in time of national emergency," and "It is a matter of national interest to develop and conserve the work skills of all women." At a National Conference on Equal Pay for Equal Work, a part of the national Defense Planning effort, Labor Secretary Maurice Tobin claimed that it was time to "blast way the fog of unrealistic, even romantic thinking about equal pay for women that still remains among various groups."[31]

The perspective of the 1980 decade suggests that these statements were logical conclusions based upon the principle of gender equality, but in truth they were exceedingly radical for the time in which they were made, and they were statements made by national leaders for important economic and political goals. Their implicit, and as yet unrecognized, rejection of the old custom of separate and unequal labor markets prepared the way for the ultimate acceptance of new feminist ideologies.

But these changes remained in the future, Women still needed to create a stronger and more committed labor force that would be essential to the continued operation of the economy. Their participation in the war emergency contributed to the development of the women's labor force by improving skill levels and lengthening work lives. Factory employment of women increased from 3.8 million in 1950 to 4.7 million in 1953. The ordnance, metals, apparel, rubber, and chemical industries had to be extensively expanded.[32]

The Korean War requirements, however, were more limited than those of World War II. Young men who had not yet joined the work force provided most of the servicemen. Thus women did not directly replace men on the production lines. Instead, women filled jobs created by the expansion demanded by modern defense mobilization.

Requirements of war and defense mobilization kept women almost continuously involved in the work force from 1940 until 1955. Wartime work experiences gave women a chance to be involved in the mainstream of society. World War II, its immediate aftermath, and the Korean War were the introductory chapters in a new story for married women. In this period women proved that they could undertake a modern work role that would not disrupt family life.

As several historians have shown so clearly, when the war ended, women could not keep the range of jobs they acquired during World War II, and they returned by necessity to the more limited gender-defined work role that already had developed in the 1930 decade. But, despite these important limits, many effects of war employment on women contributed to the further development of their work role. The rhetoric of government recruitment could never be expunged from the record. Emphasis on women's capabilities provided a new context for further development of their work role.[33]

In addition to the change in rhetoric about women's capabilities, the partial reduction of gender-stereotyping at work provided women with some new occupations. But perhaps most important, war mobilization gave many women the opportunity to work for pay, and the effect of work experience on future choices of work is strongly positive. War and defense mobilization encouraged women's work for at least fifteen years, and by 1955 women had found new work motivations based on the need for family goods and services as the first baby-boom children reached young adolescence. Like work for war production, a family-dependent reason for work also did not challenge the value system, and thus it was within the parameters of acceptable behavior.

The demand for women in war work was one of the major forces that encouraged new work behavior for women. Exogenous forces interacted with women's internal motivations to create a succession of positive impacts on their developing work role. This occurred in spite of the prevalence of negative opinion regarding married women's work for pay and the lack of supportive ideologies for new activity.

The Relationship of Work and Fertility

Work expansion and fertility increase began as relatively independent trends pursued by different women, although both trends were affected by similar economic and cultural variables. Child-bearing remained women's most basic role, and women's work developed in a form that accommodated a married female population whose younger members were committed to motherhood and to direct maternal care of children. The size of the work force, its age distribution, and the nature of work itself remained compatible with a strong emphasis on child-rearing.

The majority of jobs available to women encouraged relatively easy entrance to and exit from the work force. Qualities required by women's supportive and nurturant home role transferred easily into women's jobs like schoolteaching, nursing, selling, and stenography that required similar attitudes. Most women devoted at least fifteen years to child-rearing, the years between twenty-five and forty that men devoted primarily to career development. The dominant pattern of work participation before and after child-rearing reflected the achievement of a gender-consistent dual role that included changes of emphasis throughout the life cycle.

For women whose children were grown, the shift to women's jobs in the modern workplace appeared to be an ideal solution, one that provided a serial role including both fertility and work at different points in the life cycle. Family commitment in the appropriate years could be preceded and followed by paid work participation. This pattern provided extra income in the early years of family capital formation and in the later stages of child-rearing when family costs were at peak levels.

The serial role had begun tentatively in the 1930 decade and was strengthened by the need for women workers in World War II and the rapid economic growth after the war. But, perhaps most important, the concentrated emphasis on fertility during the baby boom strengthened the shift to work roles in middle life. Women reached the age of parity two years earlier than women before 1940, and thus had more time left for work. The expenses of a cluster of older children at similar ages encouraged women to seek extra family income.

The work force reflected the emphasis on fertility, not only in the age levels represented, but in the socioeconomic level of many of the women employed. The Long data and the census data show that the primary group employed in this twenty-year period were those women who finished high school. These women were part of the middle-income portion of the population, and they showed the lowest fertility rates during the baby boom. Freed from home responsibilities for more years than the upper- and lower-income groups, they took jobs earlier and at a more rapid rate.

By 1960 we can see the incipient decline of fertility, the emergence of new economic motivations for women's work, and, perhaps most important for the future, the emergence of a more committed female work force. Women were working for longer periods, acquiring greater work experience and more commitment to work. Work skills improved, and the increase in commitment to work can be shown by the decrease in absentee rates, a decline in voluntary resignations, increased union membership for women, and an increase in full-time year round work participation. By 1960 women were more willing to spend time and money on training for jobs—another development that supports the assertion of women's greater work commitment at the end of this period than at the beginning.[34]

Women's participation in the "emergency labor reserve army" declined in the later years of the 1950 decade since no new national crises required additional labor mobilization. At the same time, the "taste for paid work" had increased. Mothers did not wait for their children to leave home before entering or reentering the work force. At first most mothers postponed work entry until all children were at least twelve years old, but by 1960 we see still low, but increasing entry rates for women whose children were between six and twelve years old.

By 1960 the female labor supply was approaching the maximum level that could be absorbed by the demand for women workers. The gender constraints on work would soon become seriously restrictive, especially for the small group of women who would choose to work in prime adult years. Married women who worked in prime child-bearing years after 1960 expressed a lower level of job satisfaction than a similar group in earlier years. If the number of women desiring jobs continued to increase, the demand for their labor would also have to increase to keep labor supply and demand in balance.

The decline in the pace of improvement of women's wages relative to the improvement in men's wages suggests the impact of the increasing supply of women workers, and the successful male invasion of women's professions shows in another way the ominous, if still minimal, trend of decline in women's relative position in the work force. And, finally, the widening of the earnings gap between men's and women's wages between 1955 and 1960 shows in still another way the pressure on the available jobs in the women's work force. The earning's gap between men and women increased substantially between 1955 and 1960, as women's average earnings in 1955 were 63.9 percent of men's earnings, while by 1960 this percentage had dropped to 60 percent.[35]

The serial dual role was ultimately dependent upon a protected women's labor market, easy entrance to and exit from the labor force, and women's acceptance of the wages and opportunities available to them in a restricted labor market. Ironically, fertility itself undermined the innovation of serial duality by creating increased demands for consumption goods within the home. For mothers, baking cookies after school with the children soon was replaced by paid work to provide older children with summer camp, private schools, and fashionable clothing.

In 1960 most of the later baby-boom mothers were still at home with their small children born in the 1950s and their new babies born in the 1960s, but the changes in the women's work force showed the beginning of an inexorable trend. The earlier baby-boom mothers already had chosen a new path, that of paid work. Rising expectations, desire for goods, and new definitions of family "needs" led in the next period to a continuation of the changes still tentative in the late 1950s.

Nevertheless, during this period women achieved a productive dual role that included work and family. By 1960 the balance had begun to shift in a direction that threatened the permanence of the serial dual role. Cultural and economic factors specific to the period encouraged family creation and work participation. War, defense, prosperity, and economic growth stimulated both trends, but ultimately fertility itself increased the pace of work participation.

Serial duality achieved in the baby-boom period provided a more satisfactory solution to women's needs than they had found before 1940. The baby-boom family included a resurgence of some of the 19th-century ideals of the importance of a productive and supportive family life. The commitment to child-rearing, a return to a higher quantity of children while still expanding the quality of their upbringing, provided a challenging response to the loss of the traditional family. This alternative was preferable to the other choice—that of continuing to produce the small families of the 1920s—because it responded to the sense of limits on family life that so many people experienced in the depression decade.

The expansion of women's work role, concealed as well as encouraged by the massive emphasis on family, provided the basis for future change at the same time that it enriched the opportunities for women throughout their life cycle. The taste for fertility ultimately created the taste for work, and this may be the most important element of the relationship between work and fertility. Women shared in the productivity, growth, and expansion of the period with increased fertility, mother-intensive child-rearing, and more participation at work, and the new work and fertility patterns offered a more positive sense of gender.

CHAPTER 10

The Changing Context of Fertility: 1960-1986

Fertility rates had turned downward by 1960, but this year also marked the arrival of the largest number of babies ever born in the United States in one year. The oldest baby-boom children had reached child-bearing age, expanding the supply of potential mothers, a group that still included the birth cohort of the 1920s producing their final children, and the cohort of the 1930s in prime child-bearing years.

The election of John F. Kennedy to the presidency—the youngest president ever elected in the United States—showed the emphasis on youth in another way. When Dwight David Eisenhower left the White House—at age seventy, the oldest surviving president—the 1950s ended with its concern for military virtues, gender distinctions, and strong family values. In its place a new decade began, one that would be devoted to a different set of ideals. The youth protest movement advocated free speech, sexual freedom, and the end of restraints. At the same time, the feminist and civil rights movements revived, and this time they would succeed in achieving many of their basic goals.

The year 1960 also marks a major change in the lives of American women. The relationship between the work and fertility curves changed direction, this time to a significant inverse relationship. Work-force participation accelerated, and by the middle of the 1970s fertility rates fell to levels as low as those during the Great Depression. The inverse relationship between fertility and work participation was not new, but the magnitude of the change of direction after 1960 suggested that new and significant factors were affecting women's lives. For the first time, substantial numbers of women in prime adult years pursued paid work instead of fertility and mother-intensive child-rearing.

At the same time, however, some of the decline in fertility and the increase in work were predictable extensions of long-term trends. Fertility had declined continually between 1790 and 1936, a fact which suggests that lower fertility rates after 1960 only marked a return to a more normal modern pattern of fertility. The upward trend of work rates for women also had extensive historical support. When older married women moved into the work force after 1930, a new phase began in modern work for married women. After 1960 the increase in the number of women working continued the same trend at a faster rate.

Other consistencies abound in the 1960s; for many baby-boom family patterns remained similar to those of the previous period even as several different birth cohorts reached new stages in the life cycle. The baby-boom families begun in the 1950s achieved their full development in the 1960s with the birth of their third and fourth children. The maturing of the later baby-boom families occurred at the same time as the members of the birth cohort of the 1940s reached adulthood, married, and began to create their own families in ways that strongly resembled the family styles of the baby boom.

In the 1970s the baby-boom children born in the 1950s reached adulthood. Here occurred the real break with the recent trend in family creation. The family behavior in adulthood of the younger members of the baby-boom birth cohort contrasted strongly with that of their parents and of the birth cohort of the 1940 decade. The birth cohort of the 1950s chose to minimize the role of family creation in their own lives. Their new choices led to profound changes in fertility, marriage, and family patterns.

The attitudes, beliefs, and customs regarding fertility and family that can be summarized as the "context" of fertility changed more significantly after 1965 than women's work environment. The households of 1980 differed markedly from those of 1960, 1940, 1920, or

1900, and this change implies a rejection of emphasis on high fertility and family values. More than half the households in 1980 had only one or two people. In 1955 households for young people consisting of only one person had been almost unknown, but after 1970 many young adults lived in nonfamily households. Frequently two unmarried persons of opposite sex lived together in a pseudomarital relationship. In 1985 only 7 percent of all households fit the "standard" description— breadwinning father, homemaking mother, and one to four children under eighteen. In the rest of the 20th century, between 19 percent to 25 percent of the households had fit this American paradigm.[1]

Another important change has been the increase in the number of women as head of household. As the divorce rate moved toward the staggering figure of 50 percent in 1986, the large proportion of single-parent families included mostly female heads of household. Some of these women were single mothers by choice, but most of them were divorced or women whose husbands had left home. Men frequently rejected active parenthood in the case of divorce, although custody of children was granted more often to men than in the past. But, a single parent, usually female, often had to bear the full responsibility of breadwinning as well as of child care. Most impoverished families had women as heads of households.[2]

Rhetoric about the importance of family burgeoned, but, at the same time, consensus fragmented even upon such apparently simple concepts as the definition of a "family." In 1980 President Carter tried to keep his campaign promise to call a family conference at the White House, but the definition of "family" proved too elusive. When planning for the conference began, the profound disagreement on the meaning of a "family" became starkly clear. No one could agree on what categories of people should participate in the discussions or what topics were relevant. Was it legitimate for two lesbian women to participate as "parents," although they clearly represented an infinitesimal minority of the population? Questions of this sort revealed the range of unprecedented problems involved in family definition.[3]

In contrast to the changing context of fertility, women's work environment remained remarkably similar to that of the preceding period. To be sure, new participants entered the work force, but most women remained at substantially the same jobs as in earlier decades.

The media often gave massive publicity to the "revolution" in work. This fanfare contributed to the high visibility of the occasional woman in a nontraditional job, thus creating the illusion of great change in the work force. But the real change consisted of the increased volume of work participation, not in the variety of jobs in the workplace.

A more ambiguous break in the relationship between women's work and child-rearing occurred after 1960, ambiguous because it continued an earlier trend but at a much different level. In the later years of the 1950s mothers began returning to work sooner than before after they finished rearing their children. After 1960 this trend accelerated. Women increasingly rejected mother-intensive child-rearing to hold paying jobs. In prime adult years more women began to leave young children at home or in day-care centers and entered the labor markets at younger ages. Young women frequently chose to postpone having children, and young mothers often returned to work only a few months after childbirth. This trend suggests that young women were developing an increased interest in work and less inclination toward domesticity.[4]

After 1970 a decreasing emphasis on marriage and more frequent divorce matched the decline in domesticity. Women who might have preferred to remain in the home realized the hazards involved in an exclusive commitment to homemaking and child-rearing. The mere existence of rising divorce rates encouraged married women to develop careers or jobs in the interest of self-sufficiency. Thus the work force increased not only through the entrance of large numbers of divorced women, but also through the addition of many married women concerned about the possible need to support themselves.[5]

At the same time, the rate of first marriages declined, and the median age at first marriage moved upward for both genders. The interval lengthened between marriage and the first birth. And by 1980 a rising percentage of married couples had no children at all.[6]

A 1986 demographic study on marriage showed the problems inherent in marriage postponement or divorce for college-educated women born between 1946 and 1958. Opportunities for marriage or remarriage dwindled for this group since women customarily marry men a few years older than they are: The continually rising birth rates during the baby-boom years led to a marriage "crunch" as women born in 1956 searched vainly for a male partner from the smaller birth cohort of 1953. The available pool of marriageable men was also limited by the large proportion of homosexuals, estimated at 11 percent. Homosexual women are estimated to comprise only 3 percent of the women in similar age ranges. The consequences of the marriage crunch for fertility will be important. The study suggests that two out of ten educated women between the ages of 29 and 41 will never be wives and mothers.[7]

Many of these women may never have intended to be wives and mothers. Thus the decreasing availability of partners of appropriate ages is only part of the story on declining birth rates. For many women full-time paid employment appeared to be a more attractive choice than mother-intensive child-rearing, domesticity, and full time homemaking. Instead, they chose marriage without motherhood, living alone, cohabiting without marriage, or, in still small but rising percentages, planned motherhood without marriage.

The combination of new trends in society underscored the existence of marital instability and women's need to be self-supporting. Divorce became more common at all age levels and increased in frequency. New sexual alternatives began to replace marriage for some young people as society either tolerated or ignored pseudomarriages, communal living, and the homosexual way of life. Only a small minority of the population pursued these alternative life patterns, but the fact that they were condoned at all presented a challenge to the viability of the traditional roles. When women realized that work might be essential for survival, the job market assumed new relevance for all married women, regardless of their stage of life. Women responded to the new social realities by modifying their roles, and a significant inverse relationship between work and fertility appeared.

Fertility: 1960–1980

Fertility rates have dropped consistently since 1957. At first they turned downward gradually, but after 1965 they declined more rapidly. In the late 1960s and after 1976 two brief periods of relative stability provided temporary plateaus. The decline in the birth rate from the high levels of the baby boom for all religious, ethnic, occupational, and educational groups is the key to this lowered fertility. The baby-boom parents had shown cumulative fertility that had a mildly inverse relationship to family income; in the 1960 decade a similar pattern persisted. However, current fertility briefly maintained the U-shaped curve typical of the baby boom. After 1965 the fertility curves again resembled the distribution (inversely correlated with income) characteristic of the cumulative fertility measures.[8]

For special reasons, some groups had shown unusually high fertility in the baby-boom period, but after 1960 they no longer followed this unique behavior. Birth rates for Catholics declined steadily, and by 1975 native Catholic and non-Catholic fertility patterns converged. Birth rates for Catholic Hispanics, however, showed the high rates characteristic of immigrants to the United States in the early part of the twentieth century. Many Hispanics combined the traditional ethic of large families with fervent practice of Catholic teachings against birth control. Thus birth rates in many southwestern states have remained higher than in other areas, largely because of the increasing Hispanic populations.[9]

Black fertility rates remained consistently higher than white fertility, but since 1960 they have changed in a parallel relationship to the steady decline in white fertility. Illegitimate births were more numerous in the black population than in the white population, and census data suggests that blacks practiced birth control at only a 50 percent rate, in contrast to the 60 to 65 percent of the white population.[10]

The extraordinary high fertility rates of young married women disappeared as the baby boom waned. The fertility of women between the ages of twenty and twenty-nine was still higher than that of other age groups, but it returned to more normal modern levels. The extreme differentials between the fertility of the youngest women and other age groups that had been characteristic of the 1950 decade disappeared, and comparative fertility by age of mother returned to patterns similar to those of the 1920 and 1930 decades.[11]

A more extensive analysis of the consistent decline of fertility between 1960 and 1980 suggests the existence of two separate periods. In the first period, the baby boom waned, but the birth rates still resembled those of the baby boom in several important dimensions. The first and relatively brief period included the fertility of the last prewar birth cohort, those born late in the 1930s or early in the 1940s.

After 1965, when the baby-boom children entered the child-bearing ages, the contemporary pattern in fertility appeared.

The Waning of the Baby Boom. The fertility pattern of the first five years of the 1960 decade included many similarities to the fertility behavior of the baby boom. Early marriage, relatively close spacing of children, and high marriage rates persisted—facts that suggest that family goals for many young people resembled those of the baby boom. The transitional birth cohort (those born between 1939 and 1945) began their families in a context similar to the baby-boom period. A prosperous economy and still low unemployment rates provided an economic environment encouraging to child-rearing. The transitional cohort married early and finished producing their children at about the same time as their older brothers and sisters. But their families usually were smaller. The older group had produced three or four children, but after 1960 the two-child family returned as the more frequent practice.[12]

The birth cohort of the 1930s—those primarily responsible for the baby boom—also finished child-bearing during the first five years of the 1960s. Because of their early start in child-bearing, much of this birth cohort had already reached parity. However, some of these parents, who had started their families at later ages, had the third or fourth of their closely spaced children in the first five years of the 1960s. By 1965 higher-order births were declining. Women between thirty-five and thirty-nine years began to show substantially lower birth rates than those of the same age group during the baby-boom years and in the early years of the 1960s.[13]

The baby boom continued for five years in the 1960s. Fertility patterns still resembled those of the baby-boom decades because the couples in the birth cohort of the 1930s were completing their families at the same time that the transitional cohort began family creation. But when the younger birth cohort (those born during the baby boom) reached the prime child-bearing years, the decline in fertility accelerated. At this point, the new generation firmly rejected the baby-boom family style, and a new pattern of work and fertility developed.

The New Pattern of Modern Fertility. The new large birth cohort, the people born after 1945, reached the child-bearing years after 1965. They behaved very differently from the previous cohort. They avoided early marriage, early fertility, and family commitment. Instead, higher education, youthful dissent, and sexual alternatives to marriage attracted the youth of the upper middle class. Many young men served in the armed forces and suffered a period of readjustment. This cohort tended to prolong their youth until age thirty and either postponed assuming traditional adult roles or rejected them completely. Neither education nor armed service was necessarily incompatible with early marriage and fertility; the baby-boom parents had combined both roles in the 1950s. However, youthful unemployment rates—high in the late 1960s and throughout the 1970s—correlated with the rejection of early family commitment.[14]

Fertility declined for young adults throughout the society, but fertility rates for the educated and prosperous members of the middle class declined more rapidly than for any other group. This factor challenges the validity of a simple economic explanation for the rejection of family creation in this period. The rate of economic growth did not decline until after 1970, and even then absolute levels of prosperity remained high. After 1960 the relationship between economic factors and fertility behavior resumed the strong inverse relationship characteristic of the early decades of the twentieth century. This change also suggests the limitations of the Becker-Schultz model of rational fertility behavior. The most prosperous young people rejected fertility despite their access to resources, while the less affluent still frequently chose to raise children instead of purchasing other consumer goods.[15]

Fertility behavior and attitudes appeared to differ from those of the recent past in several other important dimensions. The structure of attitudes, behavior, and assumptions about fertility that developed after 1965 clashed with the fertility context characteristic of the earlier decades. One example of this is the handling of unexpected children. Fertility often appeared to be merely an inconvenient byproduct of sexual activity.

Illegitimate children accounted for a growing proportion of additional births. By 1975, 14.2 percent of all births were to unmarried women, in contrast to the 4 percent rate in 1950 or the 5.3 percent rate of 1960. Earlier cohorts had hurried to the altar or the judge to make legitimate the results of premarital conception. In contrast, the postwar birth cohort accepted the alternatives of adoption, single parenthood, or irregular family structures for the rearing of illegitimate babies. The usual explanation for the rise in illegitimacy is the well-documented increase in permissiveness toward adolescent sexual activity. But this explanation fails to explain the rejection of the more traditional solution—immediate early marriage.[16]

At this time technical deterrents to fertility had become widely available and were easy and convenient to use. New methods of preconception and postconception control of fertility had achieved widespread acceptance. Thus it is surprising that there was a sharp rise in illegitimacy because unwanted pregnancy could have been prevented through the use of the new technology.

The increase in the number of babies born out of wedlock was matched by increasing numbers of babies born by accident. Both accidental and illegitimate pregnancy constituted an increasingly large share of fertility in this period. This circumstance suggests the emergence of a significantly less positive attitude toward family creation. Indeed the new behavior raises the possibility of a profound attitudinal shift toward fertility—one that past generations, who felt that having babies was a serious responsibility, would never have tolerated.[17]

The new acceptance of abortion also suggests an important change in attitudes about fertility. Since the mid-19th century, abortion had never been condoned, much less encouraged. By the 1970s, however, abortion had become a relatively well-accepted method of birth control, despite the opposition of a large vocal minority. Legal abortion and sterilization may account for as much as 40 percent of the decline in fertility. Of course some of this pregnancy would never have occurred if abortion had not been available. But the acceptance by society of these radical alternatives to child-bearing indicates that their direct impact is only a part of the profound change they reflect. Underneath them lies the rejection of family values long espoused in modern western society.[18]

Other developments in regard to the handling of fertility—the structure of child-rearing, for example—also suggest important changes of attitudes. Married young people postponed having babies instead of starting their families quickly. Women between the ages of twenty and thirty chose to remain at work instead of leaving after a few years to raise children. Especially after 1970, more and more mothers stayed at home only briefly after their children were born. Even those who chose full-time motherhood when their children were very young returned to work when the children entered the first grade of school. This pattern sharply contrasted with the pattern of mother-intensive child-rearing chosen by the previous generation.

Perhaps this was merely the continuation and extension of a long-term trend. In the recent past, mothers increasingly returned to work after their children were twelve years old. But the mothers of the 1970s returned to work in their prime adult years. This behavior revealed a major shift in women's priorities. Active motherhood declined, both as a vocation and as an ideal. This trend was parallel to the decline in fertility, but, more important, it indicated a profound difference in attitude. Child-rearing became a part-time pursuit at the same time that fertility became a more random event.

The argument that the low birth rates of the 1970s showed only the postponement of fertility, not its rejection, perhaps has some validity since the birth rates of the women over the age of thirty have risen slightly in the 1980s. However, most optimistic conclusions about fertility levels are based upon responses to opinion surveys. Young people's verbal assurances that they expect to have children may lead to conclusions that are too traditional. Studies have shown that parity rarely achieves the level married people verbally advocate early in marriage.[19]

More recent studies have concluded that 25 percent of the baby-boom birth cohort will remain childless. Young people expect to have slightly more than 2,000 children per 1,000 women, but this is scarcely a high birth rate even if achieved. The potential parents of today desire fewer children than any past generation, and they have frequently postponed realization of their relatively modest child-bearing plans. Since older women of child-bearing age find it difficult to conceive, they often bear fewer children than they would like to have. Failure to achieve even the predicted low rate is highly possible. However, less than 6 percent of the potential parents claim to have rejected fertility completely. Thus we can assume that children retain value despite the important decline in fertility.[20]

Other changes in customs in this period, however, imply that children have become less valued than in earlier years. A more negative attitude toward children appeared as shown by the frequent rejection of children as acceptable tenants in motels and apartments, and the use of contemptuous terminology such as "rug rats" to describe young children and "holding pens" to characterize institutional arrangements for child care. Even the legal system has shown less toleration of young offenders, for they are often tried as adults without the special protections reserved for children.

Toys of the 1980s suggest that children are no longer viewed as the charming and innocent creatures of earlier decades. In contrast to the idealized Shirley Temple doll of the 1930s, the Sweetie Pie of the 1940s, and Chatty Kathy of the 1950s, what doll appears in the toy stores in the 1980s? The Cabbage Patch doll, which hardly fits the popular image of the beautiful child. The popularity of this toy model of an awkward, homely, and somewhat androgynous child suggests that we have lost our view of children as beautiful, ideal, and clearly gender-defined. This change may be a positive one in the direction of realism that will make parenthood less demanding, but we cannot ignore the implications of this important cultural change. Dolls reflect assumptions about the children they portray.

The changed attitudes about children suggest a declining taste for fertility, and the fertility rates clearly support the validity of this assumption. The rising cost of child-rearing alone appears to be an inadequate explanation for the decline because prosperity continued to increase throughout the 1960s. Tastes changed before costs rose enough to explain a major part of the decline in fertility. The return of differential fertility after 1965 revealed an increasing diversity in society, a move away from the homogeneous fertility behavior of the previous forty-five years. Thus, both tastes and costs may vary more across the population than was characteristic of the baby-boom period.

The taste for children has clearly suffered a severe decline in this period, as shown by the attitude change in society and the surveys on the subject of the desires of young adults for family creation. One study based on survey data shows that the climate of opinion was not pronatalist in this period. A majority of those interviewed favored legal abortion, said that the "presence or absence of children was irrelevant to perceptions of personal happiness and satisfaction," and refused to define couples who were voluntarily childless as "selfish."[21]

The impact of rising costs is more difficult to assess. The dollar cost of children probably did not move upward very much until after 1970. One study in 1984 shows a clear decline in preferred family size between 1962 and 1977 among a sample group interviewed in 1961 about their fertility expectations. Their final parity was 27 percent below their expectations recorded when they were childless in 1961. Either their tastes changed or the rising cost of children undermined their ability to realize their fertility desires. However, the rapid economic growth in the 1960s suggests that on the average the real cost of children did not move upward until after 1970. Thus in the 1960s, the fertility decline probably related more closely to tastes than to costs, but in the 1970s and 1980s both factors were important.[22]

The positive economic environment of the 1960s challenges the assumption of simple economic causation for fertility decline. Economic growth per capita and personal disposable income continued to increase. Surprisingly, even perceived improvement exceeded actual economic gains throughout this decade of falling birth rates. When public opinion pollsters asked people what the minimum yearly income to support a family of four people might be, their responses lagged far behind the actual improvement in average incomes throughout the 1960s. Not until after 1969 did the perceived increase in the minimum income necessary for a family of four people exceed the actual improvement in family income. If this measure is a reasonable surrogate for the perception of prosperity, the results in the 1960s decade would suggest that people knew they had plenty of money to have children if that was their preferred taste. (See Figure 8.1 in Chapter 8.)

The Janowitz data, however, which measure directly people's perception of their own expectations of improvement in the coming year, shows a shift downward in the 1960s from the high point in 1956. This shift matches closely the onset of the fertility decline, but it is at odds with the evidence of the perception of the minimum income cited above.

Several factors could have affected the individual perception of improvement for the next year and not have affected the more abstract question of the necessary minimum income for the family of four people. Taxes increased substantially in the 1960s as two presidents tried to create the New Frontier and the Great Society. Despite the fact that personal disposable income (after tax income) still rose despite higher taxes, people's concern about their economic prospects in the future may have increased at the same time that they actually had more money in hand. Inflation emerged as a major threat to prosperity in this decade, and although recognition of its impact lagged behind its reality, people may have implicitly realized that their larger incomes did not buy as much as they expected.

In the 1970s some clear negative trends marred the economic situation, and the fertility rate moved downward at a faster rate than in the previous ten years. Inflation emerged not only as a serious economic problem but also as an important campaign issue in all national elections. The rate of economic growth moved downward, and recessions appeared simultaneously with inflation. Economic instability affected the choice of fertility negatively, and by the end of the 1970s indicators of a real decline in incomes had appeared.[23]

Changing demographic factors also had implications for decreases in fertility rates. Several studies suggest the varying ways in which the rising marriage age affects fertility. The study cited earlier by John Modell showed that a single factor—the choice of later marriage—alone provides evidence of a changing taste for fertility. He correlated the norms for the ideal marriage age with norms for timing of child-bearing and family size. Those who believed in early marriage also favored a larger family size than those who preferred later marriage. Thus the new custom of later marriage by an increased proportion of the population also reveals their acceptance of a lower taste for fertility. The Modell study showed that the two beliefs (later marriage and small families) occur together.[24]

This result was shown in another way by Jay Teachman, who established the fact that as people get older they expect to have smaller families. In this period, married couples used contraception earlier in their marriage than they did in the baby-boom period, and this factor, when augmented by aging and inertia, encouraged the acceptance of a new lower norm for family size.[25]

A study by Linda Waite and Glenna Spitze showed that a substitute activity replaced the enthusiasm for early child-bearing. For women, even the chance of marrying decreases with the "increasing availablity and attractiveness of alternatives to the role of wife and the costs of assuming it." The alternatives to assuming the role of wife became clearer to women in their twenties and thus lead directly to postponement and rejection of marriage.[26]

The effects of later marriage on fertility may be even stronger than these studies suggest. Since marriage and child-bearing require separate choices, the link between them might appear to have little relevance in explaining the drop in fertility. One might assume that a person who wanted a larger family would also choose early marriage because these beliefs occur together, as John Modell has shown. But, very simply, this choice would not always have been available, given the changing customs in society. Both marriage and child production required participation with a suitable partner, and early marriage was often rejected for reasons that had little to do with rejection of parenthood. The emergence of the new stage of life in the post-adolescent years—that which has been called "youth" in the 1960 and early 1970 decades—was negative to fertility, probably without the conscious intent of its participants. Fertility declined as a high-priority choice, but the choice of later marriage then enforced its own limits on family size.

The most negative effects on fertility in this period, however, are probably the direct and indirect results of the large size of the baby-boom birth cohort. The birth cohort size affects both tastes and costs. A direct cost effect and a relative income effect has been shown by Richard Easterlin. The high unemployment rates for young men were a result of the "worker glut" caused by the entry of extraordinary numbers of workers in the work force at the same time. Easterlin argues that the cohort effects on income and employment have been the primary cause of the decline in fertility.[27]

Another study by Clifford Clogg and James Shockey shows the dramatic increase of the mismatch between occupation and schooling of the baby-boom cohort. This mismatch has characterized the entire period from 1960 into the 1980 decade. Thus, in addition to high unemployment for young men, a situation of underemployment also exists in these two decades, perhaps not as negative to fertility as unemployment, but clearly related to it through the proved impact of the relative income hypothesis. Those who were employed at lower levels than their education had prepared them to expect felt that their income and status were inadequate when compared to their peers, thus providing a negative cost effect on fertility through the perception of inadequate resources.[28]

Other cohort effects have been extensively documented by many studies, and they range from problems of employment to descriptions of psychological stress. One important negative psychological effect of large cohort size has been shown by Elwood Carlson. He suggests that large cohorts have had "imperfect socialization." When there are too many children per adult, expectations and beliefs become "less realistic and flexible in the face of adversity." Other researchers have shown the high suicide rates of the large cohort and the greater psychological stress of the young adult cohort of 1976 as compared to the smaller cohort of young adults in 1957. The feelings of confidence in the future that the baby-boom parents embraced as young adults were lacking in their children when they came of age, simply because of the massive size of the younger group.[29]

Many of the positive impacts on fertility present in the earlier period were conspicuously lacking in the years after 1970 and showed decline even in the 1960s. Cohort effects turned negative for the new large cohort, and economic factors, sometimes ambivalent in the 1960s, became more clearly negative after 1970. And if we look at the effects of the culture, we find that the later baby-boom children were not raised in a period of emphasis on traditional values. They lived in homes in which family values were praised, but the world outside the home appeared to approve alternatives to the family, such as communal living and irregular sexual arrangements. The conflict between the values of their homes and those of the outside world created an ambivalence that was impossible to resolve.

Children for the baby-boom birth cohort had become expensive consumer goods with high maintenance costs in an uncertain economy with high unemployment, serious underemployment, and high rates of divorce. The confidence in the future and the set of traditional values associated with parenthood had been undermined by new experiences and the effects of involuntary membership in large birth cohort. After 1970 estimates of the cost of child-rearing in current dollars show massive increases, a substantial rise in the real cost of child-rearing beyond what had been perceived as necessary in the baby-boom decades.[30]

Fertility decline relates closely to the accompanying increase in work participation for women. The two variables are integrated more closely in this period than in either previous period. Between 1900 and 1940, fertility and work participation had almost separate histories, and each affected the other indirectly. After 1940 the relationship moved closer as work increased in a way that protected the maternal role but still left women with opportunities for paid work in several stages of their lives.

But after 1960, when increasingly higher percentages of women in prime adult years entered the work force, fertility and work merged so closely that they can hardly be analyzed separately. Women's experience in the work force has become an integral part of the history of fertility.

The New Workplace

The women's work force doubled in size between 1960 and 1980. The numbers are staggering—from 22 million women in 1960 to 44 million in 1980. In no earlier time period had there been an increase in the labor force of such magnitude.[1]

In addition to the unprecedented size, the women's work force changed in another important way. After 1960 it no longer expanded in a manner that allowed fertility and mother-intensive child-rearing to remain as the primary goals of women's lives. Women of child-bearing ages entered the work force in unprecedented numbers; some were mothers who had rejected only direct child care, not fertility, but others chose complete rejection of motherhood in favor of paid work. In 1985, 62 percent of all mothers were working, as compared with the already high figure of 44 percent in 1973.[2]

Participants

Married women at all age levels joined in the expansion of the female labor force, but the women in prime child-bearing years, those between the ages of twenty-five and thirty-four, were the conspicuous newcomers. In 1960 only 36 percent of the married women in this age group had occupied paying jobs outside the home. Twenty years later, 65 percent of them had joined the labor force. This age group began this period with the lowest percentage of work participation. By 1980 they were almost as likely to be working as their younger sisters, women between the ages of twenty and twenty-four, who showed the highest rate of work participation.[3]

The youngest women had been a major portion of the women's labor force young since the beginning of industrialization, and their high rates of work participation after 1960 showed only the continuation of a long historical trend. But women in prime adult childbearing years (those between twenty-five and thirty-four) had historically been at home raising children and pursuing domesticity.

The change in work rates for women between thirty-five and forty-four was similar, although less striking in its magnitude. Substantial numbers of women in this age group had already moved into the work force by 1960 when 43 percent of them worked for pay. By 1980 their participation rate of over 65 percent exceeded that of the forty-five to fifty-four year-olds, the age group with the highest rates during the previous period.

Participation rates for "married women with spouse present" doubled from 31 percent to 60 percent between 1960 and 1980 for all those in child-bearing ages, i.e., women between twenty and forty-four. The change was greatest for mothers of young children. As the percentage of working mothers rose, the gap between their participation in the work force and that of their childless sisters significantly narrowed. In only twenty years, the working mother was no longer in the minority; instead, her behavior had become the norm. This change had important implications for fertility. Fertility no longer provided a powerful deterrent to work participation; women were discovering ways to pursue both roles simultaneously. To be sure, mother-intensive child-rearing showed a substantial decline, but fertility did not necessarily preclude work for pay.[4]

Each successive birth cohort in the twentieth century has shown increasing attachment to work, beginning with women over forty in 1940 and continuing with ever younger women over the next forty years. The trend already observed at the end of the baby boom of a return to work at earlier ages after child-rearing was followed by a new trend; young women remained in the work force longer before child-rearing. By 1980 many young women workers returned to work within a few weeks after childbirth.

Not only did the contemporary women's work force grow larger than it had been in earlier decades, but it showed fewer distinctions by marital status. This is probably not surprising because of the increased proportions of single and divorced women in the population and in the work force, and increased proportions of married women working outside the home. The greater frequency of divorce and the new pattern of later marriage decreased the chance that marital status would act as a deterrent to women's decisions to work or their ambition to build careers. In recent years more women, even if they planned to marry, anticipated spending some portion of their adult lives as single or divorced.[5]

The Civil Rights Act of 1964 and its amendments in 1972 lent legal support to the removal of gender and marital class distinctions in the workplace. No longer could employers make private judgments about the legitimacy of married women working. The legislation required employers to hire and promote women without reference to their marital or maternal status. And, while it was by no means fully enforced, the legislation did contribute to the rising employment opportunities for women.

Educational Level of Women Workers

Another pronounced change in the women's work force from its composition before 1960 has been in is educational level. For the first time, participation rates were highest for women with substantial education. More educated women had been entering the work force even before 1960, but the next two decades saw the full development of this important trend. One immediate effect of the increased education of the labor pool was the emergence of more rigorous educational requirements for jobs. Education served as a filter for job access in an increasingly crowded labor market.[6]

This factor also had the effect of decreasing the homogeneity of the women's work force. Income disparities increased among women of widely varying educational levels. In this respect the new women's work force closely resembled the male work force, which had always included men of widely varying incomes and educational levels.[7]

Many of the more highly educated women workers in this period were young and recently educated women, but the increase in the educational level of the women's work force resulted also from the entry of substantial numbers of highly educated middle-class women in their middle years. They entered jobs of relatively high status, if not always high income. Most of them were baby-boom mothers or mothers of the early 1960s.[8]

Entry into work roles for middle-class women represents a new phenomenon. As nonprofessionals, in the recent past they had defined their major role as homemaking. They had no strong economic motivations, for they were already at the top of the income distribution because their husbands were in peak career years. Work motivations for this group of women, then, were less traditional than for other groups, based more on ideological grounds or a search for self-actualization.

Work Commitment

Married women of all educational levels showed continually increasing commitment to work by new behavior that resembled the work commitment of men and single women. By 1977, 48 percent of all married women worked, only 10 percent less than the work rate for single women (58 percent). The percentage of all males over the age of sixteen who worked for pay declined from 84 percent to 78.5 percent between 1960 and 1978. At the same time, the work rate of married women in the same age group increased from 35 percent to almost 50 percent.[9]

Women's commitment to work increased substantially in this period, building upon the trend that had appeared before 1960. After 1970 the rate of women's dropping out of the work force during recessions was substantially lower than it had been in the recessions of the 1950 and 1960 decades. Women no longer provided a "buffer stock to cushion the swing" from recession to boom. At the same time, women's unemployment rates rose, compared to those of men, a change that showed that women chose to remain in the work force when they experienced involuntary unemployment. They sought other jobs (the measure of unemployment) as opposed to leaving the work force, the prevailing practice before 1965.[10]

Another indication of women's greater work commitment was the rapid increase in the percentage of women working full time. In 1975 three-quarters of the working women held full-time jobs; in the later years of the 1960s, only 60 percent had occupied full-time jobs. In 1960 a woman could expect to work twenty-three years, on the average. By 1970 her work life expectancy had increased to twenty-six years. Thus the percentage of experienced female workers rose even with the rapid growth in entry rates for new women workers. This surprising factor underscores the frequency at which women combined periods of employment throughout their life cycles. "New" workers who entered the labor force between the ages of thirty and forty-four tended often to be returning to work after an absence instead of entering the job market for the first time.[11]

Work Motivations

Large numbers of women of all ages and economic and educational levels shifted from the private sphere of homemaking, child care, and social service to full-time employment outside of the home. Why did so many women change their priorities? The reasons for this change of emphasis elude simple analysis, but a wide variety of suggestons has been made to explain this new behavior. For the first time ideological reasons emerge as a prime possibility, as the feminist movement succeeded in gaining new legal protections for women in the work force.

This success led to the widespread belief in another explanation for women's behavior: that a more hospitable and varied workplace had replaced the limited labor market of earlier decades, attracting women with the new variety and desirability of jobs open to women. And, finally, a third category of explanation has emerged for women's work behavior: that of economic motivations. Various kinds of economic motivations have been suggested, explanations that range from the historically precedented one of economic need to more complex motivations that include rising expectations and the pressure to achieve an appropriate income relative to one's peers.

Economic motives alone appear to be inadequate explanations for a change in work behavior of this magnitude, especially when we observe that economic circumstances varied greatly between the 1960s and the 1970s, and women's increased entry to the work force characterized both decades. Economic factors had the most direct impact after 1973, as inflation increased and the economy grew more slowly. In the 1970s the increased employment of women served to expand GNP; without women earning incomes, a decline in growth might have appeared much sooner. Women in those years unquestionably were motivated by the desire to retain economic gains already made and to improve the family standards of living. But in the 1960s the economy did not decline. On the contrary it showed continuous growth in all measures—per capita GNP, personal disposable income, and the rate of economic expansion.

A factor that should have been strongly negative to women's increased work in both decades is the lack of substantial change in wage levels for women. The increasing rewards for work in real dollars show little improvement in either decade when compared to those of men. Women's earnings between 1955 and 1970 show a much lower rate of increase than those of men in the same years. Substantial improvement appeared in men's earnings, increasing the gap between men's and women's earnings, a factor that might have actively discouraged women from work entry, as it had in earlier decades of the twentieth century.[12]

The improvement in family income resulting from men's wages between 1945 and 1960 had produced for women a strong lack of incentive to work. The research on the effect of family income changes on women's work by Sobol and Mincer clearly established the negative impact upon women's work of family income improvement from other sources. However, this factor does not on the average appear to have engendered a serious negative impact to women's work entry after 1960.

A more detailed analysis of the relative improvement of men's wages partially explains this aberration. In all but the highest level of professional and managerial jobs, salaries for white-collar workers failed to

match the relatively greater rise of wages earned by blue-collar workers. Thus the improvement in the middle-class breadwinner's pay may
have been less than that of his blue-collar counterpart.[13]

Middle-class families observed a relatively lower level of improvement in family income as contributed by the man of the family than
did the blue-collar families. This factor may have encouraged more
middle-class women to enter the work force in order to contribute to
the greater relative improvement of their family income. They chose
a paid work role as a result of a relative decline in the rate of improvement of family income. This kind of economic motivation can be defended in the 1960 decade despite the still rising levels of absolute
family income for all social classes, and this argument is supported by
the increased percentages of middle-class women entering the work
force in the 1960 decade.

By the 1970s rising expectations made additional family income more
desirable to all social classes. Popular perception of the minimum resources necessary for family maintenance in current dollars showed a
more rapid rise than did the real cost of living in the 1970s. This
factor created a perception of need for additional income in families
who actually lived at a higher level of absolute income than similar
families in the 1950s. But a crucial factor in analyzing change is that
the decision to increase family income through work participation by
wives occurred while women's wages remained at levels that were
insufficient before 1970 to attract women in child-rearing years into
the work force.

The argument that expectations rose in the 1970 decade is based
upon the rise in the perception of the required minimum income to
support a family of four people. After 1969 this perception rose at a
much faster rate than the rates of real economic growth, thus suggesting that perceived "needs" (a surrogate for economic expectations) rose
faster than the still-growing economy. Higher economic expectations
increased the value of paid work for wives in comparison with other
alternatives such as volunteer work, homemaking, child-rearing, or
leisure. (See Figure 8.1 in Chapter 8.)

In the middle years of the 1970 decade, economic motivations for
women's work became more direct. In 1974 and 1978 inflation ex-

ceeded the average real increase in income, an effect that suggests that more than half of the families were suffering economic decline. People on fixed incomes found their incomes eroding seriously, but even those whose incomes rose faster than inflation discovered "bracket creep." Their new incomes, higher in current dollars than before, only led them into higher income-tax brackets, leaving them with only small gains in purchasing power. Thus families had increased motivations to seek a second wage earner, although the income-tax structure did not encourage this choice either. But some of the additional income remained in the family's possession despite the structure of the income-tax law, which penalized the two-earner family.[14]

Work participation for married women in prime adult years accelerated during the 1970 decade of slow economic growth and of some economic decline. The coincidence of these two trends suggests the increased importance of economic impacts upon work rates for women. A comparison of the average income of families of only one earner to those of two earners suggests that by the end of the 1970s two earners had become necessary in order to achieve a continual real improvement in family income.[15]

Economic motivations have shown increasing urgency in the later 1970s and 1980s, as national income per capita has only risen through major increases in the size of the work force. Without women's entry into the workplace, median family incomes would have shown clear decline. During the baby-boom years economic growth did not depend upon rapid increases in the work force at the cost of fertility rejection. But the proportion of adult workers to (unproductive) children has increased substantially in the last two decades, and only this change has prevented a decrease in per-capita gross national product. Only the participation of wives in the work force permitted many American families to retain the standard of living achieved in the early 1970s.[16]

As illustrated in Figure 11.1, families in which both the husband and wife work have higher average incomes than families in which only the husband works. In 1960 families with the wife working had 25 percent more income; by 1983 the amount had increased to 47 percent. The increase is due in part to higher wages and more hours

FIGURE 11.1

Impact of Wife's Earnings on Family Income.

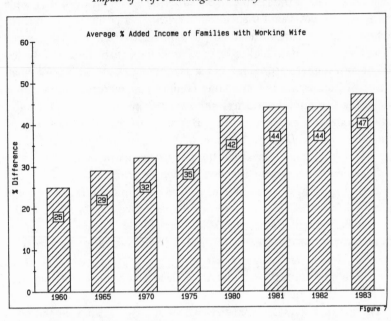

Source: Statistical Abstact of the United States: 1986, p. 453.

of work for women, but it is also due to a social change—wives of such higher-income husbands as professionals and executives were working in increasing numbers.

Economic motivations broadly based upon prevention of economic decline for the family are new for women in the most recent decade, but they do not explain the work increase that occurred before 1975. In past decades, most women during prime child-rearing years, in cases of severe economic deprivation, had chosen to work only on a temporary basis. Even in the depression years of the 1930s, women's place had been clearly recognized as in the home, despite the occasional necessity of work in serious emergencies. Mild recessions in the 1940 and 1950 decades had caused no work increase for women and, in fact, often displayed a pattern of women dropping out until the economy had recovered. Most of the increase in women's work before 1960 had occurred during periods of positive economic growth, when the demand for women in the workplace exceeded the supply of female workers. And even at these times women in prime child-bearing years had not been the group to fill the labor gap.

Therefore, even if the work increase for women in the 1970 decade was a response to reasonable economic motivations, it showed new and radical behavior. Only a striking decline in the perceived value of women's traditional role (fertility and mother-intensive child-rearing) could have elicited such a strong response to the economic situation. In the recent past, similar family financial conditions would have been viewed as only mildly unfortunate. Certainly the conditions were not sufficiently serious to undermine the perceived utility of women's responsibilities in the home.

The Workplace

Another explanation for women's assumption of new work roles is that the work environment had become more attractive and hospitable than in earlier decades. There is some historical precedent for this more positive rationale for the growth in female work participation. Higher wages, a more varied range of jobs, or even increased access to traditional men's positions might have caused more women to shift the balance between home and work in favor of paid work. In a limited way similar factors had encouraged women to choose to leave home for the workplace in the 1920s and 1930s, and more strongly during the years of World War II, when not only higher wages but a temporary decline of sex stereotyping in the workplace had combined with patriotism to increase women's work participation. However the argument of greater work attractiveness, objectively measured, appears to be seriously inadequate to explain the magnitude of the work increase after 1960.

The jobs that women found still resembled those of the earlier periods. Indeed, the number of new workers concentrated the female dominance of a few job slots, although a widely publicized scattering of women to non-traditional areas appeared. The intensified concentration defines the key trend. In 1960 most women worked in clerical areas, the lower-paid manufacturing jobs, and in service occupations. The 1980 occupational data show almost the same distribution of women among these categories. In fact, clerical work, a notoriously low-paid area, occupied 35 percent of the working women instead of the 28 percent in 1960.[17]

Moving away from broad categories, we find that more specific occupational distribution reveals the same continuity of sex stereotyping. Secretarial jobs were primarily reserved for women, and they provided a major job category in the women's work force. This occupation in 1978 included a substantial 8 percent of all working women. In 1967, 6.7 percent of working women were secretaries, and in 1960 secretaries comprised only 4.8 percent of the women's work force. Some of the increase in participation in the occupation of secretary may be a result of the greatly increased supply of new workers, who used this job as an entry-level position. However, most secretaries do not move upward in position, although they may move upward in wages and status. The secretarial route offered an opportunity for upward occupational mobility for black women. In 1978, 5 percent of all secretaries were black; by 1985, however, more black women had acquired secretarial jobs.[18]

Other examples show the same lack of change in sex stereotyping, or at best somewhat ambiguous improvement. Women made substantial progress in capturing the primarily male occupation of bank-telling in the period between 1960 and 1978. Almost 80 percent of the bank-tellers were female in 1978, in contrast to 60 percent in 1970 and only 30 percent in 1960. However, this "progress" in job acquisition was not matched by improved wages.[19]

The increasing size of the female work force did not result in any substantial improvement in managerial occupations, even in areas such as education that had employed substantial numbers of women for fifty years. In 1978 only 34 percent of the school administrators were women despite substantial increases in the total number of people in this occupation. This percentage was almost the same as it had been in 1960 and 1970.

Many occupational areas remained closed to women, particularly in craft occupations in which entry was controlled by labor unions. Almost no change occurred in these areas, despite the great publicity given to the occasional woman who worked in a "hard hat" occupation. Even crafts like television repair, which required small detail work at which women were believed to excel, remained almost entirely in the hands of men. Between 1969 and 1979 female participation in craft occupations increased by one-half of one percent.

Women continued to lose ground to men even in the pursuit of their own traditional professions, and the limits on their participation now were exacerbated by declining demand. The demand for school teachers, librarians, and nurses no longer increased as it had in the baby-boom decades, when workers in these areas had been urgently needed to respond to the requirements of a child-laden population. Demand remained relatively high in the 1960s but declined after 1970 as the percentage of small children in the population moved downward. But successful invasion by men of women's professions increased even as demand for participants declined.

In addition, the educational gap at the advanced-degree levels between men and women that had increased in the 1940, 1950, and early 1960 decades contributed to the professional disparity in the 1960 and 1970 decades. By 1980 some change began to show in the summary figures of participation in the professions. Women appear to have made successful inroads into the accounting profession, for only 21 percent of the accountants were women in 1972 and by 1980 women held 36 percent of the accounting positions. The percentage of women physicians rose slightly (from 10 percent in 1972 to 13 percent in 1980). And the impressive appearance of an increase in the percentage of women lawyers and judges from 4 percent in 1972 to 13 percent in 1980 must be viewed in the context of the continued domination of the partnership positions in law firms by men.[20]

Even in the newest industrial sector, that of high tech, women held inferior positions. Data entry, a lower-level clerical task, rapidly became an exclusive female preserve. The higher status job of computer programming, however, was captured by men, despite a very promising short period in the early days of computers when most programmers were women. Studies have shown that in management or technical-professional positions in high-tech industries, men are even more likely to dominate than in older industries. Researchers have suggested that the gender discrimination of the parent fields of mathematics and engineering may have been carried into the new field of computer technology.[21]

The possibility that the increased attractiveness of work was based upon improvement in earnings has some validity, for women's wages in real dollars showed a small increase over the period before 1960. At least one study suggests that the rise in wages for women between 1960 and 1980 has been the dominant factor in the increase in work participation. But, as we have seen women's wages did not rise as fast as those of men.[22]

The statistics on women's work participation between 1960 and 1980 show an apparent contradiction—massively increased enthusiasm for work by all classes and ages of women, despite little improvement in job choice and income, the most obvious rewards of work. The increase in participation and the increasing commitment to paid work by all ages of women was not matched by any substantial improvement in the job market.

Women's motivation and their expectations of work become immensely important, then, in assessing the dimensions of the change. Many of the work motivations defined as important in the past are inadequate to explain women's new behavior. The role of women as the "emergency reserve labor army" has no impact in the 1970s, a time of excess labor supply due to the appearance of the baby-boom children at entry level in the work force. Neither national emergency nor recession-inspired employment can explain the expansion of the women's work force, and for most women economic need was lacking at the level that would have brought earlier generations of women into the work force.

The expansion of women's work participation appears to be as irrational as it was unexpected. At least one economist has expressed amazement at the rapid pace of the new acquisition of a work role for many women despite relatively minimal economic rewards. The disappearance of traditional economic motivations and the lack of improvements in the workplace reveal the necessity for analysis of other possible work motivations.[23]

The strong resemblance between the workplace of the 1970s and that of the 1950s did not deter masses of women from seeking their fortunes within it and altering their priorities toward an increased reliance on work. An understanding of their decision requires analysis of the rejection of the home and the emergence of different economic motivations. The choice of work by many groups of women appeared to be a mass phenomenon, but in reality the motivations differed profoundly for various groups of women. The common factor for most women in this period has been the choice of the workplace at the expense of child-bearing, mother-intensive child-rearing, homemaking, and domesticity, and this factor provides the key to understanding the revolution in the workplace.

CHAPTER 12

Women's Rush to Work: Necessity or Opportunity?

The movement into the work force of many new women workers can be understood only by analysis of the different work motivations for each group of women. The appearance of a mass phenomenon is misleading because it suggests the existence of similar motivations for all the new workers. Women's reasons for choosing work have usually been different from those of men, because they have been primarily responsible for care of the home and the children. Despite some sharp statistical change, only a small proportion of the new work entrants were following new and radical behavior. Most of them chose work in historically precedented patterns, but at a more rapid pace of entry and in unexpected numbers.

The history of the women's labor force in the twentieth century shows that growth has occurred by the gradual entry of new groups of women whose motives have varied, but who have all internalized a value system that emphasized the importance of the alternative career of home and hearth. Thus every group of women has had to include their home responsibilities in the decision process about work. In the 1960–1980 period the motivations remained diverse among different groups of women, despite the massive scope of the increase in work participation, and women still made their decisions with an implicit recognition of the demands of their role in the home.

Dividing the new work entrants into groups by age, education, occupation, family income, and work motivation provides a structure that leads to a more complete analysis of the expansion of the women's work force after 1960. The history of the married women's work force suggests the most useful categories for this approach.

Many of the new workers were already within age and income groups that had long histories of work participation. For example, many women over forty in the lower-income portion of the middle class, women who had completed secondary school, had been at work for almost thirty years before 1960. New work entrants from this group had a substantial precedent for choosing to enter the work force. They were only following a well-established trend.

Young married women of all educational levels also had long work histories throughout most of the twentieth century. Work in the years before child-rearing had been a frequent and well-accepted practice. Women with children whose husbands had abandoned the family or were out of work comprise another group of women workers for whom substantial work histories already existed.

Groups of married women whose work histories began in the most recent period, however, include women of university education, both young and middle-aged, who developed new work motivations. Younger women of this group chose careers instead of short-term jobs before child-rearing, and older women of this group wanted "second careers" instead of leisure and social service later in life. And a final new group of workers included many mothers in prime child-rearing years who chose work instead of mother-intensive child-rearing.

Groups of Women with Long Work Histories

Women of the Lower Middle Class. Work entry for one large group of married women, those of high-school education in the lower-middle-income portion of the population, can best be understood by recognizing the continuation of a trend already well established in the previous period. This socioeconomic group had provided the greatest proportion of the new entrants into the work force in the 1940–1960 period. With a high-school education and in some cases further training for specific jobs, they did not enter the professions or qualify for jobs that required university degrees. The married women's work force in the baby-boom period consisted mainly of urban women who had completed high school, whose fertility levels were lower than women of either higher or lower income, and whose husbands had blue-collar or lower-paying white-collar jobs. Catholic women of this socioeconomic group, unlike Protestant women, often pursued higher fertility, but their work behavior remained similar to the rest of the group.

On the average, however, this group never made the commitment to high fertility in the baby-boom period, and it provided the major exception to the production of the three- or four-child family. Thus, many of these mothers were ready to enter the work force after child-rearing at earlier ages than the more prolific mothers of higher and lower income. At the same time they were less committed to mother-intensive child-rearing because their family traditions had often included the working-class model of involvement by female members of the extended family with child-rearing. Grandmothers and aunts had participated more actively in raising children in this family style than in the families of the upper middle class. Thus mothers could enter the work force when their children were still in childhood.

The increased participation of this group of women in the work force after 1960 continued the established trend of the previous twenty years. They cut their already low birth rates slightly and entered the work force sooner after child-rearing than in the previous period, but these changes were relatively minor and only intensified their already widespread custom of combining child-rearing with a strong emphasis on paid work.

A key point in understanding work entry in the 1960–1980 period for the women of high-school education is that they needed no new motivations to attract them to the work force. The persistence of the 1950 style workplace even in the 1970 decade had no negative impact. The available jobs were satisfactory. Bank-telling, stenography, computer data entry, retail selling, and other types of service and clerical work offered enough income, sociability, and in some cases sufficient challenge to be interesting. The old advantages of easy entrance and exit were still there in 1970, as they had been in 1950. Family needs might dictate temporarily dropping out of the work force, but the skills were easily transferable to new positions when circumstances changed.

This group of women did not demand a workplace that provided career satisfaction, frequent promotions, or the possibility of successful competition with the male gender. Some women at this job and educational level, of course, did develop ambitions for improvement, and the female labor market was not so rigid that upward movement within its confines could not be achieved. Secretaries could become skilled at using word processors and, in so doing, command larger salaries; a good saleswoman could become a department manager; a competent waitress might move into higher salary and status as a dining-room hostess.

The workplace as it existed could and did attract a large number of workers who found it basically satisfactory. No other situation could possibly explain the volume of entry into the work force. For this group between 1960 and 1985 the economic motivations were similar to those of the baby-boom decades: women worked for improvements in the home, fashionable clothing, educational opportunities for their children, and consumer durables for a higher standard of living. The double income could place a family firmly at a middle-class income level.

The women's work force in 1980 still included women of high-school education as its largest single group. The massive entry of women with university degrees did not disturb this basic similarity with the work force of the 1950 decade, for women of high education comprised only a small proportion of the population. Even if all the college graduates worked for pay in the work force, the vast majority of workers would still be those of high-school education, and this majority of workers was behaving in historically consistent ways, shifting only slightly from past behavior to include more work commitment and less emphasis on fertility. Motivations, goals, and job choice remained similar to the those of the past.[1]

Working-Class Women. Working-class women, unlike the middle-class group described above, found new reasons for entering the labor force after 1960. First, and most important, new jobs became available to this group of women because their educational level increased substantially. By 1980 the median number of school years completed for the total female population over the age of twenty-five exceeded 12 years. In 1940 this figure had been as low as 8.1 years, and even in 1960 the median of 10 years of school completed showed that many people still did not finish secondary school. The increased educational achievement of women in the lower socio-economic group opened new jobs for them in the work place. Clerical and sales occupations that required high-school completion as a qualification became available to a wider spectrum of women because of the rising educational level of the population. The increased demand for new workers in these areas was met by a larger qualified labor pool.[2]

Extensive advantages for working-class families followed the increased work participation made possible by greater educational achievement. Middle-class status frequently accompanied the wife's entry into a white-collar job, and the additional income provided the higher standard of living associated with middle-class status. Property ownership, acquisition of consumer durables, and family vacation trips followed the increased income earned by the mother of the family. The very perception of being middle-class was possible only because the number of two-earner families had increased.

The male head of the household who held a blue-collar job was achieving higher income himself in this period, and the residual disapproval of working wives that one might expect him to have was undermined by the increased upward social mobility that resulted from her work as well as his increased wages. His father and grandfather had prevented their wives from working because the jobs available for working-class women in earlier decades had frequently included harsh physical labor. This alternative had been rejected in all cases except those of the most abject poverty. But in 1970 a machinist or a craftsmen could be proud of his wife's secretarial position and the greater family status and income it provided.

Other working-class women found manufacturing jobs. In the most recent twenty-year period, women have captured a larger share of this declining category of work. In 1960 about 25 percent of the jobs in the total labor force were in the manufacturing sector. By 1980 this percentage had shrunk to 20 percent, but women held 35 percent of these jobs, as opposed to only 28 percent in 1960. The declining need for great physical strength in manufacturing was probably responsible for this change, for employers could hire women to work at lower wages than men would accept. If work could physically be done by women at lower wages, employers would make this choice. The declining power of the male-dominated labor union was also a contributing factor to this gender shift within the work force.[3]

Mothers Without Husbands. A group of women whose work motivations are historically precedented but in a new modern form are those between ages twenty-five and thirty-four "without husband present." The need to support themselves and their young children provided a clear and simple motivation for work entry. The new circumstances included the increasing size of this group in the most recent decades.

The married women's work force in past decades had not included many women of this age group, for they had customarily remained at home with children and the family. But in the early part of the twentieth century, women who had been abandoned by their husbands had entered the work force to support themselves and their children. In a small work force they provided a large percentage of the workers.

During the baby-boom decades, this age group provided the smallest percentage of workers, but those without a husband present usually worked for pay even if they had no children. However, in the years between 1964 and 1977 the percentage of this age group, married but with husbands absent, increased from 17 percent to 27 percent. The motivations for work entry for this group of women included strong economic need in the absence of an employed husband.[4]

Older Women. Work entry for other age groups in the population are easily explained by historically precedented motivations. For example, many women over the age of forty whose children were grown and who were not seriously over-qualified for the available jobs in the work force found work a satisfying alternative to leisure or full-time housekeeping. The continuation of this trend, which had begun as early as the 1930 decade, presents no problems in understanding the work behavior of women in this age group and educational level in the period after 1960. Work for older women had become accepted behavior during the baby-boom decades. Women who had no desire to behave outside established norms could take a paid job without feeling any conflict with their role.

Young Women. Another age group, young women, also chose paid work in its historically precedented manner. Young women, those between the ages of eighteen and twenty-four, have chosen paid work in the years between school completion and child-bearing throughout the twentieth century, first as unmarried workers and then as young married women. This trend of work participation for young women continued after 1960, although with increasing frequency they remained unmarried until at least twenty-five years of age.

The existence of historically precedented motivations and the continuation of long growth trends in the women's work force can explain a large proportion of the increase in the women's work force between 1960 and 1980. Younger and older women whose domestic requirements were low because they had completed child-rearing or not yet begun to raise their families, women of all ages who needed to support themselves and their families, and women who had completed their secondary education and found the workplace satisfactory—all are similar to groups that had entered the work force in earlier periods. Thus the expansion of this kind of work behavior should not be seen as surprising or radical.[5]

New Groups of Working Women

Other categories of married women, however, who had not worked in the past chose to enter the work force in the period between 1960 and 1980. They were engaged in revolutionary new behavior. Paid work for married women with husband present and employed, women in the prime child-rearing years, those between twenty-five and thirty-four years old, increased to levels unprecedented in the twentieth century. Mothers of children under the age of six years had a 50 percent work-participation rate in 1985, and the women in this age range without any children comprised a larger percentage of the total than in any other twentieth-century decade.[6]

Fertility has been rejected in favor of paid work by some women, and for others fertility did not provide the level of deterrence to work participation that had been customary in earlier decades. In the baby-boom period a trend of earlier work entry after child-bearing appeared for women in this age group, but rejection of fertility to permit paid work was not practiced at that point.

The other group who followed radical new work behavior were baby-boom mothers of the upper middle class, women over the age of thirty-five who had completed child-bearing and most of the years of child-rearing. Entering the work force in unprecedented numbers after 1965, this group of women had completed college or university training and were part of the upper socioeconomic level of the population. Women of this age and educational level in the past had not entered the work force. Without traditional economic motivations, they had felt no need or desire to work at jobs for which they were over-qualified. A few exceptions to this were women who practiced women's professions and who reentered their profession after a child-rearing period of some years. But in the past most women in this social class had chosen social service or leisure in the years after the age of forty.

The motivations for both groups practicing new work behavior have no clear historical precedents. Rejection of child-bearing, or mother-intensive child-rearing by women in prime child-rearing years, and work for women who had every reason for enjoying a peaceful middle age in the home they had created, cannot be explained by economic motivations that would have been relevant to women in past decades or by any immediate new attractions of the workplace. The spur for both groups came from the other side of women's balancing act between home and work. In the absence of new delights in the workplace, the prime motivator lay in the declining attractions of the home.

The Decline of the Home. Plentiful evidence exists for the proposition that the status of the family home was in serious decline. The social class that had been the prime defender and innovator of new family models—the upper middle class—now participated in the rejection of the baby-boom family style. The young adults who had been the baby-boom children chose to reject the family model of their parents. The components of this model—early marriage, early fertility, and close spacing of children—almost disappeared after 1970.

This development might have implied only a return to the 1920-style family, a choice similar to the one made by the transitional generation between the baby-boom parents and the baby-boom children. But other factors suggested the beginning of a more profound change in household orientation. The new social acceptance of sexual alternatives to marriage, toleration of abortion, and, unlike past practice, the ever more frequent choice of the one- or two-person household enlarged the variety of options for young people.

The new household choices were more characteristic of the upper middle class than of youth of other of socio-economic groups, as the data on fertility and household formation suggest. Differential fertility returned after 1965 as fertility rates again correlated inversely with income and education. The relationship is a strong one, and thus reveals a significant change in behavior for upper-middle-class young adults. The U-shaped curve disappeared, but not because the birth rates of the middle-income group had risen. On the contrary, their birth rates declined from the already comparatively low level of the baby-boom era. The upper-income group had to make the greatest change in fertility behavior for the linear relationship to reappear. From this same group of upper-income young adults came the creators of the new single-person household, an alternative not often chosen by similar groups in past decades.[7]

The scope of the behavior change by upper-income young adults provides strong evidence of a massive change in attitude concerning the importance of creating the family home. No longer did the home occupy the position of highest priority for young adults of the upper middle class as it had thirty years before for their parents. The more frequent choice of paid work for young women in this group logically accompanied the change in focus on family formation. Historically, young women had worked until marriage or the birth of the first child, but now marriage and child-bearing lay further in the future for educated young women. In some cases paid work may not have been their first choice, but the new practice of remaining at work after child-bearing suggests that paid work occupied a new high priority position for most women.[8]

At the same time, the baby-boom mothers of the upper middle class, now middle-aged, were making new choices of paid work and increased educational achievement. The home no longer was perceived as the major location of sanctuary, personal development, and companionship. Wives and mothers sought new outlets as their role at home was in decline.

The new behavior of the women of the upper middle class—both the young and those in middle age—is primarily based upon the rejection of the home as a sufficient single focus for all of life. Both age groups selected paid work as an alternative to remaining at home. The causal relationship between the process of rejecting the home and choosing paid work cannot be precisely defined, for they are interactive decisions, especially after the movement toward work developed momentum. The new trend soon acquired adherents who were following a path already taken by the more radical first group.

The process began, however, with the older women. They had their own reasons for choosing a new role in middle life. The baby-boom mothers had already prepared for this choice by early child-bearing and close spacing of children. Mother-intensive child-rearing by young mothers would, in their view, be followed by new stages of life that included different choices outside women's separate sphere. Ambitions for new kinds of success awaited only the opportunity for realization.

Motivations for new choices were also provided by the increasingly negative experiences with the baby-boom home that developed despite the innovation and enthusiasm with which it was created in the 1950s. The baby-boom parents of the upper middle class had endowed the home with its last rich and glorious bloom, but the children it produced were seedlings of a different sort.

The baby-boom children, so carefully and lovingly nurtured, chose alternatives to motherhood in their own lives and loudly and visibly rejected many of the values espoused by their parents. The devoted maternal attention that they received accentuated the need for their own stronger and more vocal effort to achieve independence. The rebellion of youth in the 1960s included both idealistic social protest and the more extreme choice of dropping out of the customary choices of modern youth. And the youth of the less radical 1970s also rejected family commitment, although in less visible forms than those of their older brothers and sisters.

The high expectations of the baby-boom children created by their child-focused homes exceeded the ability of the society to provide for them. Their own cohort size undermined the achievement of the economic goal of steady upward progress at a pace of improvement similar to that of their own parents. As young adults, they entered the work force in an economic environment still characterized by growth and prosperity, but that also included increasing costs for child-rearing and higher rates of unemployment. Nurtured in more positive and less ambiguous economic circumstances than their parents, this cohort developed expectations of economic achievement unrealistic after 1965.

The young adults' disillusionment was matched by that of their mothers, who had expected more results from their devoted efforts. Middle-class baby-boom parents, in their effort to restore family life through love, leisure, and creative interaction, forgot that the world outside the home offered serious competition in these same dimensions. Economic functions of the family life remained important, and grown children, who found their own happiness and sociability outside the home—often in irregular living and working arrangements— still yearned for a check from Dad.

Modern parents who wanted to be loved found great difficulty with the persistence of the economic relationship while the other dimensions of family life declined. Preindustrial traditional parents would have had no difficulty with this persistence, for their expectations would have included the recognition of the importance of the economic factors, and love from grown children was not expected. Child-rearing lost much of its appeal for both generations of the upper middle class— those who in its later stages were finding unexpected problems and the younger group who could not see child-rearing as the first priority in their environment, which included high economic expectations and a less positive economy.

Other problems emerged that revealed inherent weaknesses in the baby-boom family model. Although an innovative family model that had addressed many of the drawbacks of the 1920 family, it included many unsolved issues. For example, the homemaking style of the baby-boom era had been focused upon creating an appropriate environment for an interactive family life. Once children left home, the motivation for homemaking rapidly declined, except for the small minority of women who enjoyed homemaking for its own sake.

The historical trend of decline in homemaking had continued despite its brief revival during the baby-boom era when it acquired new psychological and nurturing importance. The decline in the value of a home separate from child-rearing led to the elimination of many of the older tasks. Prepared foods, microwave ovens, and the rising cost of home sewing either continued the trend of decline in tasks that women had experienced since 1900 or made less urgent those tasks that remained. After 1970, technology was no longer used so intensively to improve homemaking standards. Some of the new technologies—such as microwave ovens and frozen dinners—could be used only to decrease time spent on tasks, not to improve their quality.[9]

Parents found child-rearing to be another function continually undermined by new impacts from the outside world. This trend had begun in the early nineteenth century, with the new requirements for public schooling. From this time on parents could fight only holding actions to keep control of their children's mental and physical growth. Much of the history of the family in the past two centuries consists of the invention of new functions for parents to fill the gap left by their loss of a direct educational impact on their children. After 1960, parental educational efforts, with the widespread appearance of television, suffered a new blow in the very sanctuary of the home.

Like so many other benefits and aids for family-rearing—public school, public health, prepared foods, and ready-made clothing—television provided a seductive new addition to the home, offering new possibilities for leisure time, the appearance if not the reality of a participatory activity for the family, and an automatic baby-sitter. Television sets were in reality invaders from the outside world, bringing knowledge and information to the children that parents could not control. A few families rejected the new technology, just as some rejected public school, public health, and prepared foods, but the world outside the home contained all these apparent benefits, and children could not be permanently isolated from them. Good arguments could correctly be made for the value of all these benefits, but their common result was their encroachment upon the historic role of the parent.

One major effect of television was that it was no longer possible to protect children from knowledge that undermined their innocent view of the world. Maintaining childhood as a protected stage of life had become more difficult throughout the twentieth century, but television destroyed any remaining possibility that this could be accomplished. One result was the earlier end to childhood, the premature onset of adolescent attitudes that forced parents and children to suffer ten years of pseudo-youth instead of the six or eight years of earlier decades.

The argument could be made that the Victorian model of protected and innocent childhood was inappropriate and ultimately harmful to growth in a modern society. However, this model had been the implicit foundation of all modern family patterns, and changing it undermined the role of the parent. The conception of parental responsibility for their children's growth, problems, and failures provided a now hopelessly burdensome role for parents, since they could not control so much of their children's lives. The upper middle class sought help, but the only sources were other agencies outside the home, like the private school, a newly popular option after 1970.

Parental satisfaction as well as parental power declined as children grew up in the 1960s and 1970s. Popular public opinion reveals the high negative impact of the number of children on parental satisfaction. Thus a clear negative effect emerged, from the size of the family, on the positive feelings that parents might have about their parental role. The existence of higher-order births clearly undermined the frequency of parental happiness. In addition to a loss in possible emotional benefits, families rated in the baby-boom model of early childbearing showed economic difficulties that did not afflict families created later in a marriage. Savings were depressed, and asset accumulations reduced by 12 percent if children were born early in a marriage.[10]

Some serious negative impacts on the quality of family life were the result of the family size and spacing choices made by baby-boom parents. Disillusionment experienced in middle life by the baby-boom parents prompted them to search for new activities. Dissatisfaction is also revealed by the rising divorce rate after 1968 for parents of the baby-boom decades. As children grew older, some families disintegrated, and parents separated, often to form new or reconstituted families, usually with some changes of emphasis and partial rejection of the baby-boom family model.

Work for Women of the Upper Middle Class. The enthusiastic entrance to the work force of the mid-life mothers of the upper middle class can be traced in part to their experiences in the baby-boom family. Even those families with satisfactory development and relative happiness could not any longer provide a full and productive life for mothers of grown or rapidly growing children. Work, however, was not an obvious or logical choice for this group.

Economic need provided little, if any, work motivation. Although subject to the effects of inflation, perceived relative economic decline, and rising expectations, well-educated prosperous women found that their income was subject to the high marginal tax rate. The economic improvement for a family was minimal in families in which the husband already earned a large income. And certainly the attraction of the workplace of the 1970s, which so strongly resembled that of the 1950s, could not have been enough to encourage radical new behavior in the absence of economic motivation.

This group of women had ambitions for continued productivity. They had raised families in a new and creative family style, and they had twenty-five good work years remaining in their lives. Home was no longer challenging, and the jobs in the workplace appeared to be too limited for their educational level. What could they do to create a new role?

One answer would have been to seek further education in one of the women's traditional professions—schoolteaching, librarianship, or nursing. Some women did choose this option; master's degrees in library science were offered at many universities, and this choice of profession had status and challenging opportunities. The relatively low pay was not a strong deterrent because of other advantages. Nursing was not a practical option because of age limits on entrants to nursing schools. Schoolteaching, the most traditional of all women's professions, was increasingly unavailable. Men continued to encroach on this traditional women's domain, and the shrinking demand for new teachers further limited women's opportunities as the baby-boom children aged and the birth rates declined. The best jobs in the women's labor market were disappearing at the same time that many well-educated and highly motivated women wanted to enter the labor force.

The Role of Feminism. The response to this situation was the creation of a new ideology that not only encouraged women to leave home to work but demanded that they receive jobs in the work force appropriate to their educational level. The basic document for this movement already existed; Betty Friedan in 1962 had written a book called *The Feminine Mystique*, which described the emerging dissatisfaction with homemaking, and suggested that educated women should be following careers or activities more appropriate for their qualifications.[11]

In 1964 the embryonic feminist movement achieved an unexpected legal victory that encouraged the choice of paid work and that also provided a justification for young educated women to make such a choice at a much earlier stage in their life cycle. Equal job rights for women achieved legal support from the passage of the Civil Rights Bill of 1964. A southern senator attempted to defeat the bill by attaching an amendment supporting equal rights for women, an idea he believed to be so absurd that it would insure defeat. The tactic was ineffective because the supporters of the law in the northern states accepted the amendment. They were strongly committed to the protection of civil rights for minority groups, particularly blacks. Women did acquire the new legal rights, but the lack of debate on the amendment by the public left the population at large without recognition of the gender implications of the new law.[12]

The legal acceptance of equal rights for women, however haphazardly achieved, was based solidly upon the recognition of the increasing commitment of the women's work force. President Lyndon Johnson recognized in the women's work force a potential political bloc, and he showed shrewd judgment in signing the Title VII amendment to the Civil Rights Bill. A principle of legal support for women's work had already emerged when President Kennedy, at the request of professional associations of women workers, supported the principle of equal pay for equal work in 1962.

Title VII was followed by the establishment of N.O.W., a women's interest group that advocated effective enforcement of the new

laws. The quiet revolution in work participation that had already occurred provided support for an ideology that defended new job opportunities for women just at the time when the female job market
showed clear signs of inadequate size and opportunity.

The principle of gender neutrality in the work force benefited women
at all job and educational levels. Although the early leaders of the
revival of the feminist movement in the early 1960 decade were women
of the upper middle class, the existence of the large and increasingly
committed women's work force provided a broad base of support.
Feminism played a crucial role in women's work lives at a time when
a different group of women was searching for a new role.

The gender constraints in the economy had usually developed because of the concept of women's separate sphere, not because of any
economic or technical rationale for job separation. Changes in gender
stereotyping had occurred in the past, but most of the changes had
benefited men rather than women because society preferred that men
work rather than women. No economic forces existed that would have
provided major changes in the gender stereotyping of jobs, and, although attitudes on this subject were not inflexible, only minor changes
were possible in practice. Thus the legal system rather than the economic system provided the means to rid the work force of gender
constraints.

Real change in gender job participation, however, has been exceedingly slow despite legal protection. Men have continued to gain faster
entrance to women's good jobs, now a process protected by law and
defined as equitable by both genders. At the same time, the rapid
entry of women into most of the male bastions has been prevented by
problems of job preparation for many male jobs, including admission
to higher educational institutions, accessibility of internships, and
movement through certain approved career stages that were not always available to women.

Attempts to increase the pace of this process through affirmative
action led to the widespread practice of shunting women aside into
the less lucrative staff jobs in corporations, rather than positions in
line management or operations; in general practice within the medical
profession; and in support positions rather than partnerships in law
firms. A few women superstars did reach high positions, were widely

lauded, publicized, and sought after, and they frequently gave speeches in which they argued that any capable hard-working woman could succeed just as they had. The real truth is that the top jobs were few, and men were not going to give them up easily.

Similar problems emerged in other occupational areas. Craft positions in the male work force were often controlled by unions, and entry required procedures not easily available to women. Some of these jobs still required a level of physical strength that might have deterred women from trying to seek entry. Only gradually did women discover that they could enter occupations formerly unavailable to them, and that they were physically capable of jobs that had been restricted to men in the past. For example, a few women became long-distance truck drivers, a male bastion that was stormed by women attracted by this wandering life style despite the necessity of tolerating the disapproval of some of their male coworkers.

Many women, of course, remained within the traditional female occupations for the same reasons that they had done so in the past: these occupations provided easy entrance to and exit from the work force, and they used skills that women perceived themselves to have. But, perhaps most important, these jobs were those most easily available to women, and many women were willing to accept the jobs they already had rather than risk new and radical choices.

Feminist leaders, however, chose to support an ideology that allowed no compromise with gender distinctions. The principle of equality between the genders required women to behave more like men. The feminists believed that the exploitation of women had been created by role separation between the genders. Specifically, they argued that women should work for pay in the workplace in a full range of jobs, and they should develop characteristics usually perceived as those of men—assertiveness, visibility, and confidence. This policy of gender equality had a long history in the feminist movement; Elizabeth Cady Stanton at the founding of the movement in 1848 had taken a strong stand for this position.[13]

Despite some opposition backlash, and continual debate, the policy of equality has remained the basic thrust of the feminist movement, but it had its greatest impact early in the revival. This policy emphasized the need for women to acquire roles similar to those of men in order to achieve equality. The policy of equality was particularly supportive of the concept of a work role for women in place of their extended involvement in active child-rearing.

Young women, especially those of the upper middle class, were strongly attracted to the feminist position. Many made new educational choices. Engineering schools increased their percentage of women entrants in accord with Title VII and because of the new larger applicant pool. In 1960 (before Title VII) 171 women received engineering degrees as compared to 45,453 men. In 1970 women had reached the level of 526 degree graduates, compared to 63,000 men. In 1981 the women engineering graduates had increased to 9,165, compared to 85,000 men.

A greater increase in women's participation appeared in both law and medicine between 1960 and 1981. Medical schools in 1960 graduated only 387 women and 699 in 1970, but the number increased to 3,833 in 1981. In the same time span, men increased from 6,000 in 1960 to 11,000 in 1981. The 1960 figure reflected the operation of the 5 percent quota restriction on women, but the 1981 figure showed substantial improvement in women's representation: their percentage of the total graduates exceeded 25 percent. Law schools by 1981 graduated almost 50 percent women, a striking contrast to 1960, when women law graduates were a tiny minority of 230 out of a total of 9,240.[14]

The new perception of the workplace as the arena for acquisition of gender equality greatly increased its attractiveness for many educated young women who believed that the new laws and their new educational preparation would allow them full entry into careers formerly dominated by men. Pursuing the older role of mother-intensive child-rearing and homemaking retained little appeal for this new group of bright young women, who saw themselves as the first entrants into a brave new world. Even for young women holding the more customary women's jobs, work appeared to be providing freedom and independence, despite the inequality of low wages and occupational stereotyping.

Feminism also provided a strong deterrent to flagrant sexist behavior in the workplace and encouraged redefinition of tasks. Improvements resulted from changes in job titles, extra privileges at work, and more psychic rewards. Administrators became directors, and secretaries became administrative assistants with more status and pay. Direct supervisory jobs at lower management levels more often were given to women in offices, factories, and service industries. Changes like these represented real improvement for many women, despite the persistence of gender stereotyping on the job.

The impact of feminism has been strongest upon the women of the upper middle class. Feminism provided an ideology that justified women's invasion of the male job preserves at a time when opportunity in the most desirable jobs in the women's labor market was in decline. It also encouraged changes in the workplace that benefited all women by eliminating the more blatant examples of sexist behavior, by opening a few new job areas, and by stimulating women's aspirations to improve their job status.

Disillusionment with a full-time role in the home, followed by the revival of feminism, provided a new combination of motivations for women to work, especially for women who had completed their most demanding years of home maintenance and for young women not yet committed to full-time motherhood and homemaking. Although similar to the message of feminism in the past, the new revival of feminism achieved immediate success in the legal system, a crucial difference from the past that explained the strong impact of the ideology upon women's behavior in the 1970s.

The normalization of women's work and the long, steady growth of work for married women after 1930 gradually created a recognition and sometimes an expectation that women would choose to work for pay for part of their lives. The pioneers in the work force for married women were the women of high-school education in the lower middle class or in the working class. Their work entry in middle life in the 1930s, their mass participation in the defense industries in the 1940 decade, and their lower fertility during the baby-boom years permitted earlier entry to work in the 1950s and provided models for other groups of women to emulate.

The fertility pioneers of the baby-boom era, the women of the upper middle class, were latecomers into the work force, but they led the ideological revolution that opened all areas of the workplace to both genders. The beneficial economic implications of feminism for the whole society are immense and not fully realized. The increasing applicant pool for jobs that results from adding the other gender will increase productivity in all areas, for the employer's potential choice of workers is doubled. But the possible change in productivity requires the development of positive attitudes toward both genders and a new emphasis on the importance of merit in selecting workers, a process that appears to require more time than the first twenty years of Title VII. However, the contributing role of feminism in shifting the priorities of many women from the home to the workplace and in providing the basis for real change in the workplace has been successfully realized.

Mothers in Prime Child-Bearing Years. The motivation for the final group of new workers—mothers of young children—resists complete explanation by the variables suggested above as the major contributing factors for work entry for other groups. The massive increase of young mothers in the work force, with young children at home, is a change of staggering importance. A recent study shows the dimensions of this change. In 1973 only 29 percent of the working mothers had children under three years old—admittedly an already large number behaving in an unprecedented way—but in 1985 50 percent of the married working mothers had children at home under the age of three. These mothers had husbands and thus were not the sole support of a child. The increase in all working mothers in the same twelve-year period is almost as great. In 1985, 62 percent of all mothers (with children under eighteen) worked, as compared to 44 percent in 1973.[15]

The acceleration of movement into the workplace after 1975, including ever larger numbers of young mothers, suggests the emergence of new motivations for this group, motivations that may differ by social class. Rejection of the practice of mother-intensive child-rearing for young children has required powerful new motivations, for belief in mother-intensive child-rearing had been a strong and basic norm for all social classes throughout the twentieth century.

The strongest motivations for work by young mothers are probably economic in origin, strong enough to overcome the impact of societal norms for child-rearing. The decline in median family income that would have occurred if mothers had not continued to work, even after producing children, provides a powerful economic incentive. This motivation would not have been sufficient in past decades to stimulate such a major change, but it clearly offers a stronger stimulus than work entry just to provide continual improvement in family income. Under the new circumstances, the risk of leaving a job after childbirth was too high. Mothers were uncertain about the opportunity to return after several years had passed. This dilemma was particularly strong for the young well-educated woman whose job may have been professional or managerial. Her chance of regaining a job at the same level upon return to the work force was particularly low.

Higher education has been shown to be a determinant of delayed childbearing. Working women of high education have already made a strong commitment to work through longer preparation and participation, and this commitment works against the decision to go home to care for the child born late in marriage. For women of less education the work commitment may be of shorter duration, but the economic pressures are stronger to remain in the work force.[16]

The impact of male income on female work and fertility has been shown to be positive for fertility and negative for female work. The economic decline in the later 1970s that affected male income provided a strong motivation for female work, especially for the baby-boom birth cohort, which had high expectations of prosperity. The opportunity cost of producing a baby rose too high if mothers left the work force.[17]

Feminist leaders including Gloria Steinem defended the proposition that women's economic role in the family in recent years had been of prime importance. She suggested that the value structure that encouraged the shift to work away from the home played a major role in this change, but the importance of women as economic providers exceeded the importance of women's attitude changes in feminist directions. According to this argument, now strongly supported by economic data, ideology has receded as the primary work motivation, and women should be recognized for their essential economic contributions to the family. The principle of equality between the genders has become in a limited way an economic reality within the family as two incomes often are perceived as necessary for child-rearing.[18]

Women still earn substantially less than men, but their role in keeping the family from economic decline has made this salary differential increasingly less important as a determinant of work participation. The more relevant income variable in the work decision for women after 1975 has been the slow upward growth in female wage rates that has increased the opportunity cost of remaining at home.

The economic arguments for women's recent labor force participation are of crucial importance in explaining the new behavior of women in prime child-bearing years. The real cost of children has increased, and the cost of housing absorbs a larger percentage of family income in recent years than it did during the baby boom. These variables are effects of cohort size, as the emergence of the large baby-boom birth cohort into adulthood put pressure on scarce housing resources. The parents of the baby-boom children, the smaller birth cohort of the 1930s, did not find the same scarcity of housing in the 1950s, and they paid for housing at comparably lower rates, although it is important to recognize that the housing was of lower quality than would probably be acceptable to the same social class in the 1980s.

Indeed, many young mothers believed that they had no choice except to work if they wanted to have children. In the 1980s, the argument that work is a deterrent to fertility may have to be reversed. Women's work provides essential resources that allow the option of child-bearing. Many of the young mothers in the work force may be there precisely because they need the job to support the child.

The rapid increase of young mothers at work, despite strong norms opposing this practice, reveals the emergence of a new set of options available to a young married woman. She may choose between work without child-rearing or work with child-rearing, but child-rearing without work may be an impossible choice. This new set of limited choices reflects not only the higher costs of child-rearing but also the higher expectations of the appropriate standard of living that the baby-boom birth cohort acquired in their families of origin. The merging of work and fertility in a new and direct positive relationship offers the best explanation of the massive increase in work for young mothers in the 1980 decade.

However, it is important not to emphasize the role of economic explanations for women's work without also recognizing the historical changes in the impact and importance of economic motivations. Despite the importance of the economic arguments for the acceleration of change after 1975, other variables played crucial roles in the change of focus after 1960 to paid work instead of domesticity. The decline of homemaking—a long trend diverted only temporarily during the baby boom—returned again as the baby-boom family model disappeared. Several historians and social scientists have emphasized the dependence of social status on productivity in the contemporary world. As a woman's functions declined in the home, her status also declined.[19]

In 1970 young women began to see very clearly the limitations of the home as a sufficient focus for their life roles. The inexorable shrinking of women's functions in the home led to new emphasis on other forms of economic productivity. Internalization of the work ethic appeared to be a preferred substitute for full-time motherhood.

The increase in work participation and the decline in fertility predated the economic decline in the 1970 decade, a timing problem that suggests the need to reject the economic arguments alone as sufficient explanations for a change of such magnitude. A perception of the declining value of the home and the successful emergence of a new ideology also played major roles in women's changed behavior of the last two decades.

The long trend of growth of the women's work force provided an alternative for women who found the home too limiting for their skills and ambitions, but women's recognition of the importance of the dual role has always led to adaptations and combinations of work and fertility. Even today, fertility has not disappeared, and young women who work for pay and care for children struggle to do both roles well. As women rejected the home as the primary or exclusive focus of their lives, they retained a strong belief in its importance. Their acceptance of eighty-hour work weeks hardly reveals a rejection of the home. Although women in the 1980s who work for pay spend less time on housework than women in the 1960s who remained at home during the work day, the mothers of today still do the irreducible minimum of housework, and they care directly for the children in the hours spent away from the workplace.

The work motivations for different women vary profoundly, and each group that has entered the work force in the twentieth century has had its own set of reasons. Older women have found the work-place a preferred alternative to leisure and social service, and after 1965 the ideology of equality between the genders encouraged the better-educated older women to find new careers. Older women of lower educational levels had already chosen the workplace for almost five decades.

Only for two overlappng groups can we characterize work partici-pation as a new phenomenon. In the 1970s young professional women in a variety of new careers and occupations developed a commitment to work earlier in their lives than any other group. Their reasons var-ied somewhat by social class and education, but a combination of de-sires for self-actualization, improved productivity, and mainstream participation provided the initial impetus to work, and important eco-nomic motivations followed quickly upon this choice.

For many, the choice of child-bearing accentuated the economic reasons for work, and in this decision young mothers of all educa-tional levels and occupations found a common experience. An implicit recognition of the implications of their own cohort size, the possibility of divorce, the potential need to support the family with no help from a husband, and, since 1975, the shrinking economic pie have superseded the more emotional and psychological reasons for work that were im-portant early in the 1970s. The young working mother has become the work symbol of the 1980s, just as the middle-aged factory riveter symbolized female work in the 1940s and as the unmarried working girl provided the model for the nineteenth-century women's work force.

Thus, for many young women work begun as an opportunity soon became an economic necessity as cohort effects intensified and the economy changed. For women in families of low income or for women without husbands, work has always been a simple necessity. For oth-ers, particularly the middle-aged baby-boom mothers of the upper middle class, work was not an economic necessity; instead it was an opportunity created by their own application of feminism. But even for this group work has come to be viewed as a necessity, not in economic terms, but to provide satisfaction and pride in continuing to be productive after children have grown. Opportunity and necessity combined for all women as families became committed to maintaining the standard of living provided by women's work. For young mothers the burden (or the opportunity) of economic production may weigh most heavily, for they have adopted a new modern role whose strongest precedents lie in the traditional society of the past.

At the same time, the young adults must also be the innovators in family life. And the young women born in the baby boom, already the pioneers in a work revolution, find themselves in uncharted territory. Rejecting the baby-boom model invented by their parents, they are searching for the third version of the modern family, one that allows the mother to be absent from home and at work. Since both of the first two versions of the modern family were solidly based upon the foundation of mother-intensive child-rearing, the new family paradigm must be different in important new ways. The diversity of family types in the 1980s and the return to differential fertility suggests the emergence of a time of experimentation, a period from which the third version of the modern family may emerge.

CHAPTER 13

Women at the End of the Twentieth Century

Women in the 1980s live in a very different world from women of 1900, but their search for productive work roles would be immediately understood by any woman from the turn of the century. The success of modern women in finding new roles in the workplace rather than in the home might be unexpected, since in 1900 the decline of work at home was not yet apparent. Women still remained within the separate sphere, concentrating their work efforts in the home.

The greatest difference between the lives of women in 1900 and those of the 1980s is, of course, the obvious one—a large percentage of married women no longer remain at home pursuing full-time domesticity or child-rearing. In 1900 only prosperous women with servants could pursue a career outside the home, and few chose this option. Most married working women lived in poverty, dependent upon older siblings or grandmothers to care for small children while they worked for money urgently needed by the family.

The frequent absence of the mother from the home in the 1980s suggests the need for the development of a new modern family model, a process that a woman from 1900 would understand for she also was a participant in the development of a new family paradigm. But our great-grandmothers lived and worked in a separate sphere, a world dominated by emphasis on domesticity. In the later years of the twentieth century women have lost this separate sphere and must adopt new strategies in family building.

Women and the New Modern Family

In the 1980s some married couples still choose older family models. The new family strategies are pursued primarily by working mothers who must be away from home during the work day. The 1986 data on the percentage of working mothers of small children reveal the necessity for the new experiments. Only 20 percent of the families in 1986 have one earner; almost 50 percent have two earners—with few exceptions the wife and the husband. Of the 20 percent with only one breadwinner, some are single-parent families with the mother as head of household. Working mothers comprise nearly half the female population involved in active motherhood.[1]

Working mothers find few precedents for a new family model. A newly employed group in the work force, they find themselves at the same time in the role of innovators in child-rearing procedures. Mass support by society for their efforts is missing. Society in the later twentieth century lacks the generalized commitment to intensive family-rearing that characterized the baby-boom era. And no longer do women of all educational and income levels pursue domesticity and intensive child-rearing in similar styles.

However, the diversity of family styles at the end of the twentieth century, even though in strong contrast with the middle decades, resembles the family diversity of the nineteenth century and the early decades of the twentieth century. As the first modern family model was emerging as the norm for society, differential fertility and diverse family structures abounded. Not until 1920 did diversity begin to decline in favor of the new norm.

Diversity, adaptation, and innovation in families have substantial precedent, but the new frequency of the absence of mothers from home during the work day demands extensive change from the older family styles. New strategies for child care include some older methods now more extensively used—day-care centers for children in groups, greater participation by fathers, and help from grandmothers and aunts.

New approaches to domesticity include a more practical and limited approach to housekeeping, and extensive participation by the whole family in tasks.

Each of the earlier modern family models appeared as a result of innovative responses to new needs. The first version allowed greater emphasis on the individual development of children's personalities, a goal that had become important to modern people and was not emphasized in the traditional family. In the second version, the baby-boom model, some of the quantity that had been lost earlier in the trade-off for quality was replaced and new activities developed for mothers. Today there are good reasons for minimizing quantity again, and mothers have found a new activity—paid work—outside the home.

Romanticizing the earlier models that were based upon female-sponsored domesticity will only lead to a halting pace of experimentation and innovation. The new paradigm may emerge to be only one alternative in a society still characterized by extensive diversity of family styles. But the development process must occur for the family to remain a strong unit of love, nurture, child production, and companionship, goals still appropriate and possible in the later twentieth century century.

Women and the Workplace

Women's search for productivity in the twentieth century led also to the workplace. The trend toward paid work for married women shows no decline; it moved upward at an ever more rapid pace after 1900. No group of women who chose to work ever disappeared into the home again. By 1980 a large proportion of married women had returned to full-time economic production, a natural role for women throughout historical time.

Success at restoring a lost portion of women's historic role has been largely the result of women's own efforts. They created new work roles in the twentieth century in ways that did not directly confront the dominant value system of domesticity. The creation of the women's labor market required active participation by women, otherwise the jobs they found would have been held by men. Married women faced a double burden in choosing to work, for the irreducible minimum of homemaking and child-rearing did not disappear.

The society at large participated in this change, mainly by not interfering very effectively when women chose to work. As long as the home was preserved and men could hold the most powerful positions, women's work was tolerated or encouraged for economic reasons. Only twice did political action play a major part in women's increasing work role—in the government recruitment campaign for defense workers during World War II and the inclusion of women in the provisions of Title VII of the Civil Rights Law of 1964—but these actions by the federal government were immensely important in the growing trend of women's work. Women's work in World War II showed women's capabilities and commitment, and this success undermined the arguments of the detractors of their abilities. Title VII made it illegal to discriminate against women in educational institutions and the workplace, a commitment not always honored in practice but effective as a spur to women's ambitions and motivations.

Another important input to women's developing work role was the revival of feminism after 1965, which brought highly educated women into the work force and challenged the concept of the separate labor market. This action was based upon a long foundation of growth of the women's labor force and the resulting inadequacy of the gender-separate labor market that had become apparent by 1960.

The developing participation of women in the work force has been a result of at least three factors. First, women throughout the century have sought productive work roles at home and in the workplace. A growing economy encouraged limited work participation by providing opportunities for women to work. Government action in the middle and last periods lent support to working women through recruitment efforts that affected attitudes toward women's work, contributed to the development of an experienced work force, and after 1960 provided a legal basis for women's entry into jobs usually reserved for males.

Finally, and perhaps most important, ideological flexibility within the society, although it often appeared to be severely limited, nevertheless was sufficient to permit change in women's work roles. Changes were slow in coming, and they were most effective when the basic value system was not directly challenged. Only in the last period was the value system itself directly confronted and elements of the new ideology adopted by the society at large. But all three periods witnessed growth in the married women's work force, and change in the relationship between work and fertility.

Women, Work, and Fertility, 1900–1986

The work and fertility curves since 1900 provide a framework for identifying major change in women's roles. The declining birth rates in the first period did not match an increase in work rates of the same magnitude, which suggests that women's major activities declined. The middle period included the growth in both work and fertility, only to give way after 1960 to severely declining fertility combined with higher rates of paid work. Each period has its own history, its own unique trends and themes, but they are always linked to the longer history of American women. Throughout the twentieth century women have searched for ways to be productive in the family and in the workplace, a process that has included a variety of attempts to find women's place in a free and modern society.

Most interpretations of women's history in the twentieth century have emphasized the successful resurgence of feminism in the 1960s. This ideological renaissance led to new opportunities in the work force and rejection of major emphasis on the home. By this criterion, the first sixty years of the twentieth century were characterized by women's confinement in the home, oppressed by a value system that rejected emphasis on other activities. Even apparent victories like the passage of the suffrage amendment and women's successful participation in the work force in World War II changed women's lives very little.[2]

This standard interpretation, stressing dramatic recent change, does not neglect earlier way-stations, but it stresses that promising possibilities for change faded before solid success could be grasped. Educational victories won in the late nineteenth century—such as admission to medical schools and graduate programs—never gave forthright direction to women's increased entry into the male bastions. Barriers effective in practice, if not enshrined in law, emerged to prevent real change. The promising momentum of the ideological resurgence of feminism in the 1920s lost direction in the 1930s, when women rejected self-actualization outside the home because of harsh economic realities.

The period between 1945 and 1960, according to this general line of argument, marked the low point of the century, as women were thrust out of the work force after World War II. They went home to raise even more babies than usual, leaving the good jobs for men and providing a major stimulus to the economy with the burgeoning birth rate. This Victorian resurgence after a period of promising work-force participation in World War II left women again at home, this time trapped by prosperity instead of by poverty.

In this interpretation, real progress emerged through ideology, as feminism reappeared to challenge the stronger emphasis on the home. Supported by federal law enforcement after 1964, feminism led women successfully away from the stultifying home role and their position as secondary citizens without equal gender rights and opportunities. The later years of the 1970s become the high point of women's lives in this feminist interpretation of women's history, when the Equal Rights Amendment appeared virtually certain to succeed, and women were moving rapidly into new careers, rejecting, or at least down-playing, marriage and fertility in the pursuit of equality.

In the often contrasting and occasionally complementary interpretation suggested in the past twelve chapters, other events and trends in women's lives take precedence over the role of feminism, the rejection of the home, and women's success at invading male bastions. Women's successes are defined more broadly; they include improvements and change within the home, and they are not always dependent upon ideology. Women's successes at inventing a new family role and increasing their productivity at home and at work surpass the more limited achievements of ideological redefinition. In this view, rejection of the home has dangerous implications for the female gender, who throughout history have played a major role in socialization of children and have dominated child-bearing.

The periodization suggested here, using women's major activities of fertility and work as the definitive variables, suggests new insights into the nature and timing of change. The first forty years of the twentieth century included major losses for married women. Their productivity and achievement declined in comparison with the past. The home itself became a unit of shrinking value—fewer children were produced, improvements in quality became dependent upon outside sources, and work that produced income at home almost disappeared. Alternative work roles outside the home remained elusive, and little progress was made in enriching and creating new tasks at home.

Success in this period for women was based upon their achievements in disseminating the values of the modern family to various groups in the society, the practice of the new knowledge of child care, and the provision of stability and socialization to children in the decades of intensive economic and political change. In return, women received a higher standard of living, a lower infant and child mortality rate, improved gynecological care, and a longer expected life span. But their role in educating their children continued to decline as more children went to public school for an increasing number of years. Women's role at home was limiting mainly because of the loss of important and urgent functions.

At work, women gained some modest new ground as the female labor market stabilized, with occupations at various levels firmly defined as women's work. Some older women found a work role after child-rearing was complete, a major achievement that allowed the women's work force to grow without challenging the primacy of the home. The principle of emergency work for women became firmly established in this period as married women worked during the economic depression of the 1930s and when poverty threatened their own families. The growth in the size of the women's labor force and the greater participation of married women began the long process of the normalization of married women's work in the context of industrialized society.

Older women entered the work force even more rapidly after 1940, encouraged by recruiting efforts for the defense needs of World War II. The seemingly aberrant middle period, with its concomitant expansion of fertility and work, provides the key to understanding women's history in the twentieth century. Searching for a modern productive role led women to new efforts both at home and at work. For a few years the serial dual role appeared to be the best role combination that women could find—work and family in different parts of the life cycle. The family function remained strong; in fact it regained some of its past vigor, and work for pay could fill the years of early adulthood and middle age.

But the success of the serial dual role also provided the elements that led to its decline. By 1960 the women's labor market was stretched to its capacity, and jobs for women of higher education became increasingly unavailable as men sought employment in women's best jobs. The need for increasing resources to maintain the baby-boom family encouraged larger numbers of women of all economic levels to seek work, but the supply of jobs in the women's labor market did not expand fast enough to use the increasing supply of job seekers.

The political solution to the dilemma of the separate labor market was part of a larger search for equality in the 1960 decade. Women could be included in the civil rights law only because of their already extensive participation in the work force. Since women were perceived as a voting bloc by northern Congressmen and President Johnson, support for their inclusion emerged for political as well as for ideological and economic reasons. Feminism as an ideology, a political movement at the grass-roots level and a successful political interest group, followed closely upon the first and unexpected major triumph.

The last of the three twentieth-century periods has probably not ended, but the most dramatic changes have already occurred. The rapid growth of the women's work force will not continue, for most women have now accepted paid work as an appropriate and normal activity. A high level of work participation will probably continue, but at stable high rates. If fertility depends upon women's working for pay, high fertility will not return as a frequent choice. Multiple children cannot be raised in very many families unless the mother is at home. Costs are too high; housework demands on women would be too onerous after work. The high fertility of the baby boom depended upon a full-time mother at home. Thus the probable pattern in the near future is relative stability at high levels of paid work and low levels of fertility.

Differential fertility shows no signs of decline in the later years of the 1980 decade. Black fertility remains substantially higher than white fertility. Hispanic fertility in the southwestern states also shows no

sign of decline from high levels. Strong fertility differentials by income in the white population suggest that the historical pattern of an
inverse relationship between income and fertility changed only briefly
in one decade, that of the 1950s, and this change had no long-term
effect.

The pattern of extensive diversity in family size characteristic of
the beginning of the twentieth century has returned at the end. New
kinds of diversity have appeared as household size and composition
vary more extensively than ever before in modern times. In 1900 most
people lived in families, even though the families varied greatly in
size, but the rise of the single-person household, or the households
containing single persons of opposite sex living together, show the
new diversity of living arrangements in the later twentieth century.

The clearest example of the new diversity in the 1980 decade is the
combination of longitudinal stability in work and fertility with substantial cross-sectional variation. In contrast to the past two decades,
the dominant trend in the twentieth century had been a movement
toward more similar cross-sectional behavior even as longitudinal change
still occurred, but after 1965 strong cross-sectional differentials returned. Women's work behavior began to vary more extensively across
income and status levels, and the homogeneity of work behavior characteristic of the middle period disappeared. The same shift occurred
in fertility behavior as differential fertility returned, but this time
without any modifying pattern of substantial longitudinal change.

The existence of the new pattern only reinforces the conclusion that
a return to the baby-boom family in the near future is highly improb-
able. The baby boom occurred in a relatively homogeneous society in
which most women practiced traditional gender roles. The baby boom
was unique; economic, political, ideological, and social conditions
provided a context that would be unlikely to occur again. Dependent
upon nostalgia for the past, reverence for traditional institutions, a
level of economic growth that exceeded economic expectations, and a
female population with high dedication to motherhood, the baby-boom
family was an experiment bound to one time period.

In the 1980s women have the opportunity to achieve in a wider
variety of ways than motherhood alone. The workplace is hospitable
to women at status levels that were substantially unavailable before

1970. Despite obstacles of many kinds, including a persistent earnings gap and the widening social divisions among women, many women can choose from a more extensive range of options than ever before. Expectations exceed the reality, however, as idealism and ideology both suggest that women can have full equality in the work force and retain all the delights of the separate sphere at the same time. But, just as women's opportunities today exceed those of the past, so also the tensions of the simultaneous dual role may surpass those experienced by women in the recent past who pursued only one role at a time.

Women's own history has prepared them well for the problems and opportunities at the end of the twentieth century. Innovation at home and acquisition of work roles through either adaptation or challenge to the dominant value system suggest the acquisition of skills in the past that can be exercised in the present. But the tensions of the dual role will never disappear. Modern women who work outside the home find that the two environments—home and work—cannot easily be merged. Each place demands high performance levels and different skills, and both are fraught with uncertainties. But history also suggests that societally imposed rejection of either one of these roles has not succeeded for very long. Women themselves have sought the opportunity to work for pay and be mothers at the same time.

$\mathcal{N}otes$

1. Introduction

1. Theodore Roosevelt, "Preface" in Marie Van Vorst, *The Woman Who Toils* (New York, 1903), p. vii.

2. Daniel Scott Smith, "Family Limitations, Sexual Control and Domestic Feminism in Victorian America," in *Clio's Consciousness Raised: New Perspectives on the History of Women*, editors, Mary Hartman and Lois Banner (New York, 1974), p. 119.

3. Carl N. Degler, *At Odds: Women and the Family in America from the Revolution to the Present* (New York, 1980).

4. U.S. Bureau of the Census, *Historical Statistics from Colonial Times to 1970* (Bicentennial Edition, Part I), Washington, D.C., 1975, p. 54.

2. Women in 1900

1. William Chafe, *Women and Equality* (New York, 1977), p. 26.

2. Gladys Harbeson, *Choice and Challenge for American Women* (New York, 1967), p. 42.

3. Mildred Allings, "Recent Achievements of Women," *World's Work* (August, 1903), pp. 38–49; Lois Banner, *Women in Modern America: A Brief History* (New York, 1974), p. 37.

4. Daniel Scott Smith, "Family Limitations, Sexual Control and Domestic Feminism in Victorian America," in *Clio's Consciousness Raised: New Perspectives on the History of Women*, editors, Mary Hartman and Lois Banner (New York, 1974), p. 120.

5. Karen Blair, *The Clubwoman as Feminist* (New York, 1980), pp. 112–120.

6. Carl Degler, *At Odds: Women and the Family in America from the Revolution to the Present* (New York, 1980), p. 382; Alice Kessler-Harris, *Out to Work* (New York, 1982), p. 116.

7. Maxine Seller, "The Education of the Immigrant Woman, 1900–1935," in *Wom-*

en's America: Refocusing the Past, editors, Linda K. Kerber and Jane deHart Mathews (New York, 1982), pp. 242–256.

8. Herbert Gutman, *The Black Family in Slavery and Freedom* (New York, 1968), p. 216.

9. Richard Easterlin, *Population, Labor Force and Long Swings in Economic Growth: The American Experience* (New York, 1968), pp. 226–228.

10. W. Elliot Brownlee and Mary M. Brownlee, *Women in the American Economy: A Documentary History, 1675–1929* (New Haven, 1976), p. 24.

11. Richard Easterlin, "Factors in the Decline of Farm Family Fertility in the United States," *Journal of American History* (December, 1976), pp. 221–245.

12. Norman Ryder, "The Emergence of a Modern Fertility Pattern: United States, 1917–1966," in *Fertility and Family Planning*, editors, S. J. Behrman, Leslie Corsa, and Ronald Friedman (Ann Arbor, 1970), pp. 99–127.

13. For the emergence of a modernizing middle class in 1820, see Gerda Lerner, "The Lady and the Mill Girl; Changes in the Status of Women in the Age of Jackson, 1800–1840," *Mid-Continent American Studies Journal* (Spring, 1969), pp. 5–14. For demographic transition theory, see Wilson H. Grabill, Clyde V. Kiser, Pascal K. Whelpton, *The Fertility of American Women* (New York, 1958), p. 15, 180.

14. Brownlee and Brownlee, *Women in the American Economy: A Documentary History, 1675–1929* (New Haven, 1976), pp. 28, 29.

15. Willa Cather, *My Antonia* (Cambridge, Mass., 1926).

16. U. S. Department of Labor, 25th *Annual Report, 1910* (Washington, D.C., 1910), p. 693; Allan Pickerel, "The Family Status of Breadwinning Women," *Monthly Labor Review 14* (July, 1923), pp. 155–160.

17. "Report on Women Workers in New York State," *Monthly Labor Review 13* (July, 1922), pp. 64–72; Robert Smuts, *Women and Work in America* (New York, 1959), p. 16.

18. Gerda Lerner, pp. 5–14; Edward Shorter, *The Making of the Modern Family* (New York, 1976); Nancy Cott, *The Bonds of Womanhood, Women's Sphere in New England 1780–1835* (New Haven, 1977); Carole Shammas, "The Domestic Environment in Early Modern England and America," *Journal of Social History 14* (Fall, 1980), pp. 1–24.

19. A few examples of typical articles from women's magazines include "Home Life as a Profession," *Harper's Bazaar* (May 19, 1900), pp. 148–150; "The Restlessness of Modern Women," *Cosmopolitan* (July, 1901), pp. 314–317.

20. U.S. Bureau of the Census, *Historical Statistics from Colonial Times to 1970* (Bicentennial Edition, Part I) (Washington, D.C., 1975), p. 133; Brownlee and Brownlee, p. 3.

21. U.S. Bureau of the Census, *Statistical Abstract of the United States 1930* (51st edition) (Washington, D.C.), 1930.

22. Dee Garrison, "The Tender Technicians; The Feminization of Public Librarianship, 1876–1905," in *Clio's Consciousness Raised: New Perspectives on the History of Women*, editors Hartman and Banner, p. 158.

23. Smuts, p. 206.

24. Cather, Chapter 2; U.S. Department of Labor, Women's Bureau, *Report #30* (Washington, D.C., 1922).

25. Brownlee and Brownlee, p. 31: Leslie Tentler, *Wage-Earning Women: Industrial Work and Family Life in the United States, 1900–1930* (New York, 1979), pp. 47–52.

26. Marie Van Vorst, *The Woman Who Toils* (New York, 1903), p. 34.

27. Dorothy Richardson, *The Long Day: The True Story of a New York Working Girl as Told by Herself* (New York, 1905).

28. Emily Quick Householder, interview held in Henrietta, Texas, December, 1985.

29. Glen Cain, *Married Women in the Labor Force* (Chicago, 1966), p. 204.

30. U.S. Department of Labor, Bureau of Labor Statistics, *Summary of the Report on Conditions of Women and Children Wage Earners in the United States*, Bulletin 175 (Washington, D.C., 1916).

31. Gutman, p. 220.

32. U.S. Bureau of the Census, *Sixteenth Census of the United States, 1940*.

33. U.S. Department of Labor, Bureau of Labor Statistics, *7th Special Report* (Washington, D.C., 1894).

34. Albert Edwards, "Women as Teachers," *The Educational Review II* (December, 1911), pp. 943–945.

35. U.S. Bureau of the Census, *Statistical Abstract of the United States: 1940* (61st edition) (Washington, D.C., 1940); pp. 75, 96.

36. Elizabeth Gertrude Stern, excerpts from "I Am a Woman," in *Growing Up Female in America: Ten Lives*, editor, Eve Merriam, (New York, 1973), pp. 235–263.

3. Women and the Family: 1900–1940

1. Wilson H. Grabill, Clyde V. Kiser and Pascal K. Whelpton, *The Fertility of American Women* (New York, 1958), pp. 61–85.

2. U.S. Bureau of the Census, *Historical Statistics from Colonial Times to 1970*, (Bicentennial Edition, Part I), Washington, D.C., 1975), pp. 20, 21, 64. Donald J. Bogue, *Principles of Demography* (New York, 1968), p. 201.

3. *Historical Statistics*, pp. 55, 86.

4. Margaret Sanger, "My Fight for Birth Control," excerpts in *Women's America: Refocusing the Past*, editors, Linda K. Kerber and Jane deHart Mathews (New York, 1982), pp. 320–323.

5. Norman Ryder, "The Emergence of a Modern Fertility Pattern: United States, 1917–1966," in *Fertility and Family Planning*, editors, S. J. Behrman, Leslie Corsa, and Ronald Friedman (Ann Arbor, 1970), p. 104; Easterlin, "Factors in the Decline of Farm Family Fertility in the United States," *Journal of American History* (December, 1976), p. 221.

6. James Patterson, *America in the 20th Century* (New York, 1976).

7. Easterlin, *Population, Labor Force and Long Swings in Economic Growth: The American Experience* (New York, 1968), pp. 36–57.

8. *Historical Statistics*, p. 224.

9. U.S. Bureau of the Census, *Statistical Abstract of the United States: 1950* (71st edition) Washington, D.C., 1950), p. 28.

10. Ruth Schwartz Cowan, "The Industrial Revolution in the Home: Household Technology and Social Change in the 20th Century," *Technology and Culture* 17 (1976), pp. 1–24: Judith Blake, "Are Babies Consumer Durables?" *Population Studies* 22 (March, 1968), pp. 5–25.

11. Peter Lindert, *Fertility and Scarcity in America* (Princeton, 1978), p. 233.

12. *Historical Statistics*, pp. 126, 127, 132.

13. George Gallup, *The Gallup Poll: Public Opinion 1935–1971* (New York, 1972) pp. 329, 45; *Historical Statistics*, p. 54. Donald Campbell and Pascal Whelpton, *Family Planning, Sterility, and Population Growth* (New York, 1959) p. 153.

14. Many demographers and historians have discussed the formation of the modern family. See Carl Degler, *At Odds: Women and the Family in America from the Revolution to the Present* (New York, 1980), pp. 3–25; Edward Shorter, *The Making of the Modern Family* (New York, 1977), pp. 1–24; Ryder, p. 104. For early origins of the modern family, see Gerda Lerner, "The Lady and the Mill Girl: Changes in the Status of Women in the Age of Jackson, 1800–1840," *Mid-Continent America Studies Journal* (Spring, 1969), pp. 5–14.

15. For the concept of the home as a micro-economic unit that purchases children, see Gary Becker, "An Economic Analysis of Fertility," in Universities-National Bureau Committee for Economic Research, *Demographic and Economic Change in Developed Countries* (Princeton, 1960), pp. 209–231.

16. Patricia Branca, *Silent Sisterhood* (London, 1975), pp. 22–32.

17. Catherine Landreth, *The Psychology of Early Childhood* (New York, 1958), p. vii.

18. Michael Gordon, "Infant Care Revisited," *Journal of Marriage and the Family 30* (1968), pp. 589–593; Jay Mechling, "Advice to Historians on Advice to Mothers," *Journal of Social History* (Fall, 1975), pp. 23–40.

19. Tamara Hareven, "Introduction," *Family and Kin in Urban Communities, 1700–1930*, pp. 1–7. Mirra Komarovsky, *Blue Collar Marriage*, (New York, 1962), p. 49. Leslie Tentler, *Wage-Earning Women: Industrial Work and Family Life in the United States, 1900–1930*, p. 201.

4. Work at Home: 1900–1940

1. U.S. Bureau of the Census, *Historical Statistics from Colonial Times to 1970* (Bicentennial Edition, Part I) (Washington, D.C., 1975), p. 55.

2. Jane Silver, *Household Work in Pennsylvania*, University of Pennsylvania Monograph Series 21 (Philadelphia, 1925).

3. "Report on Women," *Monthly Labor Review 14* (July, 1923), p. 104.

4. Robert Smuts, *Women and Work in America* (New York, 1959), p. 204.

5. *Good Housekeeping Magazine* (January, 1936), p. 130.

6. *1897 Sears Roebuck Catalogue*, "Introduction," by S. J. Perelman and Richard Rovere; editor, Fred Israel (New York, 1968), pp. 260, 280, 281.

7. Stephan Thernstrom, *Poverty and Progress* (Cambridge, Mass., 1964), p. 164.

8. Carol Ruth Berkin, "Private Woman, Public Woman: The Contradictions of Charlotte Perkins Gilman," in Carol Ruth Berkin and Mary Beth Norton, *Women of America: A History* (Boston, 1979), pp. 165–166.

9. For emergence of rising standards for housework, see Joann Vanek, "Keeping Busy: Time Spent in Housework in the United States, 1920–1970," PhD dissertation (University of Michigan, 1973), and Ruth Schwartz Cowan, "The Industrial Revolution at Home: Household Technology and Social Change in the 20th Century," *Technology and Culture 17* (1976), pp. 1–24.

10. Tamara Hareven, "Introduction," *Family and Kin in Urban Communities, 1700–1930* (New York, 1977), pp. 1–20.

11. Cowan, p. 20.

12. Jay Mechling, "Advice to Historians on Advice to Mothers," *Journal of Social History* (Fall, 1975), pp. 23–40.

13. William Chafe, *The American Woman: Her Changing Social, Economic and Political Roles, 1920–1970* (New York, 1972), p. 104.

14. Sophia Breckenridge, *Women in the Twentieth Century: A Study of Their Political, Social and Economic Activities (New York, 1933), pp. 1–15.*

15. *Ibid.*

5. The Workplace: 1900–1940

1. U.S. Bureau of the Census, *Historical Statistics from Colonial Times to 1970* (Bicentennial Edition, Part I) (Washington, D.C., 1975), p. 24.

2. U.S. Bureau of the Census, *Nineteenth Census of the United States, 1970; Employment Status and Work Experience*, Tables 4 and 5.

3. Herbert Gutman, *The Black Family in Slavery and Freedom* (New York, 1968), p. 201.

4. A. I. Jaffe, "Trends in the Participation of Women in the Work Force," *Monthly Labor Review 18* (May, 1956), pp. 559–565.

5. Robert Smuts, *Women and Work in America* (New York, 1959), p. 112.

6. Jaffe, p. 560.

7. U.S. Bureau of the Census, *Statistical Abstract of the United States: 1940* (61st edition) (Washington, D.C., 1940), p. 74.

8. Daniel Stricker, "Cookbooks and Lawbooks," *Journal of Social History 10* (Fall, 1976), p. 24.

9. Ruth Milleman, "Women's Work and the Economic Crisis," *The Review of Radical Economics 8* (Spring, 1976), pp. 10–35.

10. James Sweet, *Women in the Labor Force* (New York, 1973), p. 174; Matina Horner, "Are Women Really Making Progress in the Labor Market?" *Radcliffe Quarterly 62* (September, 1976), p. 25.

11. Smuts, p. 112.

12. *Historical Statistics*, p. 172.

13. Valerie Oppenheimer, *The Female Labor Force in the United States* (Berkeley, 1970), pp. 124–126.

14. *Historical Statistics*, p. 379.

15. *Historical Statistics*, p. 133.

16. Oppenheimer, pp. 100–124.

17. U.S. Bureau of the Census, *Statistical Abstract of the United States: 1941* (62d edition) (Washington, D.C.), 1941.

18. Clarence Long, *The Labor Force under Changing Income and Employment* (Princeton, 1968), pp. 101–150.

19. Oppenheimer, p. 124.

20. Ibid.

21. William Chafe, *The American Woman: Her Changing Economic, Social, and Political Roles, 1920–1970* (New York, 1972) p. 104.

22. Lois Scharf, *To Work and To Wed: Female Employment, Feminism, and the Great Depression* (Westport, 1980).

23. Smuts, p. 101.

24. A. Albin, "Women in War Industries," *The New Republic*, (December, 1917), pp. 104–119.
25. Glen Cain, *Married Women in the Labor Force* (Chicago, 1966), p. 204.
26. Milleman, p. 20.

6. Ambivalence, Nostalgia, and Transition

1. Daniel Stricker, "Cookbooks and Lawbooks," *Journal of Social History 10* (Fall, 1976), pp. 24–26.
2. Ibid.
3. Richard Brown, *Modernization: The Transformation of American Life, 1600–1865* (New York, 1976), pp. 1–40; Alex Inkeles and Peter Smith, *Becoming Modern: Individual Change in Six Developing Countries* (Cambridge, Mass., 1974), pp. 1–24.
4. Molly Haskell, *From Reverence to Rape* (New York, 1974), pp. 210–235.
5. Frank Freidel, *Franklin D. Roosevelt* (Boston, 1952), p. 74.
6. Ruth Schwartz Cowan, "The Industrial Revolution at Home: Household Technology and Social Change in the 20th Century," *Technology and Culture 17* (1976), p. 24.
7. Haskell, p. 121; Betty Friedan, *The Feminine Mystique* (New York, 1963), pp. 1–20.

7. The Baby-Boom Family

1. U.S. Bureau of the Census, *Nineteenth Census of the United States: 1970 Population: U.S. Summary*, Table 81.
2. Arnold Weber, "The Changing Labor Market," *The Wall Street Journal*, (April 21, 1979).
3. Donald Bogue, *Principles of Demography* (New York, 1968); D. V. Glass, "Fertility Trends in Europe since the Second World War," in *Fertility and Family Planning*, editors, S. J. Behrman, Leslie Corsa, and Ronald Friedman (Ann Arbor, 1970), pp. 24–86.
4. Bogue, p. 221; U.S. Bureau of the Census, *Historical Statistics from Colonial Times to 1970* (Bicentennial Edition, Part I) (Washington, D.C., 1975), p. 65; S. G. Ross, "The Timing and Spacing of Births," Working Paper #30, *National Bureau of Economic Research* (January, 1974).
5. Lee Jay Cho, Wilson Grabill, and Donald Bogue, *Differential Current Fertility* (Chicago, 1970), pp. 25–30.
6. Ibid.
7. *Historical Statistics*, p. 9, 22, 52.
8. Arthur Campbell, "Baby Boom to Birth Dearth and Beyond," *Annals, AAPSS 435* (January, 1978); *Historical Statistics*, p. 35; John Haginal, "The Marriage Boom," *Population Index 19* (April, 1955), pp. 80–84.
9. John Modell, "Marriage Transition: Normative Aspects of Changes in World War II," paper presented at meetings of the Population Association of America, quoted in Linda Waite and Glenna Spitze, "Young Women's Transition to Marriage," *Demography* 18/4 (November, 1981), p. 681.
10. Charles Westoff and Norman B. Ryder, "Recent Trends in Attitudes toward Fertility Control," in Behrman, Corsa, and Freedman, pp. 83–102.

11. *Historical Statistics*, pp. 50–51.

12. Bogue, p. 221; *Historical Statistics*, p. 53; U.S. Bureau of the Census, *Nineteenth Census of the United States: 1970, Population U.S. Summary* Section 1, "Natality," Tables I and II.

13. Ibid.

14. Donald Campbell and Pascal Whelpton, *Family Planning, Sterility and Population Growth* (New York, 1959), p. 24–26.

15. Peter Lindert, *Fertility and Scarcity in America*, (Princeton, 1978), p. 117.

16. Lindert, pp. 124–127.

17. Lindert, p. 201.

18. Bogue, p. 84; *Historical Statistics*, pp. 8, 12.

19. Bogue, pp. 80–84.

20. U.S. Bureau of the Census, *Nineteenth Census of the United States: 1970, Population 1970 U.S. Summary*, "Detailed Characteristics," 1–675 and 1–230.

21. Ronald Rindfuss and James Sweet, *Postwar Fertility Trends and Differentials in the United States* (New York, 1977), p. 102.

22. Nineteenth Census of the United States: 1970 *Population*, "Special Report PC.2–3a," Table 35.

23. Benjamin Spock, *Baby and Child Care* (New York, 1946).

24. Peter Stearns, *Be a Man: Males in Modern Society* (New York, 1979), p. 121.

25. See "Open House the Year Round," *The Ladies Home Journal*, (April, 1961), pp. 154–156; "Small Box House is Opened Wide and Doubled in Size," *Sunset Magazine* (April, 1961), pp. 188–191; "For Home and Mother, Wild Patterns," *Life Magazine* (October 20, 1961), p. 153.

26. "Natural Childbirth: Facts and Fallacies with Evidence from Doctors," *Ladies Home Journal* (October, 1962), p. 53; "I Shared the Wonder of Birth with My Baby," *Parent's Magazine* (May, 1961), pp. 36–38.

27. Richard Easterlin, *Population, Labor Force and Long Swings in Economic Growth: The American Experience* (New York, 1968), p. 124.

28. Betty Friedan, *The Feminine Mystique* (New York, 1964), p. 67.

29. U.S. Bureau of the Census, *Statistical Abstract of the United States: 1970*, (91st Edition) (Washington, D.C., 1971), p. 104.

8. Perspectives on High Fertility

1. John Durand, *The Labor Force in the United States: 1890–1960* (New York, 1948), p. 210.

2. Alva Myrdal and Viola Klein, *Women's Two Roles: Home and Work* (London, 1956); Ferdinand Lundberg and Marynia F. Farnham, *Modern Woman; The Lost Sex* (New York, 1947), p. 33.

3. Betty Friedan, *The Feminine Mystique* (New York, 1964), p. 67.

4. Donald J. Bogue, *Principles of Demography* (New York, 1968), pp. 44–54.

5. "Women's War Work," *Monthly Labor Review 58* (November, 1946), p. 674.

6. Gary Becker and Lewis Greeg, "On the Interaction between Quality and Quantity of Children," *Journal of Political Economy 81* (March/April 1973); Theodore Schultz, "Micro-Economic Theory of Fertility," *Journal of Political Economy 81* (March/April, 1973).

7. Morris Janowitz, *The Last Half-Century: Societal Change and Politics in America* (Chicago, 1978), p. 156.

8. Julian Simon, "The Effects of Income on Fertility," *Population Studies 23* (November, 1969), pp. 120–127.

9. Morris Silver, "Births, Marriages and Business Cycles in the United States," *Journal of Political Economy 73* (June, 1965), pp. 202–214.

10. Peter Lindert, *Fertility and Scarcity in America* (Princeton, 1978), p. 86.

11. Richard Easterlin, "On the Relation of Economic Factors to Recent and Projected Fertility Changes," *Demography 3* (1966), pp. 131–153; Glen H. Elder, Jr., "Scarcity and Prosperity in Postwar Childbearing: Explorations from a Life Course Perspective," *Journal of Family History 6* (Winter, 1981), pp. 410–433.

12. Ronald Rindfuss and James Sweet, *Postwar Fertility Trends and Differentials in the United States* (New York, 1977), p. 163.

13. Ibid.

14. Richard Easterlin, *Population, Labor Force and Long Swings in Economic Growth: The American Experience* (New York, 1968), pp. 104–110.

15. Richard Easterlin, "Towards a Theory of Fertility," in *Fertility and Family Planning*, editors, S. J. Behrman, Leslie Corsa, and Ronald Freedman (Ann Arbor, 1970), pp. 125–157.

16. Easterlin, *Population, Labor Force and Long Swings in Economic Growth*, p. 74.

17. Rindfuss and Sweet, p. 192.

18. Philips Cutwright and Edward Shorter, "The Effect of Health on the Completed Fertility of Nonwhite and of White Women Born from 1867–1935," *Journal of Social History 13* (Winter, 1979), pp. 191–219.

19. Glen Elder, Jr., *Children of the Great Depression* (Chicago, 1974), pp. 9–10.

20. Glen Elder, Jr., "Scarcity and Prosperity in Postwar Childbearing," p. 433.

21. For the decline of partriarchy in the American family, see Peter Stearns, *Be a Man: Males in Modern Society* (New York, 1979), p. 44.

22. For rise in fertility of women between the ages of thirty and thirty-nine, see Figure 7.2 in Chapter 7.

23. Molly Haskell, *From Reverence to Rape* (New York, 1974), pp. 146–148.

24. U.S. Bureau of the Census, *Statistical Abstract of the United States: 1979* (100th edition) (Washington, D.C., 1981), Table 76. Church membership rose from 57.5 percent of the adult population in 1950 to 64 percent in 1960. For the reinstatement of the wartime draft in peacetime, see Kenneth Boulding, *The Peacetime Draft* (New York, 1970), p. 42.

25. Haskell, p. 208.

26. Alice Edwards, "The Context for Mrs. America," *Ladies Home Journal* (June, 1959), pp. 27–34.

27. Bureau of the Census, *Historical Statistics from Colonial Times to 1970* (Bicentennial Edition, Part I) (Washington, D.C., 1975), p. 304.

28. Ibid.

29. Peter Stearns, *Europe since 1815* (New York, 1975), pp. 207–215.

30. Rindfuss and Sweet, p. 67.

31. Betty Friedan, *The Feminine Mystique* (New York, 1964).

9. Women's Work: 1940-1960

1. Edward Waldham and Karolyn Goner, "Marital and Family Characteristics of the Labor Force," *Monthly Labor Review 95* (1972), pp. 406–409.

2. U.S. Bureau of the Census, *Historical Statistics from Colonial Times to 1970* (Bicentennial Edition, Part I) (Washington, D.C., 1975), p. 133; Carol Barry, "White Collar Employment; Trends and Structure," *Monthly Labor Review 44* (June, 1961), pp. 1164–1173.

3. Waldham and Goner, p. 407; *Historical Statistics*, p. 133; Richard Easterlin, *Population, Labor Force and Long Swings in Economic Growth* (New York, 1968), p. 204.

4. Carol Barry, p. 68; Margaret Gordon, "Introduction" to "A Symposium on Women in the Work Force," *Industrial Relations 7* (May, 1968), pp. 80–84.

5. Eleanor Beeley, "Distribution of Women in the Work Force," *Monthly Labor Review 36* (March, 1955), pp. 564–568.

6. Robert Anderson, "Occupational Change in the Hosiery Industry," *Monthly Labor Review 36* (May, 1945), pp. 1067–1068.

7. "Women Factory Workers," *Monthly Labor Review 28* (March, 1947), p. 368.

8. Valerie Oppenheimer, *The Female Labor Force in the United States* (Berkeley, 1970), p. 34.

9. "A Study of Women Engineers," *Monthly Labor Review 64* (July, 1956), p. 1057.

10. Barry, p. 1163.

11. "Employment of College Graduates of 1957," *Monthly Labor Review 74* (March, 1958), pp. 346–348.

12. "Employment of Women College Graduates of 1955," *Monthly Labor Review 64* (July, 1956), p. 1057.

13. Robert Stein and Herman Travis, "Labor Force and Employment in 1960," *Monthly Labor Review 78* (March, 1961), pp. 300–314.

14. Ibid.

15. Waldham and Goner, p. 407.

16. Clarence Long, *The Labor Force under Changing Income and Employment* (Princeton, 1968), p. 24.

17. *Historical Statistics*, p. 134.

18. Harold Wilensky, "Women's Work: Economic Growth, Ideology and Structure," *Industrial Relations 7* (May, 1968), pp. 235–248.

19. "Employment of College Graduates of 1957," *Monthly Labor Review 74* (March, 1958), pp. 346–348.

20. Daniel Bell, "The Great Back to Work Movement," *Fortune* (May, 1956), p. 44.

21. Arland Thornton, "Fertility and Income, Consumption Aspirations and Child Quality Standards," *Demography 16* (May, 1979), p. 87.

22. For increase in the opportunity cost of leisure for mothers as their children grow older, see Reuben Gronau, "The Intrafamily Allocation of Time: Value of Housewives Time," *American Economic Review 63* (September, 1973), pp. 634–635. *Historical Statistics* passim.

23. Carolyn S. Bell, "Age, Sex, Marriage and Jobs," *The Public Interest 30* (Winter, 1973), pp. 76–87.

24. "Marital and Family Characteristics of Workers," *Monthly Labor Review 74* (March, 1960), p. 355.

25. Marion Sobol, "A Dynamic Analysis of the Labor Force Participation of Married Women of Childbearing Age," *Journal of Human Relations 8* (June, 1973), pp. 497–512.

26. Jacob Mincer, "Market Prices, Opportunity Costs and Income Effects," in *Measurements in Economics*, editor, Carl Christ (Stanford, 1966).

27. Oppenheimer, p. 143.

28. George Gallup, *The Gallup Public Opinion Poll, 1935–1971* (New York, 1972), pp. 136, 326, 535, 1006, 1104.

29. Herbert Burstein, *Women in War* (New York, 1943), p. 46; "Expanding Occupational Opportunities for Women," *Monthly Labor Review 64* (April, 1953), p. 381.

30. "Women in Industry," *Monthly Labor Review 54* (June, 1942), p. 703; "Women's War Work," *Monthly Labor Review 58* (November, 1946), p. 674.

31. "Change to Peacetime Work," *Monthly Labor Review 54* (November, 1946), p. 674.

32. Robert Smith and William Allings, "The Korean War Emergency," *Monthly Labor Review 69* (January, 1953), pp. 25–27.

33. Carl N. Degler, *At Odds: Women and the Family in America from the Revolution to the Present* (New York, 1980), pp. 418–423; Karen Anderson, *Wartime Women: Sex Roles, Family Relations and the Status of Women during World War II* (Westport, 1981), pp. 154–176; Sheila Tobias and Lisa Anderson, "What Really Happened to Rosie the Riveter? Demobilization and the Female Labor Force, 1944–1947," in *Women's America; Refocusing the Past*, editors, Linda K. Kerber and Jane deHart Mathews (New York, 1968), pp. 354–373.

34. Nancy Davis and Larry Bumpass, "The Continuation of Education after Marriage among Women in the United States: 1970," *Demography 13* (May, 1976), p. 161.

35. Gertrude Bancroft McNally, "Patterns of Female Labor Force Participation," *Industrial Relations 7* (May, 1968), pp. 42–47; *Historical Statistics*, U.S. Department of Labor, Women's Bureau Employment Standards Administration, *The Earnings Gap between Men and Women* (Washington, D.C., 1976); U.S. Bureau of the Census, "Money Income of Families and Persons in the United States," *Current Population Reports, 1957–1975* (Washington, D.C., 1975); U.S. Department of Labor, Bureau of Labor Statistics, *Handbook of Labor Statistics* (Washington, D.C., 1975).

10. The Changing Context of Fertility: 1960–1986

1. Arthur Norton and Paul Glick, "What's Happening to Households?" *American Demographics* (January, 1979), pp. 22–24; Conrad Tauber, "A Changing America," *American Demographics* (January, 1979), pp. 130–132).

2. U.S. Bureau of the Census, *Statistical Abstract of the United States: 1979* (100th edition) (Washington, D.C., 1981), p. 76.

3. "The White House Conference on Families," *Child Today*, (November/December 1979), p. 30.

4. Tauber, p. 30.

5. Ibid.

6. U.S. Bureau of the Census, *Historical Statistics from Colonial Times to 1970* (Bicentennial Edition, Part I) (Washington, D.C., 1975), pp. 55, 64.

7. Neil G. Bennet, David E. Bloom, and Patricia Craig, "Marriage Patterns in the United States," discussed in *Newsweek Magazine* (June 2, 1986), pp. 54–58.

8. Ronald Rindfuss and James Sweet, *Postwar Fertility Trends and Differentials in the United States* (New York, 1977), pp. 63, 91.

9. Elise F. Jones and Charles F. Westoff, "The End of 'Catholic' Fertility," *Demography 16/2* (May 1979), pp. 209–218.

10. Rindfuss and Sweet, p. 63.

11. *Historical Statistics*, p. 102.

12. *Historical Statistics*, pp. 19, 55, 64; Richard Easterlin, "What Will 1984 Be Like? Socioeconomic Implications of Recent Twists in Age Structure," *Demography 15/4* (November, 1978) pp. 397–432.

13. *Historical Statistics*, p. 52.

14. Ibid.

15. For inverse relationship between fertility and husband's income, see Rindfuss and Sweet, p. 191. They show that cross-sectional differences in fertility by income and education increase in the 1970s.

16. *Historical Statistics*, p. 52.

17. U.S. Bureau of the Census, *Statistical Abstract of the United States: 1979*, p. 131.

18. *Historical Statistics*, p. 43.

19. Ronald Freedman, Deborah Freedman, Arland Thornton, "Changes in Fertility Expectations and Preferences between 1962 and 1977: Their Relation to Final Parity," *Demography 17/3* (August, 1980).

20. David E. Bloom and James Trussell, "What Are the Determinants of Delayed Child-Bearing and Permanent Childlessness in the United States?" *Demography 21/4* (November, 1984), pp. 591–611.

21. Ibid.

22. *Statistical Abstract of the United States: 1979*, p. 56.

23. Ibid.

24. John Modell, "Marriage Transition: Normative Aspects of Change Since World War II," paper presented at meetings of the Population Association of America, quoted in Linda Waite and Glenna Spitze, "Young Women's Transition to Marriage," *Demography 18/4* (November, 1981), p. 681.

25. Jay Teachman, "Declining Significance of 1st Birth Timing," *Demography 22/2* (May, 1985), pp. 185–198.

26. Waite and Spitze, p. 681.

27. Richard Easterlin, *Birth and Fortune* (New York, 1980), pp. 23–59.

28. Clifford Clogg and James Shockey, "Mismatch between Occupation and Schooling: A Prevalence Measure, Recent Trends and Demographic Analysis," *Demography 21/2* (May, 1984), pp. 24–57.

29. Elwood Carlson, "Divorce Rate Fluctuations as a Cohort Phenomenon," *Population Studies 33* (1979), pp. 523–536; Dennis Ahlberg and Morton Shapiro, "Socioeconomic Ramifications of Changing Cohort Size: Analysis of U.S. Postwar Suicide Rates by Age and Sex," *Population Studies 33* (1979), pp. 45–47; Joseph Veroff, "General Feelings of Well-Being over a Generation, 1957–1976," paper presented at meetings of the American Psychological Association, September 1, 1978, Toronto, Ontario.

30. Boone Turchi, *The Demand for Children: The Economics of Fertility in the United States* (Cambridge, 1975), pp. 210–212; Bruce Hall, "The Cost of Raising a Child Update," *Consumer Close-ups #8*, Cornell University Coop Extension. Estimates of the rising cost of child-rearing between 1969 and 1980 suggest that direct costs have increased from a range of $18,000 to $36,000 in 1969, in 1980 dollars, to a range of $48,000 to

$73,000 in 1980 also in 1980 dollars. The opportunity cost (market wages sacrificed by the mother if she remains at home for child-rearing) shows a commensurate rise in the same period. These figures are inflation-adjusted but not completely comparable since the 1969 figure is from Turchi, and the 1980 figure was computed by Bruce Hall. They both, however, represent estimates of the same cost—that is, the direct cost of rearing a child, including food, clothing, shelter, education, and recreation. The existence of a large increase over time appears to be valid even if the exact magnitude of this increase cannot be verified.

11. The New Workplace

1. U.S. Bureau of the Census, *Historical Statistics from Colonial Times to 1970* (Bicentennial Edition, Part I) (Washington, D.C., 1975), p. 201.
2. Elizabeth Waldman, "Change in the Labor Force Activity of Women." *Monthly Labor Review 93/6* (June, 1970), p. 14.
3. Ibid.
4. Ibid.
5. U.S. Bureau of the Census, *Statistical Abstract of the United States: 1979*, (100th edition) (Washington, D.C., 1980), p. 651.
6. Eli Ginzberg, "Paycheck and Apron," *Industrial Relations, 7/3* (May, 1968), p. 22.
7. Ralph Smith, "Sources of Growth of Female Labor Force Participation, 1971–1975," *Monthly Labor Review 99/8* (August, 1977), p. 684.
8. Paul Ryscavage, "More Wives in Labor Force Have Husbands with above Average Incomes," *Monthly Labor Review 101/6* (June, 1979), p. 40.
9. *Statistical Abstract of the United States: 1979*, p. 40.
10. Cynthia Lloyd and Beth Niemi, "Sex Differences in Labor Supply Elasticity," *American Economic Review 68/2* (May, 1978), p. 234; Christopher Lingle and Ethel Jones, "Women's Increasing Unemployment: Cross-Sectional Analysis," *American Economic Review 68/2* (May, 1978), p. 341.
11. *Statistical Abstract of the United States: 1979*, p. 41; Stuart Garfinkle, "Table of Working Life for Women," *Monthly Labor Review 78/8* (August, 1956), p. 101.
12. U.S. Bureau of the Census, "Money Income of Families and Persons in the United States," *Current Population Reports, 1957–1975* (Washington, D.C., 1975); U.S. Department of Labor, Bureau of Labor Statistics: *Handbook of Labor Statistics* (Washington, D.C., 1975).
13. U.S. Bureau of the Census, *Statistical Abstract of the United States: 1982* (103d Edition) (Washington, D.C., 1983).
14. Milton Friedman, "Taxes and Family," in *There's No Such Thing as a Free Lunch* (Urbana, Ill., 1975), p. 97.
15. U.S. Bureau of the Census, *Statistical Abstract of the United States: 1986* (107th edition) (Washington, D.C., 1986), p. 76.
16. Ibid.
17. Denis Johnston, "U.S. Economy in 1985: Population and Labor Force Projections," *Monthly Labor Review 96/12* (December, 1973), p. 8.
98.
19. Weiner, p. 45.
20. Weiner, p. 56.

21. "High Tech Emerges as a Man's World: Study," *Houston Chronicle* (July 4, 1985).
22. Barbara Devaney, "An Analysis of Variations in U.S. Fertility and Female Labor Force Participation Trends," *Demography 20/2* (May, 1983), p. 147.
23. Ginzberg, p. 22.

12. Women's Rush to Work: Necessity or Opportunity?

1. Ralph E. Smith, *Women in the Labor Force* (Washington, D.C., 1979), p. 34.
2. U.S. Bureau of the Census, *Historical Statistics from Colonial Times to 1970* (Bicentennial Edition, Part I) (Washington, D.C.), pp. 380, 381.
3. U.S. Bureau of the Census, *Statistical Abstract of the United States: 1982* (103d Edition) (Washington, D.C., 1982), p. 34.
4. Smith, p. 56.
5. *Historical Statistics*, p. 45.
6. U.S. Bureau of the Census, *Statistical Abstract of the United States: 1979* (100th edition) (Washington, D.C., 1980), p. 34.
7. James Sweet, "Components of Change in Number of Households: 1970–1980," *Demography 21/2* (May, 1984); R. Michal, Victor Fuchs, Sharon Scott, "Changes in Propensity to Live Alone, 1950–1976," *Demography 17/1* (February, 1980), pp. 221–224.
8. Diana Felmlee, "A Dynamic Analysis of Women's Employment Exits," *Demography 21/2* (May, 1984), p. 171.
9. John P. Robinson, "Housework Technology and Household Work," in Sarah Fensternaker Berk. *Women and Household Labor* (Beverly Hills, 1980), pp. 53–65.
10. M. M. Marini, "Effects of Number and Spacing of Children on Marital and Parental Satisfaction," *Demography 17/3* (August, 1980), p. 225; James P. Smith and M. P. Ward, "Asset Accumulation and Family Size," *Demography 17/3* (August, 1980), p. 243.
11. Betty Friedan, *The Feminine Mystique* (New York, 1964), Chapter 1.
12. Alice Kessler-Harris, *Out to Work* (New York, 1984) pp. 67–98.
13. Ibid.
14. Kessler-Harris, p. 56.
15. Smith, p. 45.
16. David E. Bloom and James Trussell, "What Are the Determinants of Delayed Child-Bearing and Permanent Childlessness in the United States?" *Demography 21/4* (November, 1984).
17. Barbara Devaney, "An Analysis of Variations in U.S. Fertility and Female Labor Force Participation Trends," *Demography 20/2* (May, 1983), p. 147.
18. Gloria Steinem, *Outrageous Rebellion* (New York, 1985), pp. 56–78.
19. Ibid. p. 56.

13. Women at the End of the Twentieth Century

1. U.S. Bureau of the Census, *Statistical Abstract of the U.S.: 1986* (107th edition) (Washington, D.C., 1986), p. 46.
2. For the failure of women's suffrage to bring major change in women's lives, see William Chafe, *Women and Equality* (New York, 1977), p. 37; Lois Scharf, *To Work and To Wed* (Westport, 1980), Chapter 2; and Winifred Wandersee, *Women's Work and Fam-*

ily Values, 1920–1940 (Cambridge, Mass., 1981). Chapters 5 and 6 discuss the failure of feminist ideals to affect women's decisions in the period between the wars. For the strongest case for the 1950s as the low point in women's progress, see Betty Friedan, *The Feminine Mystique* (New York, 1963). Several historians, although deploring the failure of feminism to provide true gender equality, nevertheless emphasize its important role in releasing women from primary dependence on motherhood. See especially Carl Degler, *At Odds: Women and the Family in America from the Revolution to the Present* (New York, 1980) and Alice Kessler-Harris, *Out to Work: A History of Wage-Earning Women in the United States* (New York, 1982).

Index